"The Men of Defeat: Ireland and the American South."

COTTON FIELDS *and* SKYSCRAPERS

David R. Goldfield

COTTON FIELDS
and
SKYSCRAPERS

Southern City and Region, 1607–1980

Louisiana State University Press *Baton Rouge and London*

Designer: Patricia Douglas Crowder
Typeface: Sabon
Typesetter: G & S Typesetters, Inc.
Printer & Binder: Thomson-Shore, Inc.

LIBRARY OF CONGRESS CATALOGING IN PUBLICATION DATA

Goldfield, David R., 1944–
  Cotton fields and skyscrapers.

  Includes bibliographical references and index.
  1. Cities and towns—Southern States—History.   2. Sectionalism (United
States)—History.   3. Agriculture—Economic aspects—Southern States.
4. Southern States—Race relations.   5. Conservatism—Southern States—
History.   I. Title.
HT123.5.A13G64   307.7′6′0975   82-6582
ISBN 0-8071-1029-9   AACR2

for Marie-Louise

Contents

Preface   xi

Acknowledgments   xiii

Introduction   1
City and Region

I   Pearls on the Coast and Lights in the Forest   12
     The Colonial Era

II   Urbanization Without Cities   28
     The Antebellum Era

III   The Old South Under New Conditions   80
     1861–1920

IV   A Kind of Sunlight   139
     1920–1980

Bibliographical Essay   197

Index   229

Illustrations

Map of leading southern cities, 1860   31

Map of leading southern cities, 1920   83

The Battery, Charleston, South Carolina   133

Stanton Hall, Natchez, Mississippi   134

Poverty-level housing in Natchez, 1981   135

The "Moon Walk," New Orleans, 1981   136

Hyatt-Regency Hotel, Atlanta, 1973   137

Black housing in Natchez, 1981   138

Map of leading southern cities, 1970   141

Preface

This book is primarily an extended hypothesis, a lengthy essay setting forth some ideas about southern urbanization as a regional phenomenon. It is the culmination of fifteen years of thinking, reading, and writing about the South and of living, working, and traveling in the region nearly that long. Yet this is not the definitive statement on southern cities but what I offer as the beginning of a new approach, a new perspective on a unique environment within our national midst—the southern city.

Most general works on the South contain an obligatory statement defining and delimiting the region geographically. The difficulty, as David L. Smiley observed, is that the "South defies . . . location." It is more a culture than a geography. Terms like "Piedmont," "Tidewater," "valley," "coastal plain," "piney woods," "Delta," "black belt," "low country," "upcountry," and "mountain" describe the various geographic divisions of the South and, doubtless, the peculiarities of life that exist within these segments as well; thus, there is no single geographic South. To compound matters, the census definition includes such interlopers as Delaware, Washington, D.C., Maryland, and West Virginia. Regionalist Howard W. Odum's analysis of seven hundred variables demonstrated that none of these entities (and Missouri as well) were southern. The most reasonable definition of the contemporary geographic South, therefore, includes the eleven former Confederate states plus Kentucky and Oklahoma. Since Oklahoma was primarily Indian territory until the late nineteenth century, and since its subsequent history as a southern state is marginal, my definition excludes that state. Within the area encompassed by the former Confederacy and Kentucky, the regional characteristics I discussed had their greatest impact.

Acknowledgments

Whatever fermentation process occurred in my thoughts to help produce this volume, an array of southern scholars aided me immeasurably with some vintage insights. I acknowledge my numerous intellectual debts in the bibliographical essay, but I would like to take special note here of Don H. Doyle's interpretive and bibliographical suggestions, and David E. Harrell's assistance on southern religion.

I appreciate particularly the kindness of David R. Godschalk for allowing me to use the facilities and resources of the City and Regional Planning Department at the University of North Carolina, Chapel Hill. While at Chapel Hill, I mined the thoughts of Joel Williamson in several all-too-brief conversations. My encounters with two other scholars—Stephanie Greenberg of the Research Triangle Institute in North Carolina and Bill Barnard in Tuscaloosa, Alabama—stimulated my own thoughts on the contemporary southern city as a regional entity.

I thought about and wrote portions of this book while residing in Stockholm, Sweden, as a visiting professor under the Fulbright-Hays Senior Scholar program. Stockholm may seem an exotic location to write a book on southern cities, but coming into contact with Scandinavian and European cities and urban systems provided fresh perspectives for me that I would not have received from an American vantage point. Indeed, the strong remnants of rural culture in Swedish cities and the dictum of Swedish urban historian Gregor Paulsson that "alla städer ligger på landet"—all cities are in the countryside—first drew my thoughts away from North American models of urbanization.

While at Stockholm University, I was fortunate to encounter two Swedish scholars—Thomas Hall and Ingrid Hammarström—who shared my intellectual interests and who were eager to trade ideas. I also want to thank Ingrid Sjöström of the Art History Institute of Stockholm University, who recommended me to the Fulbright Commission in the first place.

Most fortunate, both for myself and for the book, I have been blessed over the past decade with two good friends—Blaine Brownell and Howard Rabinowitz—who not only encouraged and contributed to my work on southern cities, but to my own personal happiness as well. These southern urbanists and I have spent countless days and nights throughout the urban South over the years talking about southern cities and about life. God knows how many brilliant ideas have been left in the hotels and restaurants of Atlanta, Birmingham, New Orleans, and Houston. I can only hope that one or two of them found their way into this book.

My wife, Marie-Louise Hedin, offered her friendship, love, advice, and reindeer stew during the preparation of this work. Her creativity, evident in the maps accompanying the text, inspired my own. Our son Erik Alexander provided a different sort of inspiration, encouraging me to send off the manuscript on schedule lest he eat portions of it. I trust that it was his appetite for knowledge and not a critical evaluation of my work that led him to such behavior.

Many years ago, when my two great loves were Duke Snider and Ingrid Bergman, I thought of Swedish women as the most perfect representatives of womankind. As one grows older, such ideals and conceptions usually fade, and this one did for me. I am dedicating this book to Marie-Louise because she not only revived that ideal, but me as well. Heja, Marie-Louise!

COTTON FIELDS *and* SKYSCRAPERS

Introduction
City and Region

Go down to Montgomery. Stand on the star where Jefferson Davis stood when he took his oath of office as president of the Confederate States of America. If you look carefully enough across the street from the Alabama State House, you will see a small brick church—the Dexter Avenue Baptist Church. Here the young Reverend Martin Luther King, Jr., gathered his followers to lead a gentle protest against the harsh racial realities of southern life. So much of southern, indeed of American history is encompassed by that view. From the sundering of the Union to the beginning of the Civil Rights movement, Montgomery was the stage where the South acted out its tragedy and its triumph. Yet you will notice that this is an unlikely setting for such momentous events. It is as if the director has told the actors to go home, and the audience has followed. All that remains is the scenery. It is pretty scenery, to be sure, if you have come in the spring before the heat dulls the vernal prism. There are camellias, plum blossoms, and the inevitable magnolias. They almost hide the service stations, the mostly empty streets, and the vacant stores. The actors have packed their grips and left for the suburbs, leaving only the bit players behind. But you can still get a good meal at the Elite (pronounced "ee-lite") Café. With the magnolias in bloom and those homemade biscuits in front of you, the frayed look of the city passes from your mind, if not from your eye. You are no longer in the city, you are in the South.

And that is the difficulty with studying southern cities as cities. A strictly urban analysis will only uncover a jumble of contradictions. What can we say about Atlanta, for example, which gave us *Gone With the Wind*, Coca-

Cola, and the Ku Klux Klan, and which boosters love to call "the New York of the South" and also "the most religious city in the country"? Nashville, for another example, is simultaneously "Country Music City, USA," and "the Athens of the South."

During the 1970s, urban experts discovered the urban South and proceeded to analyze it as they had analyzed northern cities. Historians demonstrated that urban southerners were concerned about the same issues and problems as residents in cities elsewhere and were as aggressively capitalistic in pursuing growth and prosperity. If the urban South lagged behind the urban North in the statistics of population and production, it was a lag of time, not of quality. Geographers applied their urban growth models to southern urbanization with lengthy discussions on why the central place theory or the mercantile model of growth fit the southern urban system best. Sociologists proved that South Boston was more racist than Jackson, Mississippi, and that southern cities generally were not any more racially hostile than their northern counterparts. Finally, scholars in all disciplines joined popular journalists in marveling over the Sun Belt and how the nexus of urban development had shifted to the southern rim.

All of these studies had the beneficial effect of lifting the cotton curtain that had shrouded an important aspect of southern regional development. The South could no longer be thought of simply as "planter, plantation, staple crop, and the Negro, all set in a rural scene," in the words of historian David L. Smiley. The discovery of the southern city, moreover, had significance beyond the academy. It provided a new perspective on an old region and portended well for its future. The city, after all, as southern sociologist Edgar Thompson noted, "is the natural habitat of the liberal mind." In a frequently illiberal region, the emergence of the city was significant. Southern anthropologist J. Kenneth Morlund wrote in the late 1960s that "urbanization tends to bring with it a secularization of belief in which reason plays a greater part in outlook and behavior and tradition plays a lesser part." For a region steeped in and victimized by emotion and tradition, here was an indicator of progressive change. The South, whose obituary had been written frequently over the past century, was finally expiring, with a skyscraper for a tombstone and a stock market quotation for an epitaph.

The South, however, is still the South, and has always been so. Nothing reveals this more than the southern city—the very factor that analysts have been citing as the leading agent for regional change. The problem has been that they have studied the southern city, naturally enough, as a city. Unfortunately, the model most have been using for a "city" has been the one designed by Chicago sociologist Louis Wirth in the 1920s. The city in this view is a distinctive environment, set apart from the countryside and capable of altering human behavior by the very fact that it is a city.

But the southern city is different because the South is different. In that region, the city is much closer to the plantation than it is to Chicago and New York. The study of the southern city requires an alteration in traditional views about rural-urban differences and about the distinction of the urban environment. The most helpful perspective from which to study the southern city may be the southern region. And three features have dominated the history of the southern region: rural life-style, especially that shaped by the predominance of staple agriculture; race; and a colonial economy. These three distinctive aspects of regional history have also resulted in distinctive cities.

Urbanization and agriculture have enjoyed a long partnership. Cities through history have blended rural and urban functions, and those that have lost their rural connections are of relatively recent origin and confined only to a highly industrialized and mechanized segment of the United States and western Europe. The Chinese city Ch'ang-an approached one million inhabitants during the T'ang Dynasty (618–907 A.D.), yet rural space such as farmlands, parks, and fields comprised one-third of the city's area. Even as late as the 1920s in China, market-garden farms and duck ponds were typical land-use features of the larger cities. The European rural-urban tradition is equally rich, though not as lengthy as the Oriental. The medieval city included farms and orchards. Paris' Left Bank was "semi-urban" with sprawling vineyards as late as 1200. Historians have characterized seventeenth-century London as a "pleasant country town with many gardens and broad green fields." Even after the industrial revolution, agriculture remained a part of urban life. English urban historians H. J. Dyos and Michael Wolff described the Victorian city as still tied to "its rural connections. The largest of them still conducted extensive backyard agriculture, . . . cow-stalls, sheep-folds, pig-sties above and below ground in and out of dwellings, on and off the streets, wherever this rudimentary factory-farming could be made to work."

The countryside was never far off for nineteenth-century urban residents. Eventually, however, the pall of industry obliterated the rural vestiges of urban life, and the city ceased to be merely a well-populated garden. In the American South, though, agriculture continued to characterize the region and its cities. There, the rural model of urbanization prevailed; life in the cities remained tied to agricultural cycles. As Lewis Mumford noted, there was "tidal drifting in and out of the city with the seasons." The southern city was bound to staple production, and its fortunes rose and fell with it. The architecture, landscaping, and life-style reflected the agrarian roots of southern urbanization.

But it was not only scenery and rhythm that defined the southern city as rural. It was the people above all who gave the southern city its rural atmosphere. From the colonial era and especially since the antebellum period, a homogeneous rural population of predominantly Celtic origin has dominated southern cities. This contrasts with the northern urban demography, which evidenced more diversity in its population and in its migratory flows. Not surprisingly, rural values dominated southern cities. Recent studies on ethnicity have demonstrated that immigrants' premigration cultures persisted in the city regardless of the city's adverse impact on immigrant life. In the southern city, where rural migrants did not encounter an alien culture, rural values flourished.

What are these rural values that have shaped southern urban life? Atlanta journalist Pat Watters wrote in the late 1960s that "we will not understand fully the South without according the outdoors its place of importance in the southern scheme of things." Indeed, as a rural people southerners have been close to nature. This does not imply a chummy relationship, however; southerners have battled and exploited nature. Staple agriculture, in particular, involved the conquest and continued exploitation of natural resources. The natural environment was regarded not as a treasure to be saved or savored but was there to advance the southern agricultural economy. Southern urban leaders held similar views on nature, and the mazes of railroad tracks that bisected southern cities in the nineteenth century and the industries that have polluted those cities in the twentieth reflected this exploitative philosophy.

Family and religion were southern rural bulwarks that found hospitable soil in the urban environment, too. Southern historian Francis Butler Simkins asserted that "the family was the core of Southern society; within its bounds everything worthwhile took place." Listen to the country songs of domesticity, family pride, and "mama." Southern popular music and literature are filled with heroic mothers who as teachers, lovers, and value-givers play a central role in the regional mythology, even if they are second-class citizens in the region's reality. The strength of family ties meant the weakness of the community or collective ethic in southern cities; kinship patterns determined social standing, and tradition counted more than novelty. Honor, vengeance, and pride—especially when women were involved—were, above all, family values, and they governed behavior outside the home as well as within it. Southerners believed and practiced, as historian Gerald M. Capers has noted, "the right of private vengeance."

Religion was at the center of southern family life. The southern church, historian George B. Tindall wrote, "is something unique in all Christendom in its single-minded focus on salvation, its sense of assurance, and its rejection . . . of other versions of Christian experience. It serves as one of the chief instruments of ethnic solidarity." The fierce evangelical Protestantism of the southern region bred a sense of fatalism, an entrenchment against new ideas, and a pessimistic view of human nature. It helped to make urban life conservative; change was anathema, and government provision for social services was deemed unnecessary. It also excused human exploitation, since the worldly hierarchy inevitably reflected the biblical hierarchy as interpreted by civic and religious leaders. Rewards were supposed to come in the next world.

For those who owned the requisite land and labor, staple agriculture offered significant temporal rewards. Moreover, staple agriculture provided the framework for these southern values by determining the context of both rural and urban life. As geographer Carville Earle has noted, "staples and their marketing seem to provide a key to explaining the abrupt contrasts between northern and southern urban systems." The southern city not only looked and felt like the countryside, but its very existence was determined by the nature of rural production in the region. The great southern staples of tobacco and cotton required relatively simple marketing and processing. In the colonial period, these procedures could even occur in an extremely decentralized framework that focused on individual plantations as the primary marketing units. But even when production levels and market demands required some centralization of marketing and processing activities, the places that evolved to service staple crops were relatively small. In fact, the South is overwhelmingly a region of towns and small cities.

Staple agriculture, as the most influential rural activity in a rural region, influenced the urban landscape—see the homes and gardens in Vicksburg or Natchez for examples; the rhythms of urban life —as evidenced by the gay winter social season of Charleston or the desertion of New Orleans streets in June; and the values of urban residents—their individualism, family ties, and religious beliefs. That staple agriculture helped to create relatively small cities complemented the other aspects of urban life already under its influence. When cotton and tobacco cultivation ceased to characterize staple agriculture in the 1930s and 1940s, the nature of southern cities altered to accommodate a more diverse rural economy.

Race has been a heavy burden on the southern region. Agriculture exploited the land, but the biracial society exploited the people. The biracial system required the separation, social and economic isolation, and subjugation of the Negro race. But the system also denigrated the white man, although perhaps more subtly. The biracial society restricted regional and hence urban development by devaluing human capital, black and white, and the consequent waste of human resources proved to be not only a tragedy for the people but for the region as well.

Slavery and the labor systems devised after the Civil War limited black geographic and occupational mobility. The urban labor supply, devoid of the large-scale periodic waves of immigration that characterized northern urban work forces, depended on rural economic conditions: agricultural prosperity increased rural labor demands, and agricultural depression eased the flow of labor into the cities. This was another of the many ways in which agriculture controlled the economic life of the city. By circumscribing the mobility and opportunities of the work force, the agricultural labor systems also restricted the creativity and contributions that this work force could make to the southern urban economy.

The biracial society in an urban setting restricted blacks to certain low-level occupations. Slavery meant the existence of a large body of nonconsumers, which lowered demand and capital accumulation in the cities; low postbellum wage levels, black and white, perpetuated an anemic consumer demand. In addition, the biracial society limited expenditures for education and social services that could have ultimately improved the urban economy and life-style by helping its residents become more productive. Poorer whites were victims here, too. White solidarity, especially after the Civil War, was a useful political tool in quashing the aspirations of poor whites.

In programming policies for underdeveloped countries today, econo-

mists tell us that nothing is more important than investments in human capital. Nobel laureate economist Theodore W. Schultz observed that "the decisive factor is the improvement in population quality." Three of the most
important improvements and investments are in the education, health, and
housing of the poor. The South has a dismal record in all three areas, primarily because of the dominance of rural values that place a low priority on
all three investments and because a portion of the poor, especially in the
region's cities, is black. The mingling of southern rural values and southern
biracialism to produce a lethal formula for regional and urban debility is
evident in the priority of child labor over child education; in the fear of educating blacks; in the view of disease as a religious judgment and of unhealth-
fulness as a factor of race; and in the notion that housing is an individual or
family concern for white and for black. The paucity of investments in human capital has reduced considerably the quality of the regional population
and hence its ability to contribute to the region's development. Biracialism
has restricted urban development by abusing the city's most valuable resource—the labor and intelligence of its population.

Apart from the economic debilities, the biracial society in the South created a psychological climate that inhibited the development of the region
and its cities. The capricious and authoritarian legal and customary framework that guided racial relationships bred cynicism, if not contempt, for
laws and legality in a region where private justice was rampant already.
Biracialism also contributed to the idea that labor was an exploitable resource—a legacy from the slavery era that persisted in the New South. Not
only blacks, but white men, women, and children were part of this exploitable labor pool. Class cruelty was an extension of caste cruelty.

The cities were reflections of regional racial realities. Two societies
emerged in the urban South—one white, one black—separate and unequal.
The features of that society were rigid and required strict surveillance by the
local elite. The preservation of biracialism was an objective that permeated
their policies to the point of not only weakening their cities, but of limiting
the civil rights of citizens as well. The rural values that produced hostility to
change, strong religious beliefs, individualism, and kinship bonds reinforced
the tenets of the biracial society in the city and of the ruling elite that upheld
those tenets.

But the history of biracialism in the South also indicates that blacks were
not merely anonymous victims of this tradition. They took an active role in

combating biracialism and, when success was not possible, in creating their own institutions, businesses, and communities. The family and religious institutions that succored the slave on the plantation provided the roots for a better life in the city as well. When the dismantling of the biracial apparatus began, it was not the white southerner but the black southerner who took it apart brick by painful brick. The arena was the southern city, but the songs and prayers, the devotion and determination that directed the effort came from the rural values and traditions that were also part of the black southerner's past.

The southern region has been dominated by agriculture, burdened by biracialism, and not surprisingly limited by a colonial economy. The development of a national economy centered in New York beginning in the 1840s fastened a type of regional specialization upon the South that remains with it to the present day. The South as the producer and occasional basic processor of raw materials was in economic servitude to the North not only for manufactured products but for all of the financial, credit, legal, accounting, and factoring services that attend a national economy. The regional role of the southern cities was as collection points and funnels to northern centers and as distribution points for the return flow. This system limited capital accumulation in the region, which limited investment, which reduced the opportunities for the region to develop beyond its colonial economy. And everything limited urbanization. In fact, as the national economy grew after the Civil War, southern cities shrunk in proportion.

Southern leaders recognized their region's colonial position as early as the 1840s, and for the next century and a quarter they became obsessed with the growth ethic—an exaggerated form of boosterism that doted on demographic and economic statistics and on any scheme that could possibly stimulate growth and hence lessen dependency. The regional growth effort complemented the two other main factors of southern life. It required staple agriculture and a vigorous rural sector generally for the production of indigenous capital, and it solidified biracialism by appealing to the necessity for white solidarity in the great economic leap forward and by requiring strict curbs on black freedom to squeeze the maximum labor out of this important labor resource. It was no coincidence that the apogee of the so-called New South Creed and the nadir of black fortunes in the region occurred virtually at the same time in the late nineteenth century.

The Civil War and the Great Depression were two devastating events

that revealed the region as an economic minority and as an American muta-
tion: a region that lost in a nation that knew only victory, a region that was
poor in a country of wealth. The South and the southerner have been different from the rest of the nation, and the colonial economy was the most
outward manifestation of that minority status.

Southerners sought accommodation to this status. These adjustments indicated the paradoxes that characterized both regional and urban life. One
response was the desperate attempt of urban boosters to emulate their con-
querors. Though this boosterism was in fact quite conservative and fit in
well with the region's rural life-style and biracial society, the northern model
of economic growth clearly bothered some southerners. They did not reject
urbanization, industrialization, or economic development in general. They
merely sought to place them in a southern framework in order to retain
what was best about the South while achieving progress at the same time.

The antebellum Virginian George Fitzhugh attacked capitalism and free
competition because they produced "legalized exploitation." Under capitalism, he believed, "one man's success was marked by another man's failure."
So Fitzhugh advocated active government intervention on a wide variety
of economic fronts to prevent dehumanization while ensuring economic
growth. Northern contemporaries such as Ralph Waldo Emerson and Henry
David Thoreau were also concerned about the rapid ascension of the machine over man: "Things are in the saddle / And ride mankind," Emerson
wrote. But northern philosophical warnings did not provide any clues on
how the two might be reconciled and had little impact on urban and industrial progress. In the South, where progress was much less certain and where
philosophy more closely reflected life, southerners struggled with the dan-
gers and necessity of what southern theologian Albert Taylor Bledsoe called
"materiality."

After the Civil War, writer Edward A. Pollard sought a balance between
the material and the ethereal in the southern personality. He warned: "The
danger is that [southerners] will lose their literature, their former habits of
thought, their intellectual self-assertion, while they are too intent upon re-
covering the mere material prosperity." In the 1920s, author Thomas Wolfe
scorned the "cheap Board of Trade Boosters and blatant pamphleteers" of
his native Asheville, yet he also cautioned against a retreat into "cheap
mythology." Four decades later, Pat Watters complained about the "pellagra
of the body, mind, and soul" that overtook those imbued with traditional

beliefs, yet bemoaned "every misbegotten and misguided effort of the South to catch up to something that was essentially sorry and shabby in the rest of America."

So southerners suffered the fate of a permanent minority. The host culture was an incongruent though necessary presence that conflicted with traditional values, and the indigenous culture included numerous vestigial appendages that were incompatible with the majority society, yet comforting and familiar in their own manner. Northerners wrestled with the conflicts between progress and tradition, too, but they did so within the context of success. For southerners, nothing seemed to work. William Faulkner saw only a choice between the tired and weak ideals of the Yoknapatawpha aristocracy or the ways of the Snopeses who "out-Yankeed the Yankees." Thomas Wolfe loathed the "dusty little pint-measure minds" of Asheville and looked to New York as the South's urban inspiration, but, as Eugene Gant discovered in *Of Time and the River*, the golden city proved to be a false idol after all.

In 1930, Virginian Stringfellow Barr confronted John Crowe Ransom, a member of the Nashville Agrarians, a group of southern literati who sought a return to the simple virtues of a simple past. Writing in a depression-ridden region, the Agrarians challenged the assumptions of the New South prophets and their prescriptions for industrial and urban growth. To the Agrarians, it seemed appropriate to retreat to the comforting past and wait until the world came to its senses. The Agrarian movement could only have taken place in the South, because only in that region would the notion that a society could actually opt out of the twentieth century attract serious attention. It was a charming, quaint notion, to be sure, but also a reflection of how deeply disappointed the Agrarians were that the South seemed to be losing its traditions without anything to show for it except a colonial economy and a bankrupt philosophy. So they took their stand for the past. Poet Stephen Vincent Benét's words seemed to encapsule the Agrarians' cause; "there is a melancholy pride / In never choosing the winning side."

But Barr was clearly troubled, also. Here was no "cheap Board of Trade Booster" but a noted southern critic and philosopher. He saw the coming industrial and urban revolution as a golden opportunity for the South to save mankind: "The South faces a brilliant chance for a new industrial experiment that will rehabilitate her economically without wrecking her spiritually." Here was perhaps the final chance for the South to come to terms with progress on the region's own terms. How would Barr achieve this momentous compromise? He urged the South to enact legislation to protect both communities and workers from the industrial abuses common in the North. Such mechanisms as collective bargaining, workmen's compensation, and pensions would ensure the smooth transition of southern society into a humane machine age. But, as Ransom was quick to point out, these were greater violations of southern traditions than industry itself: "Neither Mr. Barr nor anybody else will ever succeed in regulating into industrialism the dignity of personality which is gone as soon as the man from the farm goes in the factory door. . . . He [Barr] stands for the strongest unionism. . . . And the grand finale of regulation, the millenium itself, is Russian communism."

The irony of it all was that the very traditions Ransom defended facilitated rather than impeded the most abusive aspects of urban and industrial development, and Barr's suggested responses both contradicted tradition and would have removed a major inducement to progress. The South retained its traditions amid the cities and factories and molded both to its own distinctive image. So Progress and Tradition were actually two sides of the same southern coin, and their affinity accounts in part for the affinity of southern city and region.

The worlds of the cotton field and of the skyscraper are essentially the same. They both sprang from rural traditions dominated by staple agriculture and its values; they both nurtured a biracial society; and together agrarianism and biracialism supported a colonial economy that was quickly and expertly exploited by a region not burdened by its past. The southerner seems to have taken literally Agrarian Robert Penn Warren's dictum that "if you could not accept the past and its burden there was no future." The southerner carried the burden of his past into the present and left its legacy for the future. In no other region is the past so much a part of its present, and its cities so much a part of both.

I ❧ Pearls on the Coast and Lights in the Forest
The Colonial Era

Like pearls on a string, the cities of colonial America lined the Atlantic coast from Boston to Savannah. We recall the maps in those otherwise forgettable textbooks of our childhood years: the cities in geographic single file, clinging to their watery niches. The distance between Boston and Savannah, though, was more than in miles. The New England settlers wrote to their British comrades across the sea of a wilderness that was abundant but very difficult, a challenge appropriate for testing the mettle of God's chosen. The letters from the southern latitudes likened the country to paradise—a lush, easy place where modest effort brought forth great rewards. It was not only a different way of looking at the world that separated northern and southern colonies; they were in fact different worlds.

Climate, geography, and geology facilitated life in the colonial South; they inhibited it in the colonial North. The rivers in the southern colonies ran deep into the interior, creating luxuriant bottomlands as they ran their courses. The mountain spine that divided eastern America from the Ohio country was conveniently deep into the southern interior. Even here, there lay a fertile valley—a highway for travel and a soil for cultivation. The climate, though a bit uncomfortable during the summer months, allowed a long growing season. The kaleidoscopic beauty of late October in the lower Shenandoah or the colorful floral array of Charleston in late March lifted southern hearts when New England was painted gray. Climate and geography made the South distinctive. The civilization, more particularly the urban civilization that grew from these natural conditions, would indelibly bear the character of land and weather.

Several decades ago, historians debated whether cities or farms were the first settlements on the American frontier. Richard C. Wade's book on the trans-Appalachian frontier of the late eighteenth and early nineteenth century was among the most influential statements on the subject. He contended that cities, not farms, were the spearheads of civilization on the frontier. Wade's "cities," however, were for the most part military outposts, artificially sustained by eastern supplies and capital. Were it not for the farmers who followed closely on the heels of the departing Indians, these settlements would have returned to forests. An agricultural surplus was necessary for the emergence of cities.

As British policymakers discovered ruefully, however, the existence of an agricultural surplus was a prerequisite but not a guarantee for urban development. Yet the British had several good reasons for wanting their colonists to "plant in towns." First, they could not conceive of civilization as they knew it to exist without towns. The colonies, in the midst of the wild frontier, could easily lose the trappings of Western culture and assume the manners and tastes of their surrounding environment. Second, the colonists as individual settlers were vulnerable against enemy attack—Indian, French, or Spanish. The English mind, only recently removed from the reality of walled cities and fortified towns, equated urban life with security. Anxious Carolina proprietors wrote to some prospective settlers in the 1660s: "we must assure you that it is your and our concern very much to have some good towns in your plantations for otherwise you will not long continue civilized or secure, there being no place in the world either of these without towns."

Finally, there were commercial-administrative reasons why the English government and its New World representatives urged the growth of towns. From their European experience, they saw towns, at the very least, serving as marketplaces—convenient gathering points—for agricultural and industrial production. The towns facilitated and financed production in a reciprocal arrangement: as the farms grew, so did the cities, encouraging expansion of cultivation, which in turn stimulated urban growth. In addition, the commercial legislation, weighted toward the mother country in a colonial economy, was most readily administered at urban focal points. The difficulties involved with overseeing the economic activities of a diffuse population were obvious.

Besides simple encouragement, there were periodic schemes designed to promote urban settlement in the face of an apparent southern colonial resistance to do so. In the 1660s, when the nonurban appearance of the Chesapeake colonies (Maryland and Virginia) was a source of both incredulity and concern in official circles, the Carolina proprietors published lengthy directives for the creation of agricultural villages that would also function as commercial centers. The combination of farming and urban activities was common throughout Europe and, as New England demonstrated, appeared in the New World as well, where such settlements solved the problems of food supply and commercial-administrative function. Later, in 1730, Governor Robert Johnson of South Carolina, looking more to security than to commercial-administrative problems, recommended the establishment of ten frontier towns to protect and thereby encourage interior settlement.

These plans, and the more general official encouragement, were unsuccessful. And here the influence of the distinctive geographic and climatic conditions of the colonial South is evident. The rivers that spread like fingers from the coastal plain to the interior discouraged concentrated settlement. The fertile lands along the winding rivers proved ideal for agriculture, and their abundance from coast to fall line enticed thousands of settlers. For the traditionally land-starved Englishman, the plentiful supply of good land made huddling together in small villages unnecessary, unattractive, and unremunerative.

In addition, these rivers were navigable deep into the interior. This allowed the planters to market their own crops, removing one of the primary functions of towns. Ships, even oceangoing vessels in the Chesapeake colonies, sailed up to the docks of individual farmers, unloaded their goods from England, and took on tobacco or rice. The planter doubled as merchant, eliminating the middleman and therefore maximizing his profits (and risk as well).

This scenario was especially apt for the Chesapeake colonies, where the Chesapeake Bay and the rivers of the Virginia colony were like so many miniature seas. The respective colonial governments of Maryland and Virginia, in futile attempts to override nature, passed fourteen acts promoting town growth during the last half of the seventeenth century. By 1710, the failure of urban settlement was so complete that officials permanently abandoned legislative town-building efforts. As the Reverend Hugh Jones wrote in 1724, "neither the interest nor inclinations of the Virginians induce them to cohabit in towns."

The situation was much the same further south. The Carolina proprietors' agricultural village scheme failed. The abundance of good land, especially on the irregular coastal plain in North Carolina, resulted in scattered farms rather than the hoped-for villages. Governor Johnson's military villages fared little better in South Carolina sixty years later. Only one of Johnson's ten towns—Orangeburg—was permanently established. The nine others simply could not counteract the centrifugal tendencies of the population, even on the hazardous frontier.

If towns were to emerge in the colonial South—and they did—legislation and wishes were obviously poor incentives. The same geographic pattern that encouraged dispersed settlement would also dictate the nature and extent of the urban settlements that eventually emerged amidst the farms. As the Chesapeake and Carolina regions settled into staple production patterns, which abundant land and accommodating soil made possible by 1700, towns developed to service staple agriculture at various levels. The type of staple agriculture in turn determined the type of urban settlement.

The connection between staple production and urbanization was apparent with tobacco, the leafy monarch of the Chesapeake. The weed's popularity in Europe was such that as early as the 1620s tobacco grew in the streets of Jamestown, the forlorn first town of the Virginia colony. The marketing demands of the crop complemented the Chesapeake's geographic condition. Tobacco marketing in the colonial era did not require intermediaries. When the tobacco fleet arrived from England in October and November, the planter simply packed his crop into hogsheads (roughly four hundred pounds each) and rolled them to the nearest dock (frequently his own) where he bargained with the captain for the price.

By the early eighteenth century, however, Europeans had developed a discriminating taste for tobacco that required more quality control at the colonial end of the trade. Also, tobacco cultivation had become so extensive that the individual deals struck between captain and planter were becoming less feasible if the ships were not to remain in the colonies most of the fall and winter. Perhaps most important, the tobacco trade had become big business by the 1700s. London and Liverpool merchants were not content to entrust their profit margins to itinerant captains or refractory planters, so they sent agents to the Chesapeake to establish bases of operations to end the uncertainties of the traveling tobacco show.

The result in town building from these initiatives was quite small. Geography again limited what might have been an urban boom under the new arrangements, because the continued availability of good cropland, especially in Virginia, restricted population in the towns. Moreover, the numerous estuaries and rivers that dotted the Chesapeake made communication difficult if a traveler's or a cargo's destination was not along the same river. In order to negotiate the 120 miles between Williamsburg and Annapolis, for example, more than a dozen ferries and considerable hours were required. Hence the market area for the farms along these winding riverine highways was small, and as a consequence the towns that marketed the tobacco from these farms were also small. In fact, shipping tobacco was the only function performed by these communities. This activity did not serve as a base for developing other urban functions because such functions were unnecessary given the geographic conditions of the Chesapeake colonies and the relatively uncomplicated marketing requirements of tobacco.

But urban Chesapeake was to get new life in the 1740s with the introduction of a new agriculture. The decline of tobacco prices and the increased food demands in Europe encouraged the cultivation of wheat in certain areas of the Chesapeake colonies. The marketing of wheat, unlike tobacco, required several procedures that could be conducted best in central locations, *i.e.*, towns, and the processing and subsequent storage requirements of the crop facilitated the growth of larger urban settlements. Baltimore was a direct beneficiary of wheat cultivation, being able to tap the wheatfields of Pennsylvania and western Maryland. In the Piedmont and Valley regions of Virginia, where farmers began to shift to grains, Richmond, Fredericksburg, and Staunton grew as wheat markets to supplement an unstable tobacco trade. Whereas the tobacco trade had rarely sustained towns of more than three hundred residents, the wheat trade succeeded in building cities like Baltimore that exceeded six thousand people by the time of the Revolution. In the 1780s, tobacco regained profits and favor in southern and eastern Maryland and in Virginia, so these areas remained overwhelmingly rural.

The interaction between geography, staple cultivation, and urban development was equally apparent further south, where the string of pearls on the Atlantic thinned out considerably. There was Norfolk, a struggling little seaport of six hundred persons in 1775, existing as a rendezvous for the British navy and by the grace of royal commercial regulations. Williamsburg also appeared on the map, but despite its importance as a colonial capital, it could never generate more than two hundred permanent residents, and the only trading of importance conducted in Williamsburg was of a political nature. That Williamsburg achieved a reputation beyond its meager numbers is a tribute to the people who occasionally visited there to pass laws and swat mosquitoes and to its unique town plan, which introduced Baroque civic design to the New World.

The city, planned by Theodorick Bland, provided an excellent interplay between government buildings and street layout. The linear pattern featured one major thoroughfare—Duke of Gloucester Street—along which were located the major structures and activities of the community. At one end of the street, at the College of William and Mary, the linear pattern broke off into branches, a common Baroque device. However, Bland's interesting plan was insufficient to sustain a population, and only latter-day tourism has rescued the community from weeds.

Williamsburg was an interesting but insignificant (in terms of urban development) knot on the strand, and there was virtually nothing to fill the strand in the neighboring colony of North Carolina. The hazardous shoals of the Outer Banks precluded the emergence of an important seaport, and the small ports, more administrative than trading centers, like Edenton, New Bern (the colonial capital), and Wilmington served only their immediate hinterlands in the fertile coastal plain, much as the small Chesapeake tobacco ports did. Geography more than crop cultivation accounted for the colony's urban anemia. The navigable rivers flowing into backcountry North Carolina emptied into South Carolina, so the lumber and wheat cultivation that characterized interior North Carolina ultimately benefited the urban growth of Charleston.

Charleston was the major southern colonial urban center, with a population of ten thousand by the time of the Revolution. Its development reflected the history of crop cultivation and geography in the Carolina region. The city's early growth resulted from the deerskin trade, which demanded extensive storage facilities and produced sufficient capital to enable the city to become an important credit center as well, moving beyond the level of simple marketing functions. With this foundation, as well as an extensive commercial network in the backcountry, Charleston merchants helped to develop the rice, slave, and lumber trades that generated relatively rapid urban growth after 1730. When England allowed South Carolinians to export rice directly to southern Europe in that year, Charleston merchants reaped the benefits. Rice, like wheat, required extensive marketing, storage, and processing facilities. Finally, as the hub of rice cultivation, Charleston was also the leading slave market in the colonial South. The human cargo provided additional capital for its merchants, which in turn enhanced the city's influence as a credit center.

Rice cultivation spun a culture of its own in Charleston. City and country merged in the Carolina capital. The rice planters, some of whom had begun their careers in Charleston and all of whom had economic ties to the city, built comfortable townhouses of brick or cypress and yellow pine to complement their spacious country homes. Indeed, some interesting architectural forms appeared late in the colonial period as the planters attempted to duplicate the comfort and privacy of their plantation homes on a city lot. The result was a home with narrow street frontage and the ubiquitous porch or veranda extending back on the side of the long lot. These lots were sufficiently deep for servants' quarters, stables, a kitchen, and the usual garden. The symmetrical, well-proportioned exterior design of the houses and the hand-carved woodwork and paneled rooms in their interiors reflected the influence of the Georgian architecture then popular in England. As a combination urban plantation home and Georgian townhouse, the Charleston residence of the rice planter was a home away from home in more ways than one.

Charleston was a seasonal residence. Its life beat to an agricultural rhythm —vibrant in the winter months, languid during the rest of the year except for a few months in late summer when the "sickly season" in the low country brought planters and their families to the city. The activities during the winter season swirled about the planters in a perpetual round of balls, theater performances, dinner parties, and concerts. It was as if these sometime city residents were absorbing all of the social life they could to last them through the isolation of the growing season, when there would not be another white family for miles.

By the mid-1760s, the St. Cecilia Society had become a major focal point of Charleston social life. It was a men's club much after the London fashion. Initially, the society was a music appreciation association, but its concerts soon became secondary to the balls that followed them. These affairs were the highlights of the Charleston social season, a season that moved a dazzled St. Jean de Crèvecoeur to proclaim the Carolina port as "the most brilliant of American cities."

All was not dancing and frivolity in the rice capital, however. By the time the St. Cecilia Society had organized its first ball, the merchants of Charleston had been organizing a wide network of commercial partnerships that helped to link the backcountry with the coastal capital. Recalling the strand of pearls along the coast, it is perhaps easy to forget that urban civilization penetrated the interior forests of colonial America and in some instances would rival coastal counterparts in the nineteenth century.

Backcountry Carolina settlement began unpretentiously as military garrisons in the early eighteenth century. The forts soon expanded their security functions to supply soldiers and frontier traders. They were also convenient collection points for the important deerskin trade to Charleston. Here too, the nature of the deerskin trade—the need for storage and processing facilities—stimulated urban growth. After the 1730s when the deerskin trade declined in importance, these backcountry towns easily shifted to marketing wheat, hemp, and indigo to Charleston merchants.

Charleston entrepreneurs did not wait for backcountry resources to pour into their laps, however. After years of organizing the deerskin and later the rice commerce, they learned that organization meant efficiency. They nurtured the frontier outposts and lined their own pockets with the profits.

Camden, South Carolina, located 125 miles northwest of Charleston along a major trade road to the backcountry deerskin commerce, was one such Charleston protégé. Charleston merchants sent agents to the interior town, much as London merchants sent representatives to the Chesapeake tobacco towns, to serve as formal links between coast and backcountry and to ensure an orderly, steady flow of commerce in both directions. By the 1740s, Camden had transcended its initial function as a collecting point to engage in some minor industry. When the transformation of the backcountry from trapping to farming resulted in wheat cultivation in the Camden area, merchants in Camden erected mills to process wheat, which they then shipped to Charleston.

The growth of Camden reflected the growth of functions. No longer an appendage of Charleston, it was becoming an urban settlement in its own right with the development of backcountry agriculture. The town boasted a sawmill, a circuit court, a warehouse, two meetinghouses, a jail, and some fine residences. Commercial, industrial, and administrative functions had transformed the backwoods outpost into a full-fledged trading partner with Charleston.

The Camden experience was repeated throughout the colonial South wherever a primary coastal center, linked to the interior by roads or rivers, helped to build commercial bases in the backcountry. In Virginia, communities like Alexandria, Norfolk, Richmond, and Petersburg, located at the heads of river navigation, were no rivals to imperial Charleston, but they too stimulated interior development in such towns as Dumfries and Colchester, downriver from Alexandria, and Leedstown and Hobbes Hole, down the Rappahannock from Fredericksburg.

Here, in outposts of fifty to one hundred citizens, the line between rural and urban was surely blurred—a characteristic of a frontier society. Frequently, these types of communities began as mere extensions of a plantation where an enterprising planter had established a gristmill, some warehouses, and a country store for the benefit of neighbors and the profit of himself. In fact, descriptions of larger plantations, especially those in the Carolina low country, read much like accounts of small towns. One such plantation, not atypical, included a dairy, a large gristmill, a sawmill, and a store stocked with the latest inventory from Charleston. The clearing in the forest, the farm with a gristmill and a store shared characteristics of both urban and rural environments, but were neither.

By the 1750s, however, a remarkable wave of immigration to the Carolina backcountry established and expanded previously marginal settlements into full-fledged urban places with their economic livelihood firmly grounded with the farmers in the surrounding countryside. During the 1750s, settlers from western Pennsylvania and Virginia streamed into backcountry Carolina attracted by land and the security against Indian attack. Immigration increased during the 1760s to include an ethnic mix that still characterizes these backcountry areas today. The German and Swiss settled in already-existing outposts such as New Windsor and Saxa Gotha; the Scotch-Irish in Ninety-Six and the Waxhaws; and the Welsh Baptists, Irish Quakers, and French Huguenots in similar interior settlements, giving the backcountry a unique international flavor.

The development of Saxa Gotha indicated the vagaries of backcountry urbanization. The town was one of Governor Johnson's frontier settlements of the 1730s, but it languished until some seventy Swiss families moved there in the 1740s, and soon a church and school appeared as landmarks of civilization. The town's location on a river that penetrated further into the backcountry led to the establishment of a gristmill once farmers began cultivating the surrounding region. Charleston merchants also established their interests in the town by the 1760s, and inns, warehouses, and homes soon filled out the growing community. By that time, the story of Saxa Gotha was similar to the evolution of Camden, though on a much smaller scale.

By the time of the Revolution, similar urban settlements had evolved as far as three hundred miles from Charleston. Considering the distances and the primitive transportation available, the ties with the coast were quite tenuous. The very distance from the coastal capital forced, in effect, the creation of central locations in the interior to supply the frontier population, serve as temporary security, and eventually serve as a marketplace for surplus agricultural production. Nevertheless, when the British attempted to force the backcountry to capitulate by blockading Charleston, they understood that however independent these backcountry communities seemed, their lifeline to Charleston—for capital and goods—was unmistakable. For Charleston, the Camdens and the Saxa Gothas enabled that pearl of the Atlantic to maintain and increase its luminescence.

The diligence of Charleston merchants in establishing commercial links to the interior received additional inspiration when a rival city appeared on the strand to the south of the Carolina port. Savannah was indeed a gem of the ocean. At least, that is what its imaginative mentor, James Oglethorpe, had in mind when he planned the city in 1733. The outlines of his good sense can still be seen in the tree-lined streets and periodic interruptions of parks and rest places. Well into the nineteenth century, Savannah was one of the few cities in the country that provided sufficient open spaces for its citizens.

The same ideas that influenced the Carolina proprietors and South Carolina's Robert Johnson affected Oglethorpe: the belief in the importance of urban settlement, yet the recognition that rural features were necessary to temper the urban landscape. In Oglethorpe's view, the city and the country could be mutually reinforcing environments. The result—a middle landscape—would integrate the best from both worlds. Oglethorpe grew up with a generation that was beginning to see the problems of concentrated urban settlement. Indeed, a half century before Savannah appeared on the Georgia coast, William Penn had designed Philadelphia as a "green garden town" with spacious lots, an orderly gridiron street pattern, and five squares that served as America's first public parks.

Oglethorpe was aware of Penn's plan—Savannah copied the Philadelphia gridiron street pattern—and sought to improve upon it. The city was constructed of building-block units, or wards, each of which contained ten or a dozen house lots with an open square at the center. Since the city controlled surrounding lands, the expansion of Savannah could be easily regulated with the simple addition of wards as the need arose. This allowed for considerable expansion without the formless sprawl that was already evident in Philadelphia. In order to provide food for the community and to inject pastoral activities and values in the urban milieu, Oglethorpe surrounded the city with garden plots and larger farms. As one contemporary observer described it, "each Freeholder . . . has a Lott . . . beyond the Common of 5 Acres for a Garden. . . . Each Freeholder of the Tything [ten houses equaled one tything] has a Lott or Farm of 45 Acres. . . . Beyond . . . commerce Lotts of 500 Acres; these are granted upon Terms of keeping 10 servants."

As both city and countryside developed, the idea of the urban farmer became less plausible. The collection of plots and farms into larger units and the permanent residence of citizens either on the farm or in the city were becoming more common by the time of the Revolution. The city itself, however, with its relatively slow growth, was able to preserve the basic features of the "green garden town" plan, the disappearance of which had so frustrated William Penn.

English settlers were not the only southern colonists who appreciated the middle landscape ideal. The French in their European communities had compromised urban and rural life-styles. The wide avenues and formal gardens that were characteristic of urban planning during the reign of Louis XIV, as well as the smaller, less formal squares, were simultaneous attempts at the elegant and the pastoral. The French influence in the colonial South was confined to the Gulf Coast, an area that remained of only peripheral concern to the empire. After the establishment of Mobile in 1710, the French embarked on their most ambitious scheme in the area with the founding of New Orleans in 1722 by Jean Baptiste Le Moyne, sieur de Bienville. He held lofty aspirations for the city at the Mississippi delta. He intended a great capital, and his plan reflected these intentions. The focal point of Bienville's city was the *place d'armes*, a formal open ground now called Jackson Square. The formal *place*, a common French planning device at the time, was centered perfectly on the river and dominated by St. Louis

Cathedral. Later, government buildings and apartments of wealthy and prominent citizens joined the church on the *place*. Architecture historian Christopher Tunnard has called this grouping "the most important architectural plaza in the United States."

New Orleans did not achieve the hoped-for grandeur. The siting of the town may have been militarily efficacious, but for almost every other purpose it was unfortunate. Settlers constantly battled floods, tropical diseases, and virtual isolation from other settlements. The potentially rich farmlands in the area were hardly worked, so the city's economic potential went largely unfulfilled during the colonial period. Still, as early as 1727, there were nearly one thousand people in this mainly administrative and military outpost. By the late eighteenth century, Americans were arriving in significant numbers, bringing with them more aggressive business methods and staple-crop cultivation.

The isolation of New Orleans, though extreme, was not unique to that city. By the time of the American Revolution, urban civilization existed in the colonial South, but certainly not in an integrated urban network or a well-defined urban system with a distinctive hierarchy of urban places. Transportation, whether by roads or rivers, was problematic and seasonal. The type of steady reciprocal commercial flow characteristic of an urban network was missing in certain areas. Indeed, in some regions, towns of any size were missing. All settlements were small, with the exceptions of Charleston and New Orleans, and limitations on size implied limitations of functions that would preclude the evolution of an urban hierarchy. The frontier environment, in addition, was too unstable to support an urban network. Settlements were founded and frequently disappeared. Finally, the metropolis or primary city so necessary for the development of any system was absent.

Despite London's general failure to encourage urban settlement during the seventeenth century, the commercial policies of the eighteenth century had some impact on the growth and decline of towns. In 1691, when monarchs William and Mary designated certain ports of entry in Virginia, urban growth suddenly blossomed in that once-barren environment for towns. When royal officials attempted to pump some life into the sagging tobacco trade during the 1740s by consolidating tobacco shipments in certain Maryland towns, those communities not favored by the legislation literally disappeared.

The pattern of urbanization in the colonial South was similar to urban development in feudal Europe, which is not surprising considering the primitive surroundings and the lower-order economic activities. That pattern was decentralized, revolving around relatively parochial economies. The pattern reached an extreme in the Chesapeake, where geographic configurations produced a new economic region every ten miles or so. The towns of Virginia and Maryland, though in the same geographic area, probably had more communication with London than they had with each other.

It appeared that a network of some sort was in the process of creation by the 1770s. The river towns in the Chesapeake had established ties with smaller places along the river system. In the Valley of Virginia, a series of towns evolved by the 1760s with ties both to the coastal communities and to the towns in the western backcountry. The functional and size distinctions between these places were not sufficiently great to warrant the term *hierarchy*, however. These links, moreover, were irregular, and there was rarely contact with towns in other colonies.

In the Carolinas, the connections between low country and up-country, especially in the case of Charleston and its partners, were more developed, but they had little communication beyond the Carolina region. As with the Virginia towns, the distinctions between the dozens of settlements on the Carolina frontier were so minor that a hierarchical structure did not exist. The basic materials were there, however: coastal cities and backcountry towns that would later evolve into a system with connections beyond the region.

This development seemed evident, given the evolution of the urban South during the colonial period. Urbanization went through three general periods. During the seventeenth century, urban development was slight. The abundance of fertile land, the limited nature of staple-crop cultivation, and geographic patterns counteracted the directives and intentions of royal officials. The first half of the eighteenth century was the seedbed for sustained urban development in the colonial South. Staple cultivation burgeoned—wheat and rice production in particular—and increased manipulations by England's merchants and legislators stimulated urban growth. Finally, beginning in the 1740s, the establishment of Charleston as the colonial South's most important city, the growth of backcountry towns and cultivation, and the links between coast and frontier marked the third stage of urban development.

Urbanization throughout much of the period, though, was insignificant—indeed all of colonial America remained overwhelmingly rural up to and considerably beyond the Revolution. Even the appearance of urban settlements during the late colonial era was quite modest, certainly when compared with the more precocious northern towns, which benefited from a more diverse agricultural hinterland and, especially in New England, the relative scarcity of good climate, geography, and soil. Yet the colonial period is a crucial era for southern urbanization because the themes that characterized the distinctive development of the South's cities up to the present first appeared at that time.

To begin with, whatever direction southern urbanization would take in the post-Revolutionary era, it seemed evident that the peculiar characteristics of the region—its geography, climate, and crop cultivation, for some major examples—would mold the character of its cities. If the region were distinctive, so would its cities be distinctive. The colonial era had demonstrated that within the same colonial empire, very different patterns could emerge.

Second, a biracial society was emerging. Certainly, blacks, both free and slave, resided in areas outside the colonial South. The black population was greater in the South, however, and here staple-crop agriculture, particularly such labor-intensive crops as tobacco and rice, encouraged the use of black labor. The abundance of land—and large tracts of it—made the use of gang labor feasible and efficient. In a colonial society where labor was scarce, the African provided an excellent adaptation to soil, climate, and geography. Such a fixed capital investment ensured adherence to staple agriculture.

Slavery, however, was an urban institution as well. In the colonial era, when the line between slavery and freedom was unclear, the urban slave probably enjoyed more freedom than he would at any future time. Southern urban residents were just beginning to cope with the implications—legal and philosophical—of a biracial society by the time of the Revolution.

A practical and more immediate consequence of a biracial society was the creation of a class of low consumers. What towns existed maintained low functional levels in part because the demands and the capital of the surrounding population—in some areas over three-quarters slave—were limited. The relative absence of towns, especially of major ports of entry other than Charleston, discouraged the immigration of a free population. The growth of Boston and Philadelphia in the eighteenth century resulted in great part from the demand generated by the free white families who required provisions, implements, and livestock during their first years in the New World. This is not to say that slavery discouraged or retarded urbanization; slavery, after all, existed throughout colonial America. But it is evident that the large slave population and the relative absence of free migration reinforced the shallow urban development already evident in the colonial South.

The importance of the metropolis in determining the urban and economic future of a region was a third theme that first emerged in the colonial era. By the eighteenth century, the colonial administration in London had sufficient influence to enhance or inhibit urban growth in the American colonies. The power of legislation, especially commercial legislation, was understood in the colonies. Where possible, detrimental laws were avoided, but where this was not possible, oblivion and economic ruin were realistic concerns. This point was evident with all colonists, regardless of region, and more so in the cities where the economic stakes were highest. When avoidance was impossible, or when threatening measures seemed imminent, revolution was the alternative. Of course, the origin of the American Revolution was not as simple as that. But the colonists' long experience with the real and potential power of the metropolis was a crucial factor in fomenting revolutionary sentiment once that power was used in an adverse way.

The metropolis could affect urbanization in more subtle ways as well. Capital accumulation and consequently credit were constant problems in colonial economic life, and some colonies resorted to inflationary paper money to "solve" the difficulties of inadequate capital. The absence of banks in the colonial economy threw the responsibility of capital accumulation and credit upon urban merchants and planter-merchants. The system worked adequately in Charleston, for example, but ultimately the reins of capital were held in London. The coastal financiers were typically middlemen in the credit network. In fact, some planters dealt directly with London capitalists, bypassing local lenders. London had the banks, controlled the specie circulation (chronically short in the colonies), and therefore had as much influence on economic growth as the colonial financiers. This situation merely describes a typical colonial condition. It was, nevertheless, a well-remembered legacy of the colonial era. Banking, in fact, was a dominant issue during the first half century of national existence.

These then were to become the persistent themes of southern urbanization: the influence of the rural landscape and especially of staple agriculture, the presence of a biracial society, and the impact of the metropolis. The same forces, of course, affected the entire region. And that is the point. In the next period of southern history, the antebellum era, southerners would capitalize on the first, accommodate themselves to the second, and fight the third. In the process, they would become increasingly set apart from the rest of the nation, and so would their cities.

II ❧ Urbanization Without Cities
The Antebellum Era

Agriculture Is Commerce

Lovely Natchez. The phrase comes naturally, like hog jowls and hominy grits—inseparable and unmistakenly southern. Overlooking the Mississippi River, Natchez was an antebellum prototype. Its wharves were a mélange of white, brown, and black: white steam, white cotton, brown water, black men. Further back, the colors softened, the noise subsided, and the sun's broiling presence was tempered by trees, verandas, and cool lemonade. Visitors to this semitropical paradise were given to superlatives like "the best hedges and screens of evergreen shrubs . . . in America." Every home, no matter how mean, was invariably festooned with flowers and trees of various species. The grand houses of the city, those "rural residences" on "beautiful streets," furnished from England or France, lent a prosperous yet curiously rural air to this port city. Inside these urban plantation homes, high ceilings moderated the heat, graceful spiral staircases and ornate woodwork signified taste and wealth. Thousands of cotton bales and hundreds of slaves had purchased these mansions. Lined up along the leafy, flowered Natchez streets, their flashing white pillars announced that here stood wealth, substance, and style.

Natchez was an urban hybrid. In that sense it typified the antebellum urban South, even if its impressive architectural array had few rivals. The activity along the wharves gave all appearances of urban life, but back beyond the trees a more rural scene took shape. It was as if James Oglethorpe's idea of a middle landscape—a blend of city and country—had come to some illogical conclusion on the banks of the Mississippi.

The hybrid flourished in southern soil. Travelers commenting on the distinctions between northern and southern cities frequently lapsed into rural metaphors when describing the urban South. Of course, there was much that was far from pastoral in the cities of those days, but the landscaped beauty, the scent of magnolias, crepe myrtles, and mimosa, and the architectural styles as languid as the weather and adapted to it encircled and in some cases enraptured visitors as cities elsewhere never had.

Palmettos and magnolias graced the streets of Charleston, and a walk on the Battery "to inhale the pure and cool breezes . . . and to enjoy the view" was essential on the itinerary of any visitor. The homes with their courtyards and inevitable gardens—nature growing right up to the front door—added to the country atmosphere of the city. "Savannah," one visitor wrote to his northern friends, "is a city of trees and gardens." Away from the activity of the wharf, this traveler noted an "almost rural quiet." Romance awaited those who strolled along the levee at New Orleans with only moonlight and imagination as a guide. A bit further upriver, Baton Rouge was "clothed in flowers like a bride." Even on the Texas frontier, at Galveston, "one of the most charming places—in appearance—that I have ever seen," as one traveler exclaimed, the landscaping and the elegance of the residences along the Strand bespoke the same pastoral quietude as more civilized Natchez or Savannah.

Why did antebellum southern cities retain a rural aspect long after their northern counterparts had forgotten the values of trees, the uplifting beauty of flowers, and the use of space to liberate rather than to crowd? Indeed, southern cities were distinctly horizontal—low in density and in profile. The fact that typically the ratio of families to dwellings was one to one (this, of course, said nothing about quality) in southern cities but rarely that low in contemporary northern cities underscores the middle landscape observations recorded by visitors. The reasons for the continuing agrarian prospect do not lie in the close proximity of southern cities to nature. In an overwhelmingly rural nation, this was so everywhere. Rather, agriculture, especially the type of agriculture, was one determinant of the urban landscape of the South. The influence of staple agriculture and its concomitant features of climate and geography had indeed not changed since the colonial era, though the staple had.

To understand the antebellum southern city and its distinction, one must understand cotton. Cotton was not grown everywhere, of course, but its impact permeated the region. Planters in the low country grew cotton during the colonial era, but it was not until the invention and implementation of the cotton gin that cultivation became widespread. By the second decade of the nineteenth century, cotton had extended its kingdom from the South Atlantic to the lower Mississippi Valley. The staple was particularly suited to the black soil and long growing season characteristic of the Deep South. Cotton generated capital, spun industries, created insatiable demands for land and slaves that affected non-cotton-growing regions of the South and accordingly directed the course of the southern economy. If the demand for cotton was strong, prosperity would radiate throughout the region; if demand fell, so did the economy. Not surprisingly, cotton influenced the nature and type of antebellum southern urbanization.

In 1821, Lloyds of London predicted that in a short time New Orleans would become the world's greatest port. This bold statement was not necessarily based upon the impressive aspect of the city—its frontier scruffiness vied with French insouciance as the dominant feature of its life-style—but from the fact that 300,000 cotton planters had settled within its vicinity and, in the words of the last French governor, "have no other outlet than this river [the Mississippi] and no other port than New Orleans." These sanguine observations proved correct, or nearly so. Between 1820 and 1850, the Crescent City's population quadrupled to 116,000, making it the fifth largest city in the country. For a time during the 1830s, New Orleans actually outdistanced New York as an export center and thereafter maintained a close rivalry with its northern counterpart. Curiously, however, as one looked about the cotton belt, especially in the Black Belt and the upper Mississippi Delta, there was barely any urban civilization. The quietude of Natchez was matched by dozens of other delta towns. Except for Mobile, New Orleans seemed to enjoy an urban monopoly. Of the ten leading southern cities in 1850, only Mobile and New Orleans were in the cotton belt.

Cotton, like tobacco, required relatively few services. Processing largely occurred elsewhere—New England or Great Britain—so the only requisite for the crop's commercial success was an outlet to both of these locations. New Orleans merchants organized the trade by sending agents into upriver towns to collect the crop and, in turn, supply planters with wares. The volume of cotton production and the need for quality control and price stability militated against the diffuse trade that had marked tobacco commerce in the early colonial era, but the functions of upriver towns were limited to serving as collection points for the staple. Moreover, New Orleans' early re-

Leading Southern Cities, 1860

gional dominance of cotton commerce inhibited urban growth elsewhere in the region by restricting capital accumulation, since Crescent City merchants came to control local banks as well. Finally, as the regional center for the slave trade, New Orleans had another economic monopoly to drain capital from the hinterland. So cotton and capital both flowed to the Delta port.

Nature gave and took away. Charleston might have retained its colonial supremacy, but cotton quickly ravished Carolina soil and the fickle staple moved west to fresher surroundings. The city languished and so, to a lesser extent, did Savannah. Charleston, the sixth largest city in the country in 1830, had vanished from the top fifteen by the Civil War, yet it was the third largest city in the region behind New Orleans and Louisville. The population gap separating the first and third cities, however, was enormous. Charleston had only 2,500 fewer people than New Orleans in 1820. Forty years later, with a population of nearly 169,000, the Mississippi River port had outdistanced her Atlantic counterpart by four times.

Soil exhaustion was also a factor in the tobacco staple region of the Upper South. The Chesapeake (not including Baltimore, which was tied to wheat cultivating areas) and the North Carolina tobacco belt provided little sustenance for Richmond, Lynchburg, and Petersburg. Only in the 1850s, when these cities added the processing function, did growth occur, though on a modest scale.

Yet the figures are somewhat confusing. Between 1800 and 1850, the North's urban population grew two and one half times as rapidly as its total regional population, while the South's urban population increased at a rate more than three and one half times as rapidly as the whole population of that section. Thus urbanization was in fact occurring in the antebellum South. What was not occurring, however, was the development of large cities. The urban place with under four thousand people (by 1860) was more characteristic of the antebellum South than of any other region, and the urban population of the region was, therefore, more diffuse. This was consistent with the relatively low level of functions that southern towns performed in support of a staple-crop economy. The result was urbanization without cities.

In 1857, southern writer Daniel R. Hundley met a New Yorker aboard a steamboat cruising downriver to New Orleans. After several days of gazing over the polished wood rail, the New Yorker turned to Hundley and asked abruptly, "Where's your towns?" There were, of course, towns and cities in the Old South, but none that Hundley's provincial New Yorker was likely to find familiar. Even the largest cities—New Orleans, Charleston, Memphis, Mobile—were what sociologist Edgar Thompson termed "plantation cities," entertainment and marketing adjuncts to those self-sufficient agricultural units that were the mainsprings of the antebellum southern economy. "Mere trading posts," W. J. Cash called the best of them, and that is precisely and only what they were. If travelers occasionally wrote of bustling seaports and commercial vigor, they more frequently lapsed into descriptions of the urban flora much as if they were meandering through a lush wood. And these rural towns and cities were indeed quiet and green. White-painted towns dozing in the summer sun, strewn about with hogs, dogs, and a few people; a river lazily lapping against rotted wood pilings; a languid populace briefly awakening with the arrival of a steamboat—that smoking, belching monster that likely provided the only excitement for a day or a week, unless a revival was in town—and then quickly resuming its "at ease" posture waiting for nothing more than supper.

Returning to Natchez, it is understandable how small, relatively stagnant cities and towns could simultaneously commune with nature and load steamboats with cotton. But size and rate of growth were only partial indications of how staple agriculture made southern urbanization and southern cities distinctive. The dominance of staple agriculture not only had statistical implications but influenced the character of these southern market towns as well. Travelers visiting these communities knew little about relative rates of urbanization and market mechanisms, but they knew very well that what they were seeing and feeling was quite different. They were seeing, feeling, and writing about a unique urban form—an agrarian city.

The agrarian city existed because staple-crop agriculture not only dominated the fields but came to hold the hearts and minds of the region as well. The Jeffersonian view that agriculture was a prerequisite for a republican society persisted in the South long after northerners had abandoned or modified that equation, not because Jefferson was a Virginian but because, unlike the North, the South's economy derived primarily from staple agriculture. In addition, nature had blessed the South particularly, and this blessing, in a devout society, raised agriculture from a mere pursuit to a birthright.

In the Northeast, conditions were quite different. Although Emerson wrote about the benefits of the pastoral life, the experience of his New England countrymen hardly established a romantic role for agriculture. Ultimately, northeastern agriculture, which had battled soil and climate since the colonial period, was ruined by western competition. The release of workers from unproductive agriculture created an availability of laborers for the textile mills and growing cities of the region, and by the 1840s northern writers were already contrasting the diversified northern economy with the agrarian South, despite the fact that statistics emphasized greater similarity than difference between the two regions.

For southerners, "peculiar climate, peculiar productions, and still more peculiar institutions," as a South Carolina agriculturist explained, had "rendered agriculture the fundamental determinant of the entire southern way of life." Although it is possible to dismiss some of this as agrarian hyperbole, there was empirical evidence of agricultural dominance in virtually every aspect of southern life, including the city.

Staple agriculture formed the economic base for the urban South. The proliferation of small urban places meant, among other things, that marketing staple products was the main if not the only economic activity of much of the urban South. But even in the larger urban settlements—what few existed—the dominance of the staple crop was evident. In New Orleans, visitors observed with some annoyance that conversations with residents invariably took one track: cotton prices, cotton planting, cotton climate, cotton soil, and cotton labor. Scarcely a shopkeeper or professional in the city was untouched by the economic vagaries of the staple. In Richmond, where tobacco controlled the economy, a slightly asphyxiated visitor to the city in 1860 commented that "the atmosphere . . . is redolent of tobacco; the tints of the pavements are those of tobacco. One seems to breathe tobacco, to see tobacco, and smell tobacco at every turn. The town is filthy with it."

Observers recorded impressions, but urban residents recorded debits or credits depending on the extent of staple cultivation in any particular year. The economy of Shreveport, Louisiana, demonstrated the total dependence of southern urban centers on staple agriculture. With a population of over 3,500 in 1860, Shreveport was typical of the numerous Mississippi River collection points that gathered cotton for the New Orleans market. The city's economy was actually based on three types of activities. First, cotton planters from the surrounding countryside brought their cotton to Shreveport merchants for shipment downriver to New Orleans. Second, merchants supplied local planters and farmers with items ranging from agricultural implements to patent medicines—most of which came up from New Orleans. Finally, there were a few small industrial enterprises in the community, the most important of which was the manufacture of cotton gins. This self-styled "unquestioned commercial emporium of Northwestern Louisiana" was, therefore, a creature of cotton, and its economy fluctuated to the rise and fall of cotton prices.

Indeed, the economic cycle of southern cities can be followed simply by looking at staple-crop prices. The 1850s were the most prosperous years for southern cities and not coincidentally for staple agriculture. The production of cotton doubled between 1849 and 1859, while prices rose generally. The prosperity of tobacco was less spectacular but with similar results. Across the South, rapid urban growth reflected the good years in the fields during the 1850s. New Orleans, after struggling for two decades, rebounded with a 45 percent population increase in the decade before the Civil War. The growth of cotton cultivation in Arkansas and Mississippi led to the sudden growth of Memphis—155 percent during the 1850s. And in Savannah, where tired soil surrounded a tired city, its citizens found that, with enterprise, fertilizers, and high cotton prices, they too could undergo a renaissance, which was reflected by a 45 percent growth rate between 1850 and 1860.

The connection between staple production and the urban economy was so marked that contemporary commentators discounted those places that did not have access to staple crops. The unsuitability of Atlanta's hinterland for staple cultivation was deemed a certain indication of a dismal future for the nascent railroad junction. Observers prophesied that the absence of staple cultivation ensured that "the place can never be much of a trading city," though they conceded that in due time the unfortunate town would "be a good place for one tavern, a blacksmith shop, a grocery store, and nothing else." Yet it was precisely this relative agrarian poverty that eventually saved Atlanta from being just another pretty little cotton-market town.

Not only the urban economy but the urban life-style moved to an agricultural rhythm. Towns slept from late spring to early fall and awoke with the arrival of the first cotton or tobacco shipments. Even a metropolis like New Orleans did not have a life of its own apart from the dictates of the cotton fields. "New Orleans," journalist J. D. B. De Bow wrote with some dismay, "about the first of June, begins to show evidences of waste. People inquire of steam and rail routes, and are buying trunks. The hotels look very shabby, and the parlors have lost their lustre. The streets are parched and dry." Of course, many residents were escaping another southern natural phenomenon—the onset of yellow fever season—but even if the city had been healthy, there was simply nothing to do while the cotton was still in the fields.

The tempo picked up in the fall and especially in early winter. Then the towns and cities were colorful panoplies of wagons, farmers, traveling salesmen, women of pleasure, barkers, riverboatmen, slaves, ships, and railroad locomotives. Cities arranged their yearly social and cultural calendars around staple marketing time. February, for example, was the "gay time" for a revived Charleston of the 1850s, and the horse-racing season was a particular attraction for visiting planters. The quality of cultural entertainment in the urban South was generally low. The visiting agriculturists, after all, had little to compare it with and settled for lowbrow entertainment as a welcome diversion from the isolation of the countryside. The theater in Natchez was located in a graveyard, and reports indicated that the plays were equally deadly. Occasionally great performers such as the Irish actor

Tyrone Power or American thespian Edwin Booth graced the sometimes-primitive arenas in southern towns, but it is likely that fashion rather than theater appreciation was the major motivation of the theatergoers.

The influence of the planters went beyond their physical presence during these gay times. Perhaps to escape the crowded and frequently uncomfortable hotels, but more likely to display their wealth and maintain an urban base, many planters built residences in the city. Natchez was an extreme example of the agrarian proclivity for an urban address, but other cities from Charleston to Galveston contained the planters' seasonal residences. In some of the smaller towns like Demopolis, Alabama, or Clinton, Mississippi, planters constructed year-round residences on the periphery near their cotton plantations. And of course the architecture of all these urban mansions reflected the plantation influence. The huge columned porches and plain Greek pediments reflected romantic ideals that a civilization could be built out of brick and wood in the vast agrarian environment that was the antebellum South.

The urban connection for the planter was usually more personal and warm than the sometimes coldly austere version of Greek Revival architecture implied. There existed an economic and intellectual community of interests between himself and the urban merchants with whom he dealt that was the most personal urban extension of the plantation. The identification between planter and merchant went beyond the fact that planters occasionally built homes in town and urban merchants dreamt of plantation homes in the countryside. Their mutual interests were inextricably entwined in other areas.

"Agriculture is commerce, and commerce is agriculture," the Richmond *Enquirer* declared matter-of-factly in 1859. On this axiom, planters and merchants constructed railroads together, held agricultural fairs in cities, invested in factories, and exchanged labor. When rival cities challenged each other for commerce and prestige, rural politicians rushed to their respective market partners with support for internal improvements. The urban press in turn frequently pushed agrarian interests in their columns. This does not imply that the partners did not quarrel occasionally. Farmers complained about the prices that urban merchants charged, and urban merchants wondered why those tobacco hogsheads occasionally contained more stems and less leaf than advertised. But greater distinctions existed between cities than between town and country. In the words of a Norfolk editor, "the city is benefitted with the country; their interests are often one in the same."

The leadership in the antebellum urban South was predominantly mer-cantile, a fact that ensured an environment that facilitated commerce—*i.e.*, exchange between town and country. The leaders controlled the economic and political institutions of the community and utilized both to enhance this exchange. For the accommodation of goods and persons, iron-framed mar-ket-houses and hotels were erected, "so that our customers have the best accommodations that can be afforded." For amusement, theaters and con-cert halls provided necessary diversions. A delighted farmer from a neigh-boring county recalled that Alexandria, Virginia, "used to be as dull as the d---l after night—no amusement—nothing to do—no where to go. . . . Now that some of your enterprising citizens have established a Theatre, do pray keep it—you'll see the benefits in a very little while." Finally, in the larger cities, the numbering of houses and the publication of city directories detailing clubs, amusements, and business addresses helped to orient visi-tors from the country.

The motivation behind all of these improvements was to secure and maintain the business of the countryside. All cities hoped to present the best possible face and attraction to visitors, but this desire had more urgency in the urban South. Since southern towns were relatively small, with clearly defined and limited market areas, and since, particularly after the 1840s, transportation improved throughout the region, the threat was always pres-ent that rural customers might take their business elsewhere. That option concerned merchants everywhere, but in the smaller cities and towns, with their one-dimensional and hence fragile economies, a loss of trade meant ruin.

Perhaps cynics could suggest that the pastoral beauty for which the ur-ban South was uniquely noted was, in fact, a calculated device by commu-nity leaders to make potential rural customers feel more at home. Beauty, it may be argued, was good business. Though this contention seems a bit far-fetched, there was definitely something more than met the eye in the physi-cal appearance of southern cities. "Beauty is only skin deep" is a cliché, but an apt description of the southern town.

Given a mercantile leadership, it was not unusual that local government everywhere in antebellum America was a sort of political chamber of com-merce. In the South, however, this philosophy not only became a way of governing, but a way of life. There were at least three reasons why this was so. First, although staple agriculture generated considerable wealth, only one-third of this wealth stayed within the region. Southern cities were typically not processing or finishing centers. If foreign export, as with cotton and tobacco, characterized a crop, southern ports rarely became involved in international trade. Products that farmers required were frequently manufactured elsewhere, and the credit to buy (and to grow) often came from financial centers outside the region. The low level of capital accumulation, combined with the wild fluctuations of staple commodities tied to a world market, did not create sound financial systems for southern cities. In prosperous times, southern urban politicians had limited financial resources, and in bad times they had none. Accordingly, these limited funds had to be applied selectively. And they were appropriated primarily with the hope that such application would generate more of a scarce resource—capital.

Second, blacks comprised anywhere from a quarter to two-thirds of the population in southern cities. Expenditures in social, educational, or other "nonbusiness" services could directly or indirectly assist this population, but slaves were thought to be the responsibility of their masters, and blacks in general were simply not considered appropriate concerns of local governments unless they seemed threatening. Even then, the threat would need to be quite substantial to loosen tight city purse strings.

Finally, though biracial, the southern urban population, except in New Orleans, was relatively homogeneous compared with that in northern cities. Urban immigrants were predominantly rural southerners, though Germans and Irish began to enter southern cities in appreciable numbers in the 1850s. Given the identification between rural and urban southerners and the blending of the two environments, it was not unusual for rural values like religion and strong family ties to persist with greater strength in the urban South than in cities outside the region. This was especially so when the values that underlay most churches and families stemmed from similar roots. Consequently, reliance on family, kinfolk networks, and church in times of crisis, distrust of government and its institutions, and the fatalistic acceptance of poverty, disease, or ignorance as religious judgments were important cultural characteristics that affected behavior and perceptions throughout the South.

The spread of evangelical Protestantism to antebellum southern cities indicates how common religious values pervaded city and countryside. Beginning in forest clearings and on isolated riverbanks, preaching to hardbitten, lonely pioneers, southern evangelists carried their message of man's basic depravity and the assurance of salvation to the region's cities. The great revival that excited the region in 1857 was primarily an urban phenomenon.

Evangelists sought city audiences—their numbers and wealth far outdistanced the spartan gatherings on the frontier. Evangelical Protestantism did not yet represent the major religious force in cities, or in the South as a whole for that matter, but it arrived at a time of religious ferment, when not only the church but southern society in general came to be defined in religious terms. The debate over slavery and the increased bitterness of sectional controversy heightened religious consciousness in the South. Presbyterian minister J. H. Thornwell, from his seat in Columbia, South Carolina, told his congregation in 1850 that "the parties in this conflict are not merely abolitionists and slaveholders—they are atheists, socialists, communists, red republicans, jacobins on the one side, and the friends of order and regulated freedom on the other."

Order and regulation were indeed divine dicta for southerners in the troubled 1850s, and they cast a conservative pall over southern cities, limiting literary and artistic expression, excusing official neglect of civic problems, and generally idealizing the status quo. "Every man was in his place," W. J. Cash wrote of the southern mind in that fateful decade, "because He had set them there. Everything was as it was because He had ordained it so." The South, Cash continued, was en route to "the savage ideal: to that ideal whereunder dissent and variety are completely suppressed." If difference and diversity were basic characteristics of antebellum American urban civilization, then here was another way in which southern cities followed distinctive regional ideals. Urban leaders rarely stated these values when proposing their actions—though frequently invoking Providence as an excuse for inaction. The values were, nonetheless, silent partners in the council chambers and budget committees and, because of the relatively homogeneous population, were shared by most urban residents.

Local urban government functioned, therefore, within the financial, racial, and psychological limits established by the region's rural society. Urban leaders adopted a primitive cost-benefit formula that they applied to decisions on funding for various services. Simply put, if local legislators believed the economic return (*i.e.*, strengthening the staple connection) from a particular service expenditure would outweigh that expenditure, they would fund the service; if the balance tilted in the other direction, they would reject the service request. As businessmen, they had, of course, their own biases, which affected the equation, although most sincerely believed they were acting for the benefit of the entire community.

In the matter of streets, for example, visitors were often impressed by the

neat, pastoral residential streets of the well-to-do areas or by the commodi-
ous main business streets. Actually, however, southern streets were generally
horrible. A popular story of the period that made the rounds in the southern
press told of a citizen who rushed into the street to help a man buried up to
his neck in mud. "No need to worry," the entombed victim replied, "I have a
horse underneath me." The story doubtless produced much recognition in
New Orleans, where the mud was so deep for so long that local government
never bothered investing in paving stones, believing that the stones would
sink and disappear as fast as the citizen's horse did. New Orleans had rivals,
however. One foreign visitor found Richmond's streets "the most dirty,
rough, and disagreeable streets to walk on that are to be found perhaps in
the Union." Another traveler, this one in Mobile, disagreed, claiming that
city's streets were "worse than I have ever seen." Indeed, the typical pedestrian found himself wading in mud or choked by dust, depending on the
season.

Street paving, as with other services, was a selective activity. Abutting
property owners theoretically provided a portion or all of the total cost, but
in reality most property owners refused to pay the assessment. City councils, however, would seldom allow a major business thoroughfare to go unpaved. They reasoned that such an undertaking had economic benefits for
the entire city and should legitimately be supported by the public treasury.
After all, as one southern editor observed, "there are few things which operate against a city more than bad streets, and especially when they are the
principal ones." Street paving in the poorer districts was unknown, however.

The condition of streets was a concern of local government because it
also related to a city's health. The southern climate, semitropical in certain
areas, facilitated the spread of epidemic disease. Killing frosts came later to
the South than to other regions, so the danger from epidemics lasted longer.
The comings and goings of planters, merchants, and others were, in part,
determined by the length of the epidemic season. The record of local government on disease prevention was mixed. Here perhaps more than with
other services, the conflict between business cost and the general welfare
was most evident.

Disease was bad business. In 1850, a group of southern physicians estimated that the cost of disease and death in New Orleans alone totaled $45
million annually in business and in trade. It took Norfolk five years to recover the population and business lost by the yellow fever epidemic of 1855.

During the Norfolk epidemic, all major Virginia cities, Baltimore, and New York issued interdicts against trade from Norfolk, and wharves, streets, and business establishments became deserted. No farmer wanted to trade cotton or tobacco for yellow fever or cholera.

When disease struck, local newspapers attempted to suppress the news as long as possible to avoid serious economic loss to their city. The southern urban press delighted in exposing epidemics in rival cities and in chiding their silent newspapers. Some of the most bitter exchanges in southern newspaper columns occurred over this subject. In August, 1858, for example, the Augusta (Ga.) *Dispatch* charged that the Charleston *Courier* had deliberately suppressed yellow fever statistics, and the *Dispatch* considered this suppression a "penal offense." At the same time, a Norfolk paper reported that "people are fleeing [from Charleston] in every direction." Charleston sources repudiated both stories, but several months later published the following comment: "The *Courier* decided it was not necessary to report the epidemic cases, but it is now safe for any American . . . to visit in Charleston."

A healthful image was important to a southern city's prosperity. Public health expenditures, therefore, should have received a high priority from local leaders. In fact, disease prevention received relatively little budgetary attention. The rigorous cost-benefit analysis was at work again. For one thing, there was no convergence of medical opinion on the etiology of epidemic diseases. Cleanliness (drainage of swamps and garbage removal primarily) and quarantine were frequently advanced as the most effective preventive measures, but they were expensive to implement and by no means guarantees against disease. Savannah officials expended $200,000 to drain the lands around the city and place them under dry cultivation, yet epidemic disease attacked Savannah as frequently as other cities.

Quarantine had some proven success in northern cities, but many physicians doubted that yellow fever, for one example, was contagious, so quarantine seemed irrelevant. Moreover, merchants viewed quarantine as a restraint of trade. A Charlestonian in 1858 urged that the city forego plans for invoking quarantine and concentrate on sanitation instead: "If a committee be appointed to inspect cellars, drains, yards, streets, lots . . . it will prove more conducive to the health of Charleston, than all the quarantine . . . systems which may be invented; and by leaving our trade to itself, unfettered by restrictions, we may look forward to health and wealth combined." A disgusted Charleston physician retorted: "And is the health of the city to be placed in competition with a few cargoes of sugar and molasses, introduced without care or caution, so as to afford a luxury to our people at the least possible expense of money, and at the greatest cost of human life?" In most antebellum southern cities, such questions remained rhetorical. Quarantine in some cases became "little more than an administrative gesture." Health reformers were lonely men and women in southern cities: "the leading idea," a New Orleans reformer complained in 1854, "has always been convenience for commerce."

There was little public pressure to subordinate "the leading idea" because the victims of epidemic disease most frequently were the black and white poor. If enlightened opinion no longer adhered to the view that contraction of disease was a divine moral judgment, there was more general agreement that the profligate life-style of the poor made them more susceptible to disease and that public expenditures on their behalf would only encourage such behavior.

This attitude carried over into the provision of social services. Southern cities lagged far behind their northern counterparts in public support for poor relief and public education. Orphans, the poor, and the physically and mentally ill found few public accommodations in southern cities because it was expected that private charities would provide the necessary assistance, though such organizations frequently worked with meager budgets and soon overextended themselves. Poor relief, for example, tended to be strictly seasonal (and private)—the needy received wood and food in the winter. The attitudes of the private relief agencies were scarcely calculated to provide succor. The Norfolk Association for the Improvement of the Condition of the Poor maintained that "*sound discrimination* then, is the first principle of this Association. It will give to none who will not exhibit evidence of improvement from the aid afforded." It is not clear what type of transformation the members expected to achieve with an annual budget rarely exceeding $500, but perhaps so rigorous a test meant that this sum was sufficient and that "artful mendicants" were turned away.

Southerners viewed education with the same suspicion as they viewed poverty. Education was potentially dangerous as an instigator of slave unrest, so the less knowledge floating about, the greater the security. Also, southerners tended to associate public education with social welfare, as an adjunct to poor relief. It is true that higher education often received public funds as cities supported academies, colleges, and even universities, but there was a class bias evident here, since the sons and occasionally the daughters of planters and merchants were the typical students in these institutions, which represented another mechanism for the perpetuation of the rural-urban alliance and of the leadership class.

Given the frugality, if not the austerity, of urban public service expenditures, it is surprising to discover that many southern cities were mired in debt by the 1840s. The answer was relatively simple and related to one major motivation behind the cost-benefit formula: the desire to enhance agricultural commerce. Beginning in that decade, urban leaders tapped public resources to build canals, roads, and railroads as well as to dredge harbors and construct wharves. All of these activities, especially the railroads, required huge investments, which merchants justified on the grounds that the choice was investment or oblivion. If the city failed to build a railroad, deepen its harbor, or extend its dock, rivals would. In addition, the economic benefits to be gained from better access to staple agriculture would turn temporary debits into permanent profits. For various reasons, which I will discuss later, these sanguine predictions were premature. Instead of trade, these investments generated debts.

Macon, Georgia, was an early victim of large investments in internal improvements, falling into bankruptcy in 1844 after plunging heavily into railroad subscriptions during the previous eight years. This city of slightly more than three thousand inhabitants had produced a debt of more than a quarter of a million dollars. Its coastal rival, Savannah, accumulated an indebtedness of $1,872,840 by 1860—nearly all of it as a result of railroad subscriptions during the 1850s. Finally, Richmond had a $2 million debt hanging over the city in 1857, more than two-thirds of which resulted from internal improvement expenditures. Southern urban governments were so chastened by this antebellum experience (and by postwar economic depression) that limits on bonded indebtedness and virtual abstinence from heavy capital investments marked the postwar era.

The most common reaction of urban leaders to a galloping public debt was to curtail already-limited expenditures on public services and to increase license fees and capitation taxes (a uniform tax on adult white males). Fire and police services suffered in particular. Only when a disaster occurred, such as the destruction of several shops in a Wheeling, Virginia, conflagration, did local officials restore appropriations. The property tax that afforded the majority of revenues for southern cities generally remained stable or actually declined during the readjustment period of the 1850s. Property levies, of course, would have affected local leaders the most since these people were frequently the largest property holders in the community.

Local government in antebellum America was inseparable from the business community. Filthy streets, haphazard public health planning, and spotty social services defined the urban condition in all regions. It was worse in the urban South, however, and here the difference in degree was sufficient to make it a difference in kind. In the urban South, the combination of a homogeneous cultural background, the limited capital reserve afforded by a staple agricultural economy, and the existence of a biracial society produced a sharp division that went deeper than the white-pillared mansions and paved business thoroughfares versus the muddy streets and neglected poverty in the bottoms. The antebellum southern city reflected the plantation with which it was so inextricably connected: the contrast between big house and slave shack, between broadlooms and dirt floors, and between freedom and slavery.

The presence of black men and women not only evoked a certain response from white society but influenced the relationship between whites as well. It would be a mistake to attribute the southern city's poor performance on services primarily to the biracial character of the region, but the merchants frequently seemed to run their cities as their farmer-partners ran their plantations. Inevitably, the consuming concern of both was the black man. It was this presence that helped to make the antebellum South and its cities distinctive.

Life and Labor on the Urban Plantation

During the antebellum period, the number of blacks in the South was roughly ten times that in the North. The South's four million blacks accounted for one-third of the region's population, whereas blacks constituted only 1 percent of population in the North. Blacks comprised 20 to 40 percent of the population throughout the urban South, also considerably above northern urban figures. The black population of the Old South consisted of two groups: slaves and free blacks, though frequently the dividing line between them was blurred. Slavery was primarily an agrarian institution, while free blacks were the most urbanized native group in the South. Still, it was the presence of slaves more than of free blacks that established the tenor of the biracial society in southern cities.

Controversy persists as to whether urban slavery resulted in less or more freedom for the slave. Certainly urban slavery was different. It was possible to hide in a city; even in the small southern urban communities anonymity was easier for blacks. It was not unusual for fugitives to make southern cities the first stops on their way through the underground railroad northward to freedom. The back alleys and shanties that comprised the neighborhood of poverty in low-lying areas of the urban South were a twilight world where the police only occasionally entered and thus provided shelter and seclusion as slaves mingled with free blacks and poor whites.

The police hardly acted as effective upholders of white law. Public safety and law enforcement received as little attention from local budgets as other services. If white urban residents feared slave insurrections, this fear was rarely translated into increased expenditures for police. The quality of what police service existed was dismal. New Orleans police rivaled New York's for corruption, and the police protecting Charlestonians were more of a menace to public peace than the criminals they reputedly sought. When the police were not perpetrating crimes themselves, they usually could be found either sleeping on duty or imbibing at the local grog shop. A uniformed, salaried police force was a rarity, and some southern cities did not possess even a day force. As one Louisville editor complained: "Think of the perfect absurdity of giving the peace of 75,000 people into the charge of eight men."

Under these circumstances, the life of the urban slave was easier than a reading of the laws governing slaves would have us believe. For example, laws forbidding manumitted slaves to remain in a particular state were ignored in cities and frequently waived by urban magistrates. In the early 1850s, a Richmond editor could not recall the last time a local judge had enforced that law. Legal restrictions on slave hiring practices that limited both the mobility and choice of the urban slave similarly received studied neglect, especially in the 1850s when fears of slave uprisings allegedly reached a peak in southern cities. The threat and occasionally capricious enforcement of these laws doubtless hung like a cloud over the slave population, but such periodic flurries of zealousness were unusual.

Actually, throughout the antebellum period urban slaves usually escaped from the full or even partial impact of laws designed to curtail and circumscribe their lives. Urban slavery at the end of the eighteenth century was everywhere much as historian Gerald W. Mullin described it in Richmond: "permissive, confused and disordered." Such shocks as Gabriel's revolt in Richmond itself in 1800 and Nat Turner's rebellion in Southampton County, within hailing distance of Virginia's capital, failed to alter the general pattern of laxity in Richmond and in other southern cities despite official declarations of resolve immediately after both uprisings.

The charitable instincts of the white community do not account for this seeming paradox between written law and customary enforcement. The economic situation of the southern city does. Unlike northern cities, antebellum southern cities did not experience great migrations either from the countryside or from Europe. The most likely source of labor—the oil of urban growth—was the black, especially the slave. The advantage of slavery lay both in the institution and in the slave. The institution provided a tractable and mobile labor force sensitive to demand, and the slave proved adept at a wide variety of work and at forging new relationships with urban employers. The result was a flexible institution that adapted well to an urban environment and still fulfilled the requirements of its agrarian base.

Slaves worked in factories, on wharves, in mechanics' shops, in homes, and were even self-employed in the city. Urban labor requirements varied in the antebellum South, depending on the relationship between an individual city and the staple agriculture of its region. In the cotton South, females far outnumbered male slaves in urban communities. This reflected both the low level of functions performed by urban places in the cotton South and the preeminence of agricultural labor demands. Cities in the cotton South could substitute free blacks, the scattering of immigrants, and white and black women for the black male slave work force. No such choice existed in the countryside, where free blacks and immigrants were relatively scarce. Hence, in the competition for labor, agriculture relied on one labor source, the city on several. In the great cotton boom of the 1850s, for example, male slaves became even less prevalent in cotton towns as a result of growing production demands on the farm.

In the areas north and east of the cotton belt, different patterns prevailed. Industry, especially in urban Virginia, required more male operatives, so the sex ratio there was more balanced. Also, agricultural demands were less because tobacco in particular suffered through declining prices and production in the 1830s and 1840s. When tobacco prices and cultivation revived in the 1850s, urban slave populations declined in such tobacco centers as Richmond and Louisville. Historians have interpreted the general decline in urban slave populations during the last decade before the Civil War as an indication that cities and slavery were incompatible, and that anxious southerners, viewing urban slavery as "one step toward freedom," took measures to reduce the incidence of urban slavery. In fact, two mechanisms were at work. First, agricultural demand was reasserting itself, and second, a selective process was operating, especially in the tobacco South, where those slaves particularly skilled in urban occupations (in the tobacco factories, for example) remained in the cities, while less-skilled slaves returned to tobacco cultivation.

Slave hiring was probably the most remarkable feature of urban slavery, especially in the 1850s. This primarily urban adaptation of the "peculiar institution" demonstrated that institution's flexibility and also afforded another example of the close relationship and identity of values between city and country. Throughout the South by 1860, nearly one out of every three urban slaves was a hired slave. In industrial cities like Richmond, more than 50 percent of the slave work force was hired.

The attraction of slave hiring to entrepreneurs was its flexibility. For a growing commercial or industrial firm, slave hiring eliminated the necessity of a substantial investment in a labor force. Slave hiring also had the advantage of being temporary, since contracts could last from one day to one year. It was expensive to furlough owned slaves during slack periods.

The sources of slaves for the urban slave-hiring system were varied and included widows, merchants, estates, and farmers. In the 1850s, however, large-scale suppliers emerged to provide slaves specifically for the urban labor market. These suppliers were typically wealthy planters, although some farmers pooled their labor resources and formed consortia to supply slaves to urban clients. This practice created another link in the already strong bond between city and country.

Although some employers were more severe in their treatment of hired slaves than of slaves they owned outright, the slaves probably preferred the slave-hire system. Laws existed prohibiting a slave from hiring his own time, seeking his own lodging, and bargaining with his employer, especially for bonuses, but he typically did all three. Occasionally it was possible for a slave to parlay enough income from overtime and bonuses to purchase his own freedom and even that of his family.

Slave hiring was especially prevalent in the tobacco factories of the

Upper South, and here the system evolved into its most sophisticated form. By 1860, over one-half of the tobacco workers in Virginia were hired. One Richmond newspaper estimated in 1852 that hired slaves in tobacco factories earned about $120 a year. In 1857, another Richmond editor raised that sum to $8–12 per week. Much of this "salary" resulted from overtime. The increased earnings of the hired slaves during the 1850s indicated the increased demand for their labor. Hiring rates doubled in the 1850s, and some skilled operatives brought $225 for their masters on a one-year contract.

Emanuel Quivers was but one hired slave who benefited from the prosperity of the 1850s. Early in the decade, he borrowed money at low interest from his employer, Joseph R. Anderson of the Tredegar Iron Works in Richmond, for the express purpose of purchasing his own freedom. Anderson then promoted the newly freed Quivers so that the former slave could repay the loan. Later in the decade, Quivers secured a second loan from Anderson in order to purchase his family and migrate to the West. Obviously, Quivers was an unusual man, but his story indicated at least one possibility within the slave-hiring system that would have been unlikely in the more orthodox framework of agricultural slavery.

Urban slavery, especially slave hiring, was a variation of but not a departure from slavery. In fact, the urban work routine was reminiscent of the plantation. In both factory and field, slaves used songs to set the pace of their labor. This pacing of their labor was one of the few aspects of life that the slaves could control, and as several Richmond hired slaves boasted, they received "more wages for themselves than they had earned for their masters." The farm, in fact, was never far from the life of the urban slave, since even in the factory he was engaged in initial crop processing. Frequently, the towns in which he worked were close to the plantation, and his work was an extension of the multifaceted environments that plantations had become. Finally, like the city in which he worked, he was subject to the fluctuations of staple-crop cultivation. A few prosperous years for cotton or tobacco, and his limited mobility ended.

In securing a place to live—a new experience in itself—the urban slave had several poor choices. There was no large black ghetto to repair to, and urban blacks tended to live in clusters scattered about the city. This pattern implied a degree of racial residential integration, and indeed some blacks lived in back-alley dwellings behind their masters' or employers' homes. The most prevalent black urban residence, though, was in a peripheral area, frequently on badly drained land where public services were nonexistent and housing was as poor as the land: flimsy shacks, barely furnished. Industrialists or landowners usually constructed these shantytowns to house hired factory slaves. These instant communities were often worse in environment and accommodations than plantation slave cabins.

Although whites complained about the urban slave's mobility, the slave's housing options were more apparent than real. If employed or owned by one employer or master, the slave's residence was invariably nearby. If the slave was part of a relatively large gang of hands, the peripheral shantytown was his home. In cities that were primarily mercantile, like Charleston, residential patterns for slaves were dispersed; in an industrial city like Richmond, clustering in peripheral areas was more common. As in most other aspects of his urban life, the slave bent to the winds and whims of the urban economy.

Family life was another victim of the urban economic order, which in most urban places dictated an imbalanced sex ratio. The relative scarcity of slave children was another clue to the absence of a stable family life among urban slaves. This is not to say that urban slaves, male or female, spent a lonely existence framed by dulling work and miserable living conditions. As on the plantation, the urban slave broke through the chains of his physical and social environments to build a community, however modest and insecure. As the plantation was once his home, so it was also his institutional model.

They raised their voices in song at the factory during the week and in church on Sunday. Religion was a community bond on the plantation and in town as well. The slave shed his monotonous work clothes and "appears in full-bloom on Sunday, and then he is a striking object . . . whether in silks or muslins; or beaver and broadcloth." Clothes, as one of the few vehicles of individual public expression allowed to a slave, enlivened an otherwise drab life. But Sunday was not only a fashion show, it was a day of collective worship.

Following the religious proclivities developed on the plantation, urban slaves, together with free blacks, were typically Baptists or Methodists. Christianity was a paradox for blacks. On the one hand, the churches generally supported the institution of slavery. On the other, the teachings of Christ and the Hebrew prophets as revealed in the Bible provided the slaves with a moral and psychological underpinning that counteracted the institutional church's twistings of these principles. So the church became the focal point of black urban life, a reinforcement of their humanity and a confirmation that their lives mattered.

Accordingly, wherever whites would allow it, urban blacks sought to establish their own churches. The First African Baptist Church in Richmond opened in 1841, for example, and several other churches soon appeared. The church exercised considerable influence in the black community because it was the only institution over which the blacks had control, and, since family life was less evident in the city than on the plantation, the church was virtually the only institution to which blacks could turn. It provided rudimentary social welfare and counseling services. Finally, the church was a valuable training ground for black leadership.

The church was not the only place where urban blacks congregated. Prayer and worship provided release of a sort, but for some, different stimuli were necessary to brighten their lives in the city. Grog shops, gambling dens, and taverns were located in or nearby black residential clusters. The sale of spirits to slaves, and occasionally to all blacks, was illegal, as were gambling and some of the other activities carried on in these places. As with most such urban legislation, however, these regulations received only sporadic attention from the police and then only when violence or white fears became sufficiently intense to warrant intervention. Although some whites viewed these dens as hatcheries for rebellion, it was more likely that comraderie, not revolt, was the customers' primary objective.

In church, in more secular locations, and on the streets, the urban slaves received support and companionship not only from their own number but from free blacks as well. The free black was another component in the urban South's distinctive biracial environment. The very term *free black* embodied its own contradictions. Free blacks were relegated to a sort of racial purgatory between free white and black slave, yet they were much closer to the latter. Especially after the Nat Turner uprising in 1831, southerners viewed free blacks as dangerous to the security of their society, particularly in cities where opportunities for interaction between free and slave were numerous. Southern cities reacted to these concerns by enacting laws to restrict free black mobility and to curb contacts with slaves.

That these were primarily urban statutes reflected the urban nature of the free black population, which by 1840 was four times more urban than the southern white and seven times more urban than the slave. One out of every three free blacks dwelled in cities. They tended to concentrate in the larger cities (those over 10,000 people), which offered a variety of economic opportunities and presumably more chances for upward mobility. Two-thirds of the urban black population resided in these centers.

Some free blacks evidently prospered in the urban environment. At the least, it was more remunerative than rural society. Urban free blacks owned more property than their rural counterparts, and the difference between them increased rapidly during the antebellum years. In rural Virginia between 1830 and 1860, the value of free black property doubled, but the value of such property in the city grew by six times. In Davidson County, Tennessee (the location of Nashville), free blacks held close to one-half of the black-owned real property in the state, though the county contained less than 10 percent of Tennessee's total free black population. Although most of the real estate wealth of the free black population was held by a relatively small number of individuals, the city environment offered economic promise for all free blacks.

The labor of the free black was a valuable urban resource, especially since the availability of slave labor depended on what was occurring in the fields. How much value urban whites attached to the free black labor force was nowhere better measured than by how little value they placed on the legislative restrictions upon it. When several white residents demanded the removal of all free blacks from Richmond during one particularly nervous time in the anxious 1850s, a local newspaper editor retorted: "They [free blacks] are not a bad class; their labor is needed." Predictably, however, Richmond authorities rigorously enforced a law providing for forced labor for misdemeanor violations. The chain gang evolved from the application of this law.

On the other hand, employers of free blacks openly ignored regulations requiring them to ascertain the status—slave or free—of their help. A supportive Norfolk editor warned that "full enforcement of such a law will act seriously detrimental to the thriving prospects of our city." Businessmen came to view the free black less as a social pariah and more as an economic asset, and testimonials from urban employers depicted the free black as quite the opposite of the shiftless individual that his detractors described: "They [free blacks] are more docile, less expensive, and less prone to riot than Irish laborers."

Indeed, by the 1840s, a body of occupations had apparently been set aside in southern cities and labeled as "nigger work." Their invariably low status did not diminish the importance of that labor to the urban economy. In the skilled trades, free blacks clustered in such occupations as barbering, carpentry, plastering, blacksmithing, bricklaying, and shoemaking. In Richmond in 1860, four out of every five skilled free black workers toiled in these trades. For many free blacks, however, only the most menial urban occupations—domestic work for women and day labor for men—were available. More than 85 percent of the free black work force in cities of the Upper South was engaged in unskilled occupations by 1860. In addition, there was little occupational mobility among free blacks. If anything, their economic status declined during the late antebellum period.

Relationships with white employers varied. Free blacks usually preferred short-term contracts for cash wages. Undoubtedly, they felt that relationships of a year or more in duration could eliminate the already-fine line existing between free and slave. Some employers allowed their free black workers to run up a debt and have them work it off in a version of debt peonage. Short-term contracts tended to minimize the likelihood of this imposition.

There were regional variations in the economic status of the urban free black reflecting the different requirements of the various staple regions. Free blacks in the Lower South tended to be more urbanized than their counterparts in the Upper South: one out of every two free blacks in the cotton South was urban. Their status was generally higher as well. The general prosperity of cotton cultivation drew available slave and white labor to the farm. Those free blacks who chose an urban way of life usually found more opportunities in cities like New Orleans, Mobile, and Charleston. In Charleston, for example, three out of every four free black men worked at skilled trades in 1860.

The relatively fewer numbers of free blacks in the Lower South may have helped their occupational situation. More than 85 percent of the South's free black population resided in the Upper South. The free black of the Deep South was also often lighter-skinned, and some undoubtedly "passed" for whites. In cities like New Orleans and Mobile, these individuals were the aristocrats of their race, and whites referred to them as "free people of color," setting them apart from their darker brethren, free and slave.

The free black, regardless of color or location, generally had more residential options than the slave. Free blacks were more dispersed through the general population, but clusters were evident. The poorest areas of a town—along the wharves, on poorly drained land, beyond the town limits—typically included more free blacks than other residential sections. Segregation by class was more likely in southern cities than segregation by race. It was probable, then, that poor blacks and whites carried on some interchange in the city, sharing their poverty and breaking down ever so slightly the rigid strictures that characterized the biracial society.

Free blacks frequently joined with slaves in religious and fraternal organizations. The church was the focal point of their lives as well as of the slaves', and the free blacks typically provided the leadership in these churches. Freedom had a status itself, and free blacks were more stable members of the black community. It was unlikely that they would be forced onto a farm or to another city, or even to another employer. As tenuous and as ill-defined as freedom was for the free black, it still had these important distinctions.

By the 1850s, the distinctions were narrowing, however. Laws restricting free blacks were not enforced with greater frequency, but the free black economic situation was slipping in some cities. As long as labor was scarce, the free black could always count on something to do in the city. But the slave's flexibility and bondedness made his labor attractive to urban entrepreneurs, so when slave workers were available the free black became expendable. The free black's insistence on short-term contracts, his ability to lay off whenever he wanted to, his reputation as a possible source of unrest, and the very fact he was black militated against his labor. When labor stringencies prevailed, whites lived, however grudgingly, with these perceived debilities. When the labor situation eased, the free black faced strong competition from slave workers.

What happened to the free black in the 1840s and 1850s underscored the cruelties of the biracial society—a type of society where expediency and economics determined the life-style of one of the races. European immigrants began to filter into southern cities at this time, nowhere near the numbers that crowded into cities elsewhere but enough to have some economic impact on the relatively simple agrarian economies of the antebellum urban South. The immigrants were the most urban group in the region: nearly 90 percent resided in cities. In some cities, immigrants comprised sizable portions of the population. Forty percent of New Orleans' residents were foreign born in 1860; in smaller Natchez, the figure was 25 percent, and 24 percent of Mobile's inhabitants were of foreign birth. At the same time, 36 percent of Boston's population was foreign born.

But immigrants were important economically beyond their numbers. Single males and couples in their twenties and thirties were overrepresented in the immigrant population of the urban South. They came to southern cities to work, and frequently they drifted down from northern cities to Charleston, Mobile, or New Orleans. Since immigrants initially landed in the major ports of entry in the United States, only New Orleans received significant numbers of new arrivals, but these numbers were still low relative to Boston, New York, or Philadelphia. Because of their demography and their objectives, the immigrants were important additions to a labor force that generally was in short supply. In some of the port cities, they represented one-third to one-half of the free work force, and sometimes more. In the Richmond free-labor force, immigrants comprised 65 percent of the laborers and 47 percent of the craftsmen. Little wonder that one Richmond editor called immigration "the greatest benefactor of the human family."

Though most immigrants were in unskilled occupations, they could also be found in skilled and entrepreneurial activities, as the Richmond statistics indicated. The relative absence of skilled labor in the South meant attractive wages for skilled immigrants. In addition, immigrants, especially Germans, opened small shops of all kinds, from dry goods stores to confectionary establishments. Scarcely a southern town was without a German shopkeeper by 1860. Immigrants came to dominate the commercial life of the river towns in Mississippi, and factory entrepreneurs occasionally invested in European excursions to recruit foreign weavers, spinners, and mechanics.

Leon Godchaux was not a typical immigrant, but his career reflects the type of economic roles immigrants could play in southern urban society. Godchaux, an Alsatian Jew, arrived in New Orleans in 1840 and "established" himself as an itinerant peddler in the Delta countryside with New Orleans as his supply base. He prospered and soon opened a store in Convent, Louisiana, fifty miles north of New Orleans. With profits from the Convent enterprise, Godchaux, in 1844, opened a dry goods store in New Orleans. By the time of the Civil War, he and his brother had one of the most successful retail businesses in the city. Godchaux eventually owned factories, plantations, and two retail stores.

For the majority of those immigrants below Godchaux's level, there were sufficient opportunities in the trades and factories to enjoy modest economic prosperity. Although nativism existed in southern cities, it rarely attained the bloody virulence that ran through northern cities in the last decades of the antebellum period. In a biracial society, the immigrant for the most part was counted as white—and that is what really counted. As the immigrant came into economic competition with blacks, slave and free, his whiteness proved an important advantage.

The competition was most intense in the unskilled occupations where Irish and black laborers predominated. Visitors in the South reported the shift to white immigrant labor, especially along the wharves, and even such traditional "nigger work" as barbering and domestic help were increasingly becoming immigrant occupations. White urban families, especially in Upper South cities like Louisville and Richmond, preferred Irish or German immigrant girls as domestics, thus eroding one of the few occupations available to black women. In some cities like Charleston, free blacks held their economic status against immigrant pressure. Immigrants in that city, primarily the Irish, replaced slaves in their traditional occupations during the 1850s. In this case, the Irish won the competition more or less by default because unskilled slaves were leaving the city in any case as a result of an agricultural revival. In Charleston, unlike some other cities, the presence of immigrants did not so much ease the labor shortage as replace one work force with another.

By the time the immigrant arrived in the southern city he was already conditioned to the vagaries of economic competition. New York and Boston were tough educators. But life in the urban South came a bit easier. Race, the need for labor, and the relatively few immigrants residing in southern cities reduced the hazards of competition and allowed a more stable lifestyle to develop. Family life replaced the "rootless unmarried man" in the Irish community in Charleston during the 1850s, for example. In 1850, over 70 percent of the Irish immigrants in that city lived in a family. Charleston's Irish tended to remain in the city longer than the Irish in cities of similar size in the North. Most significant, immigrant institutions developed and flourished, lending a foundation to the growing sense of community.

The Irish in New Orleans were indicative of the institutional impact of some immigrant groups in the urban South. Coming as immigrants in the 1830s and 1840s, the Irish transformed the Crescent City from a predominantly black to a predominantly white city. Their vigorous Catholicism conflicted with the French-dominated hierarchy in the city, and by 1860 the

Irish had assumed leadership in the Church and opened its institutions to all Catholics. Unlike the exclusivistic French, the Irish supported free Catholic parochial schools, orphan asylums, and benevolent associations.

Few immigrant groups were as influential in their cities as the Irish were in New Orleans. Nevertheless, there were numerous opportunities for a rich institutional life for other immigrants as well. Churches and synagogues were the most evident forms of immigrant associations. The Germans usually formed singing societies—*Liederkränze*—which served a variety of social functions in addition to music. The Irish had their Hibernian Clubs, and some of these organizations, like the one in Charleston, were important in city affairs.

In the relatively homogeneous urban South, immigrants stood out from the native white population, but their difference did not isolate them from the larger community. In New Orleans, for example, which had a heavy Irish concentration—one out of every five residents was Irish—the Irish population was dispersed. This residential pattern prevailed for immigrant groups in most southern cities, though clusters were evident. Discernible ghettos, however, did not exist. The Irish tended to congregate with the blacks, but this was more a reflection of poverty than of ethnicity. Southern cities were small enough that dispersion did not mean isolation from ethnic comrades. Also, it was unusual for one immigrant group to monopolize employment in a particular factory or mercantile establishment—the type of occupational monopoly that lent itself to residential concentration. Finally, there was no apparent pressure from the native community to isolate and segregate the immigrant. Local leaders were generally positive toward the immigrant presence.

Immigrants fared relatively well in the antebellum biracial urban society. They soon discovered that adopting the prevailing racial attitudes made acceptance easier. Psychologically, it was good for a change not to be on the lowest rung of the status ladder, and there was always the presence of blacks, slave and free, to ensure that.

The biracial society, like the agrarian society of which it was an inextricable part, had a significant role in antebellum southern urbanization. Just as agrarian rhythms dominated urban seasons, they determined the labor composition of the city as well. Urban places were invaluable outlets for agricultural slaves and in turn provided necessary labor when agricultural cycles demanded. Cities were thus exposed to a constant ebb and flow of labor. Usually cities could substitute free black and, later in the antebellum period, white immigrant labor for the slave, but it was also true that in many antebellum cities a chronic labor shortage existed, not necessarily in the unskilled occupations but in those jobs requiring specific skills. Agricultural slavery was not the best school for urban occupations, though some slaves successfully learned skilled trades.

The biracial society reduced significantly the contributions that blacks could have made to urban society and economy, because enforced ignorance and low skill levels limited the creativity of a large minority of the urban population. As consumers, blacks were a small factor in the urban economy. The slave's only earnings, if he was fortunate to have earnings, came from bonuses and overtime; the free black was paid about one-half the usual dollar-a-day wage rate or else was paid in kind. Since blacks represented a very limited demand for urban goods and services, southern urban places were not likely to generate higher functions.

The antebellum southern city had an artificially low population, since the agrarian economy limited the mobility of a sizable proportion of the population. It is not certain that blacks would have fled to the cities if allowed to do so, but given the blacks' antebellum preferences and the benefits, however limited, of urban life, a larger black population probably would have resulted from unlimited mobility. Population, of course, does not necessarily raise the level of urbanization, but it makes the appearance of more functions more likely.

The biracial society worked on the city in more subtle ways. It was undoubtedly clear to blacks, slave and free, that regulations which interfered with the local conception of economic progress were generally ignored while those that did not were enforced with unstinting vigor. Free blacks often complained about long forced work sentences for relatively minor offenses, and vagrancy statutes ensured that work habits were regular. Fear of disruptions to the urban economy, not of black uprisings, prompted the respective enforcement or neglect of antiblack legislation. This was evidently clear to whites, who adopted a cynical attitude toward the law, which, like the government, was a part of economic policy.

The maintenance of the biracial society limited urban development. Two separate societies existed in the southern city, and blacks were not only unequal business partners, but they attempted to subvert or at least to slow down the factory routine, the loading on the wharves, and the building of the railroads. This is not to say that black labor was less efficient than white labor or that white labor had more incentives, but it is possible that the biracial society foreclosed the possibility of the blacks' contribution to that society beyond the sweat of their brows.

The agrarian and biracial society that was the antebellum South circumscribed the possibilities for southern urbanization as well. However, staple agriculture and biracialism were not the only factors that molded a distinctive southern urban environment. A wider world existed for the southern city and for the South as well, and both city and region became increasingly aware of this outside presence during the antebellum years. This was not a new phenomenon for the South, of course; its cities and agriculture had thrived in the broad Atlantic world of the colonial era. Now they thrived again, but the Atlantic world had narrowed and the economic focus had shifted closer to home. Southern city and region had discarded one colonial era only to be confronted with another. Like the earlier era, this one prescribed certain limits for both city and region; like the earlier one, the only alternative to removing these limits was revolution.

Hewers of Wood

Until the 1840s, the predominant character of the American economy was regional. Commercial and to a lesser extent financial transactions tended to occur within regions and, more frequently, within subregions. Beginning in the 1840s, a national economy based upon interregional commercial and financial transactions evolved. There were several reasons why this occurred. First, there were revolutionary changes in transportation and communication technology. The canal era had opened the possibilities for wider contact, but even the famous Erie Canal was primarily an intraregional highway. The railroad, however, was flung across rivers and driven over and through mountains; it conquered time and space. The canal introduced regions to each other; the railroad married them. Local merchants talked almost mystically about the "Iron Messiah," although they did not mean deliverance and salvation in the biblical sense but wheat, corn, cotton, and manufactures that would be delivered and economies that would be saved.

The telegraph, together with the railroad, sped information. For a merchant or a banker, information was as important as a crop shipment, if not more so. Prices, crop conditions, industrial output, weather—these were variables to be weighed in business transactions. The faster and more accurate the information, the better the quality of business. A national economy was nourished by information.

The growth of industry was a second important development in facilitating a national economy. Antebellum America was not an industrial nation, but manufacturing enterprises were sufficient to support a reciprocal trade between agricultural hinterlands and industrial-commercial cities. In this manner, a rough balance of trade existed that enabled the railroads and customers at each end to survive and profit. The other part of the commercial equation—agricultural produce—also underwent a production stimulus during the late antebellum decades. The settlement of the West and the millions of acres of croplands placed under cultivation generated huge surpluses of grains far beyond the need of a regional market. Growing eastern and European food demands begged for an interregional commerce. From a practical standpoint, the rapidly growing cities of the East, swelled by rural and European immigrants, required western connections to meet these new demands.

There were more subtle but equally important catalysts in forming a national economy, which involved changing methods of doing business. Some historians have termed these adjustments collectively "the Business Revolution," a revolution that involved rationalization of accounting, credit, and marketing procedures that first facilitated and then accelerated commercial transactions. The various state and federal courts provided legal underpinning for these changes by bolstering contractual obligations, circumscribing monopolistic practices, and facilitating government involvement in the economy. Merchants and financiers could expand their networks with confidence that their activities would receive a minimum of legal surveillance and a maximum of government support.

The national economy did not emerge full blown in the 1840s, of course, and even by 1860 the interregional connections were still developing. Nevertheless, the shift from purely regional economies to a national system was evident. The railroads, industrial and agricultural expansion, the business revolution, and the encouragement and support of government institutions had generated a significant change in American economic life. The horizon for the local shopkeeper, farmer, and consumer now stretched considerably beyond the nearest market town or even the regional center. And the implications were as far-reaching.

The factors that precipitated the development of a national economy spread unevenly across the American landscape, and the benefits derived from the national economy were therefore shared unequally. The South and particularly the urban South were the weaker members in the national economic partnership, which centered in New York. Through entrepreneurial skill and aggressiveness, a strategic location, and a bit of luck, New Yorkers were able to capitalize on the new economic trends to assume a commanding position in the nation's commercial and financial realm. Once in the lead, they seemed to increase their advantage geometrically, while entrepreneurs in other cities scrambled merely not to fall further off the pace.

A basic law of urban economic development was in operation, and one resigned contemporary observer explained it well: "When once a city has acquired an established character as the great commercial emporium of a country, . . . the course of trade becomes settled by flowing regularly in the same channel." Scarcely any new commercial development occurred without New York merchants and financiers knowing about and, more important, taking advantage of it. "Every new mine opened, every town built up, comes into relations with New York; and every railroad, no matter how short has one terminus here," boasted one New Yorker in 1865.

Geographers call this the "law of primacy," but southerners did not need academic theorists to tell them the implications of a national economy centered in New York. The signs were everywhere in the region, but most of all in the cities. Young agents from New York or other northern cities descended on the urban South seeking cotton, tobacco, and orders for manufactured goods and offering credit and other financial services. By the early 1850s, southern ports developed economic umbilical cords to northern ports—ties that seemed to sustain the mother much more than her children. Northern ships bobbed in southern harbors laden with riches from the soil, money from the people, and manufactures from northern factories. Most alarming were the signs that were not so readily visible.

In New Orleans, something was amiss. The Crescent City was still Queen of the Mississippi, but her realm was dwindling. The cotton prosperity of the late 1840s only partly masked the fact that crops north of the cotton belt were moving eastward over the railroad rather than southward by the river. The Mississippi was becoming a regional highway. During the 1850s, the proportion of flour moving eastward and northward from Cincinnati increased from 3 percent to 91 percent. Nearly two times as much flour and eight times as much pork and bacon were exported from New Orleans in 1846–1849 than in 1858–1861. On the other hand, cotton receipts advanced by 160 percent in the 1850s, accounting for all of the city's trade increase during those years. Though the superintendent of the United States Census exaggerated when he wrote in 1860 that "as an outlet to the ocean for the grain trade of the West, the Mississippi River has almost ceased to be depended upon by merchants," the West was lost to the South as an economic partner.

The silent drama of New Orleans' decline and all the other manifestations of economic dependence and erosion stung southerners into action. In antebellum America, growth meant progress; this was the essence of the American dream. To cities caught up in the national excitement of expanding production and territory, stagnation meant death. There were numerous examples of promising cities with favorable locations that for want of enterprise failed to reach their promise and settled into a not-so-comfortable decline. Newspapers spouted statistics, local leaders anxiously awaited census figures, and merchants measured progress in profits, skylines, and railroad depots. In such a climate, inaction was deemed a sin.

Southerners realized they were starting from behind, though they did not perceive how difficult it would be to catch up. In 1850, transplanted Bostonian Albert Pike assessed the situation for a group of merchants and planters meeting in New Orleans. Beginning in barely audible measured tones and ending in a booming crescendo that reverberated throughout the hall, Pike catalogued the colonial South:

> From the rattle with which the nurse tickles the ear of the child born in the South to the shroud which covers the cold form of the dead, everything comes to us from the North. We rise from between sheets made in Northern looms, and pillows of Northern feathers, to wash in basins made in the North, dry our beards on Northern towels, and dress ourselves in garments made in Northern looms; we eat from Northern plates and dishes; our rooms are swept with Northern brooms; our gardens are dug with Northern spades and our bread kneaded in trays or dishes of Northern wood or tin; and the very wood which feeds our fires is cut with Northern axes, helved with hickory brought from Connecticut or New York; and when we die our bodies are wrapped in shrouds manufactured in New England, put in coffins made in the North. We have our graves filled with Southern soil but it is pulled in by Northern spades and shovels.

Stating the problem, even if somewhat melodramatically, was obviously easier than solving it. But southerners realized that they must begin with their cities, for which New York was both a model and a rival. "The South,"

Virginia's agrarian philosopher George Fitzhugh wrote, "must build up cities, towns and villages." Constructing interregional railroads, especially to western wheat fields, was a prerequisite to establishing equilibrium within the national economy. Once this network was completed, "then our cities . . . will at once become receptacles of a trade and commerce which will attract capital and population. They will be cities, not in name merely, but in all the elements to give them manufacturing and commercial consequence. We may then look forward to a freedom from the vassalage to which we have been so long subjected."

There was an edge to the tone of this competitive statement from a group of Virginia railroad officials. The national economy and heightened sectional antagonisms appeared almost simultaneously, and some southerners believed it was more than coincidence. For them, city-building activities were not only good economics; they were patriotic acts as well. The rhetoric of sectionalism crept naturally into pleas for railroads and urban growth. J. D. B. De Bow drew the lines and presented the task for fellow southerners: "A contest has been going on between North and South . . . for the wealth and commerce of the great valley of the Mississippi. We must meet our Northern competitors . . . with corresponding weapons." But this was not to be a war of economic conquest; the goal was to attain economic parity. If southern economic weakness invited northern aggressions, then economic equality would remove the incentives for sectional conflict. Railroads, predicted William M. Burwell, a Virginia urban booster and future editor of *De Bow's Review*, "will result in the rapid increase in our cities . . . and the South will be restored to her former position in the Union and render that Union more stable and firm."

But railroads were not the only weapons that southerners employed to reach economic equality. Albert Pike's catalog of southern dependence made it clear that home manufacturing was essential to urban growth and to an equal place in the national economy. Plantations had functioned as small manufacturing units for decades, but not for regional or national markets. A broader, more urban effort was necessary to reduce the sectional imbalance. A Mobile editor acknowledged that domestic manufacturing was "the only safe and effectual remedy against Northern oppression." The lessons of the past were obvious: "No people," counseled a Richmond entrepreneur, "are independent who are compelled to rely upon others for industry."

Finally, the southern economic package focused on direct trade. To watch the rich southern soil yield sought-after bounties only to have them whisked away for the profits of others must have been galling. Northern intermediaries drained off natural resources and capital, so a direct relationship with European ports would not only enhance urban development of the southern port cities but would increase southern self-reliance as well. "By showing our determination and ability to conduct our own foreign trade," a Portsmouth, Virginia, editor reasoned in 1850, "we shall soon lessen the existing disparity between the northern and southern sections of the country."

The three weapons that De Bow had in mind when he hurled the challenge at his southern countrymen were, of course, connected to each other. Railroads secured western produce for southern cities, where urban merchants would load it on their own ships bound for Europe or northern ports. Local factories would supply western farmers with agricultural implements and fill regional demands as well, providing railroads with the necessary two-way traffic to sustain profitable operations. The scenario ended with prosperous cities in a bountiful region, all enjoying the benefits of the national economy and toasting a lasting Union, one and inseparable.

That the regional drama reached its denouement in quite a different manner was not through want of trying. During the last fifteen years before the Civil War, southern cities entered an unprecedented period of growth marked by railroad construction, manufacturing growth, and new export-trade ties. Between 1850 and 1860, southern railroad mileage quadrupled, while northern mileage tripled. The interesting feature about this construction boom was that regional capital financed it. Local and state governments, planters, and merchants pooled their limited financial resources to realize the dream of an interregional commercial empire. Of course, the effort bankrupted at least one city and drove numerous others to the brink, but for those cities that avoided drowning in red ink there were rewards. Savannah, an economic backwater for most of the antebellum era, raised nearly $3 million in private and public subscriptions to four railroad companies during the 1850s. The sum led Mayor Richard Arnold to boast that "in the ratio of her population, [Savannah] can challenge most cities to a comparison of the capital contributed." The heavy subscriptions resulted in record cotton receipts and the city's greatest expansion since the eighteenth century. In one decade, Savannah's cotton exports jumped from 300,000 to 500,000 bales, and the value of total exports more than doubled. By 1860, Savannah was the third largest exporting center in the South. The reason was simple, according to a local editor: "the extension of our Railroads." *Railroad*, like *God*, was always upper case.

In manufacturing enterprise, the traditionally bucolic South could point to some major gains as well. Not surprisingly, agricultural processing industries predominated. Georgia's cities had pioneered cotton textile manufacturing in the 1830s, and by 1848 there were thirty-two cotton mills in urban Georgia, with over one-third of their production marketed outside the state. In the mid-1850s, De Bow was referring to Georgia as the "Empire State of the South." Local investors—planters and merchants—again dominated. By 1851, Columbus residents had invested nearly $1,000,000 in local textile industries. In the Upper South, where tobacco and wheat cultivation were prominent, flour milling and tobacco manufacturing flourished. Richmond manufactured more tobacco than any other city in the world by 1860 and was among the nation's leading flour-milling centers. In addition to the processing industries, the Tredegar and Belle Isle Iron Works gave Richmond an industrial diversity that was unusual in southern cities. By the time of the Civil War, Richmond could well lay claim to being the "Lowell of the South."

During the 1850s, southern cities also developed new export markets, especially in Latin America. Savannah established lumber commerce with several Caribbean islands, and by the end of the decade Richmond's exports to South American ports exceeded those of all other United States ports, including New York. But the European connection remained elusive for the southern port cities.

The recitation of southern urban accomplishments could go on, but that would be as pointless as some southerners felt it was by 1860. By that date, despite impressive gains, southern urbanization was lagging farther behind northern urbanization than at any previous time in American history. Also, by that date southern cities—indeed the southern economy in general— were more tightly woven into the national economy and more subservient to New York's hegemony in that system than at any previous time. How did this happen in the face of the South's most prosperous decade of all time?

Southerners built railroads but not railroad systems. State legislatures were so overwhelmed by chartering and appropriations requests that they did the politically expedient thing and funded virtually every scheme that came before them. New Orleans entrepreneurs recognized their national decline and sought a railroad to counteract it. They received a charter but only a paltry appropriation because of dozens of similar projects that other Louisiana towns had requested. In addition, southern urban businessmen may have wrapped themselves in a cloak of regional patriotism, but their most bitter invectives were aimed at southern urban rivals. More than one interregional railroad proposal ran aground because rival cities could not agree on routes. The fierce competition for commerce had an effect quite the opposite from promoting regional urban unity.

Even when railroads received enough financial support to operate, poor management and a dearth of technical skill limited efficiency. Southern railroads typically hired northern engineers, but there were simply not enough to go around in the railroad-building boom of the 1850s. Few southern railroads achieved financial stability. The absence of reciprocal trade—crops went to the city, but few manufactured goods went back into the countryside—undermined the limited capital reserves of many railroad companies.

The railroads were far from comprehensive in their coverage of southern agricultural areas, since they were primarily transportation links between staple regions and port cities. Upcountry areas not involved in staple production were usually ignored, though these areas could have diversified the cities' commercial economy. The railroads, then, served primarily as facilitators for export because that is what usually occurred with staples. The Georgia Central Railroad brought record cotton shipments to Savannah in the 1850s, but the bales were quickly loaded on northern vessels bound for northern ports. Commercial steamship service from Savannah to New York began in 1848, and by 1856 no less than nine lines carried cotton to New York. Southern railroads were, in effect, expensive (to the South) ferries for northern merchants and helped to set the role of southern ports as intermediaries in the national economy. As one urban entrepreneur observed sadly in 1858: "We are mere way stations to Philadelphia, New York, and Boston."

The great dependence of southern railroads on staple agriculture indicated that home manufacturing, despite considerable increases, was insufficient to create a balanced regional economy. The South's industrial promise was dim to begin with. Some historians have attributed the failure of antebellum southern industry to the inadequate demand of a region where nearly half the population was enslaved. Although demand for manufactured products was not as great as it might have been in a free society, northern industrialists found sufficient demand to support their marketing efforts in the region. Again, the law of primacy worked against the South. In New

England, investments went not into the rocky soil or, during the War of 1812, into uncertain commercial enterprises, but into manufacturing. By the 1840s, southerners were used to having northern products in their homes and businesses.

It was extremely difficult for infant southern industries to compete in price and quality with established northern manufactures, and the railroads merely made it easier for northern industrialists to speed their wares to southern customers. Southern patriots paraded in homespun, but merchants' shelves were stocked with northern supplies. South Carolina textile entrepreneur William Gregg noted ironically that his goods "are more popular in New York and Philadelphia than at home," and some southern textile firms actually disguised the origin of their products and advertised them as "Lowell goods." An Alexandria, Virginia, resident summarized this absence of home patronage in his native region while visiting New York in 1860. He was somewhat startled to find more southern merchants in that city than ever before and concluded, "Southern people, despite of everything said and done, buy where *they think* they can get the best assortment, and purchase at the cheapest rate."

There were structural problems with southern industries that made it even more unlikely that southern industrialists would win consumer loyalty in the future. Southern industry, like the southern city, moved to an agricultural beat. Most southern manufacturing involved processing crops, and during the late spring and summer many of these factories shut down unless they had stocked raw materials during the winter. Eight-month operations were common. Crop failures or preferences for higher prices at other cities further stifled industrial development. William F. Fowle of Alexandria invested heavily to erect a flour mill in that city, only to be bankrupted by too little wheat. Fowle, considerably wiser and poorer, admitted that "I have lost a fortune by it. It was too large for the back country."

The lack of coordination between crops, railroads, and factories was evident in southern investment patterns. Processing industries functioned most and best during good staple years; these were precisely the years when southern manufacturers found that investment capital was scarcest. Southern industrial investment patterns were cyclical, following the fortunes of staple-crop cultivation. In poor crop years, planters and merchants shifted their capital from land and slaves to factories. In good crop years, manufacturing investments fell off drastically. In the 1820s, a rapid decline in the price of cotton and the depletion of soils in the South Atlantic states convinced planters and merchants to invest in more profitable activities, such as textile manufacturing. Articles in the Charleston *Mercury* philosophized about the Southeast becoming the industrial section of the southern region. Industrial growth occurred slowly in the 1830s but accelerated again when cotton prices dipped to their lowest level in decades during the 1840s. The *Southern Cultivator*, a leading agricultural journal of the period, warned in 1849 that "industry cannot be dispensed with in any State with impunity."

But the brave words of the forties became silent echoes in the fifties. Cotton prices and production rose, and industrial investment fell. Cotton prices set in northern markets were sometimes too high for local mills, which were forced to close. It was an anomaly of staple-crop economics that while agriculture flourished, home industry languished. Investment dollars naturally sought the opportunities that generated the highest rates of return, and only truly doleful times on the farm could distract capital to a southern industry overwhelmed by northern competition and consumer neglect.

The life and death of a textile mill in Natchez, Mississippi, encapsuled the struggle of southern industry for survival even in the very heart of King Cotton's domain. John Robinson, a Scot, opened a textile mill on the outskirts of the city in the depression year of 1842. He struggled for two years against insufficient capital, shortages of skilled labor and of machinery, and local preference for New England textile products. A local merchant bought the mill in 1844, installed a Lowell-trained superintendent, expanded the work force, and marketed his product vigorously from Vicksburg to New Orleans. Three years later, the discouraged and unsuccessful merchant sold out to two Natchez mechanics who failed as well. The mill breathed its last in 1848, and the textile industry expired in Natchez.

There were, of course, numerous examples of factories that survived and flourished. Richmond was a thriving industrial city on the eve of the Civil War. For the most part, however, southern industry failed to alter the agrarian pattern of southern urbaniztion. Southern industry was not a city-builder, as in the North, but rather a rural activity that complemented the plantation and remained estranged from the city. Rural industry was common in antebellum America, of course. The New England textile mills that nestled in the rolling countryside along fast-moving streams seemed like college campuses from a distance, but demand and production soon transformed these rural idylls into gritty cities like Lowell, Chicopee, and Springfield.

Southern industries had no need for urban locations. Demand was insufficient to transform rural sites to cities or to make much of an impact on the cities in which some factories were located. Their raw materials—staple crops—and their labor sources—frequently slaves and rural whites—were out in the countryside. Even when processing industries appeared in cities, they were most frequently found on the outskirts. Finally, the same doubts about mixing industry and cities expressed by Thoreau and Emerson concerned southerners, although for southerners it was not only the specter of what industrial cities might become, but also the fear that an urban industrial order could challenge and dislodge agriculture as the region's economic and psychological foundation.

The experience of the South's most prominent industrialist, William Gregg of South Carolina, revealed the nature of industry as an agrarian activity. When capital for industry became available in the 1840s, Gregg constructed a textile factory in rural Graniteville, South Carolina. He also built a town around the factory, the little Gothic cottages of the workers arrayed like supplicants before the massive granite factory building. With northern superintendents and machinery, Gregg worked his rural white work force, of which only one in five were adults, twelve hours a day, six days a week. The factory became a profitable enterprise and gave investors a 15 percent return on their investments, a rate that compared favorably with returns from staple agriculture. But Graniteville remained a rural company town because Gregg believed that cities would corrupt workers and he strongly opposed urban manufacturing. Of course, the type of control that Gregg exercised on his Graniteville preserve would have been more difficult in a larger urban environment.

In fact, Graniteville was an urban plantation. Just as such strange entities as rural cities appeared in the antebellum South, so were there urban farms. One sympathetic historian described life in Graniteville and Gregg's managerial style as "benevolent despotism." The town-plantation was as much a "civilizing" school for rural whites as the plantation supposedly was for slaves, but the company town was not an expansive enterprise like the plantation. With limited capital, technology, and demand, growth was also limited. In Graniteville, Prattville (Alabama), and other similar textile operations, output fell far short of similar operations in the North. In 1860, after a record cotton crop, the largest cotton-producing region in the world produced only 6.7 percent of the value of cotton goods manufactured in the United States.

Northern capital and credit, liberally extended to planters, were not evident in southern industrial enterprises. In the national economy, which depended on interregional commerce, regional specialization benefited the North. Northern merchants would market southern cotton in exchange for credit and manufactured products, so the development of an independent southern industry was not in their best economic interest; the cultivation and expansion of staple-crop agriculture was. Northern financiers encouraged southern investments in land and slaves because part of the return from such investments would accrue to the northerners in the form of commissions, shipping fees, and insurance and interest payments. The cost of an agrarian economy was high, but it was the South that bore the burden. In 1860, the Montgomery (Alabama) *Advertiser* estimated that regional specialization cost the South $110 million annually in the form of: profits from the manufacture of southern raw materials ($30 million); profits from export of southern goods ($40 million); profits of agents and brokers, and commissions ($10 million); and capital drawn from the South ($30 million). The implications of regional specialization in the form of staple-crop agriculture went even further. In a brilliant summary of the South's secondary economic status, George Fitzhugh explained the result of Nature's curse on the region's economy:

> A fertile soil, with good rivers and roads as outlets, becomes the greatest evil with which a country can be afflicted. The richness of the soil invites to agriculture, and the roads and rivers carry off the crops, to be exchanged for the manufactures of poorer regions, where are situated the centres of trade, of capital, and manufacturing. In a few centuries or less time, the consumption abroad of the crops impoverishes the soil where they are made. No cities or manufactures arise in the country with this fertile soil, because there is not occasion. The rich go off for pleasure and education, the enterprising poor for employment.

Of course, there were other factors besides Nature that fastened agrarian rule on the South, as we have seen. Nature did not forge the national economy, for one thing. But Fitzhugh was correct in outlining the limited economic options available to an agricultural region. It also explains why southern hopes for direct trade routes to Europe were as chimerical as western trade empires and industrial metropolises. Certainly, southern ports possessed attractive export commodities—cotton and tobacco, for two prominent examples—to fill ships bound for Europe. The problem was that ships returned home with ballast and little else. The market for European manufactures was not any larger than that for southern industrial products.

In 1860, New York exported 36.2 percent of the nation's value in exports, while five southern ports (Richmond-Norfolk, Charleston, Savannah, Mobile, and New Orleans) combined for 47.2 percent of the nation's value in exports. In that same year New York accounted for an impressive 68.5 percent of the nation's value in imports, while the five southern ports could manage only 6.6 percent. Southern cities, in the words of one Richmond journalist, were "*literally* hewers of wood and drawers of water" for the North.

The antebellum South was strangled by its own prosperity. It fulfilled a role in the national economy and played that role too well. The scene was just as Fitzhugh had described it: a bountiful agriculture with limited urbanization, industrialization, and international trade. To be sure, the cities shared the prosperity of the farms in the 1850s; they grew, but they did not develop. And therein lay the fundamental problem of the southern economy—it did not lead anywhere else, except to the North.

Southerners surveying their region from the vantage point of their cities in 1860 must have been as frustrated as the Richmond journalist. After the most prosperous decade in their history, Albert Pike's words of 1850 were even more accurate ten years later. But southerners were also frightened. It was one thing to see their cities as economic appendages to the northern commercial juggernaut; it was another to see that dependence in the light of growing sectional antagonisms. Political subjugation could be the next logical step from economic subservience. For at least a decade, southerners had interlaced their pleas for railroads, industry, direct trade, and urban growth with warnings that failure had implications for the region beyond being "hewers of wood and drawers of water." Loss of wealth meant loss of independence—economic and political. "It is now a well-established theory of political economy," the Richmond *Enquirer* lectured in 1856, "that the centre of trade robs the extremities of their . . . independence as well as of their wealth."

That "independence" had both economic and political connotations was evident from the manner in which southerners, especially those in the cities, had viewed De Bow's call to arms a decade earlier. In that era when the quest for riches—commercial, mineral, and industrial—was a national fever, the importance of that quest assumed immense proportions. Thus southern economic and specifically urban growth was intertwined with sectional equilibrium and political equality. This is what southerners had been reading and hearing for over a decade: from George Fitzhugh came the dictum "trade very easily effects now what conquest did formerly"; from a southern politician: "If we are ever to divide, it will probably be brought on by a war of commercial restriction"; from the Richmond *Enquirer*: railroads to southern port cities would enable Virginia "to command justice at the hands of the other sections of the confederacy"; from a Richmond merchant in the aftermath of John Brown's raid: "Commercial independence of the North is the first great object in looking about for the means of remedy and redress"; from the *Enquirer* again, a promise that southern urban growth "will pacify the nation"; and finally from a Portsmouth editor who saw sectional antagonism as "a contest for political power as a means of securing pecuniary and commercial supremacy."

But suppose the North secured "pecuniary and commercial supremacy"; then what? The examples were neatly laid out for the South of what the response to that question might be. In that momentous spring of 1861, St. George Paxton, scion of a notable Virginia family, and Dennis Leatherbury, a promising young Richmonder, sat discussing the events of the day in Paxton's Richmond home. Paxton, drawing from the wisdom of his experience, lectured young Leatherbury on the causes of the crisis that was about to engulf their lives, their city, and their region: "My dear young man, this antagonism between the sections has nothing to do with slavery. It's as old as the country and has existed since the first American Congress. It's an economic struggle pure and simple. To grow rich the North must pass certain laws—tariff, for instance—harmful to the South. . . . The North needs the South's subservience for their complete financial success, and they won't allow us to withdraw." Paxton did not elaborate on the specific points of this historic economic struggle, but Clifford Dowdy, the novelist who created Paxton in *Bugles Blow No More*, doubtless assumed they were evident to southerners of the time, even to those as green as Leatherbury.

The necessity to limit or to reduce government authority had ranked with staple agriculture as a philosophical pillar of the antebellum southern mind ever since the Constitutional Convention of 1787, as Paxton implied. At that conclave, southern delegates expressed concern that northerners would use the new federal government to pass favorable commercial legislation and to tax exports. The southerners were successful in writing a prohibition on export levies into the Constitution, but suspicions remained that the wealthier North would use the federal government to its own economic advantage. Over the antebellum years, these fears were more or less confirmed, especially in the debates over the tariff. The tariff was an especially sensitive issue in the South because, as Virginian John Randolph warned, "the constitutional power that permitted Congress to enact a protective tariff could also be used to free the slaves." In addition, as economist Thomas R. Dew reasoned, the tariff increased wages and profits in the Northeast, inhibiting the migration of labor to agricultural regions and thus limiting their growth.

There were other examples on which anxious southerners could draw to support their fears about federal involvement in the economy. The United States Army as supplier, protector, and consumer had considerable impact on the extent of western urbanization and commerce. The United States Supreme Court ruled, in effect, that even property was not inviolate if it stood in the path of economic growth—an ominous precedent for the South. The role of government in all branches seemed to be evolving in antebellum America as a facilitator of economic growth. "The government's most pervasive role," according to political historian Richard P. McCormick, "was that of promoting development by distributing resources and privileges to individuals and groups." And the riches dispensed by government were numerous: corporate charters, tax exemptions, eminent domain, river and harbor improvements, land, and railroads. Governments gave, but they rarely took away. Regulation did not accompany generosity.

State governments led the way in the economic free-for-all that characterized the Age of Jackson. They spread funds, land, and legislation like seed across a field—and much more randomly. Debt and retrenchment were frequent results, but rarely did the financial antics of state governments ramify beyond their borders. For the federal government to engage in such profligacy was another matter, however. The resources that Washington could distribute were vast and, in terms of land, amounted to a western empire. In a nation comprised of relatively separate regional economies, the impact of federal largesse would be limited. In a national economy, with all the interregional linkages that this implied, the federal government could have significant impact as the only agency with interstate powers.

It was difficult enough, southerners believed, to battle northern dominance in the national economy without the additional concern of a northern economic alliance with Washington. Of course, virtually any measure the national government advanced in behalf of the national economy would benefit northern interests most, since they were already in the most favorable economic situation. This was not favoritism; it was economics. Southern anxieties boiled not only in the tariff debates but in the discussions on the disposition of western territories, a future economic empire. Although slavery remained the focus of public debate, wider questions were involved. In an America that cherished growth, would the South be stopped from growing? If no growth meant decline and subjugation—political and economic—could the South be precluded from the West? Of particular importance was the economic role of the western territories in providing the last major link in the national economy's advance to the West Coast. The Pacific railroad would provide that link, and the generosity of the federal government would be significant.

As early as the 1840s, southern urban leaders such as De Bow and New Orleans financier James Robb were attempting to persuade Washington to favor a southern route. At a southern commercial convention in 1853 in Memphis, the subject of a Pacific connection dominated the discussions. A report on the gathering in a New Orleans newspaper indicated the importance that southern entrepreneurs attached to the project: "This [the Pacific railroad] was the Aaron's rod that swallowed up all others. This was the great panacea which is to release the South from its bondage to the North, which is to pour untold wealth into our lap; which is to build up cities, steamships, manufactories, educate our children, and draw into our control . . . the untold wealth of the gorgeous East." There was a faint air of skepticism in the report, but irrepressible southern businessmen continued to believe that the railroad would be the Iron Messiah. At a similar conclave two years later, the delegates resolved in by-now familiar rhetoric "that the construction of a railroad to the Pacific Ocean, from proper points on the Mississippi river, within the slaveholding States of the Union, is not only important to those States, but indispensable to their welfare and prosperity, and even to their continued existence as equal and independent members of the confederacy." By 1855, the translation of economic issues into political terms was commonplace in the South. With the organization of new territories and with the Kansas-Nebraska Act of 1854, Congress had removed obstacles to a central or northern route for the railroad. Southerners, in the midst of a "contest . . . for wealth and commerce," to use De Bow's words, viewed these as ominous developments.

Perhaps it was the dark Calvinism that southerners practiced that led them to such fatalistic world-views of conspiracies against them and shining dreams turned to ashes. Whatever the philosophical roots, the economic realities seemed to confirm southerners' beliefs that they were an embattled minority. At every opportunity, they sought to preach the doctrines of equality within the Union. The rhetoric of urban and regional growth rarely excluded mention of equality, and by the 1840s equality was a common theme in political expressions as well. Southerners believed that they were the true upholders of "republicanism"—a limited government designed to protect individual freedom "from the impositions of tyrannical and arbitrary power," as historian Michael Holt explained—and that they were therefore the true keepers of America's revolutionary legacy.

Indeed, as sectionalism grew and economic prospects dimmed, the analogy between southern theorists and earlier American patriots appeared in bold relief. The Revolutionary mind was, according to historian Bernard Bailyn, "obsessed with corruption and disorder, . . . hostile and conspiratorial [in] outlook," and possessed a "millenial vision of a regenerated society." On a less philosophical level, the American Revolutionists were greatly concerned about the magnitude of corruption generated by "national engagement in the market economy" and the "aggressive national policies" that engagement entailed. The Revolutionary analogy was vivid for southerners because the national economy that was overwhelming them bore many of the same characteristics as the economic order the British attempted to fasten on their colonies in the 1760s and 1770s. Even unconsciously, southerners sounded like the patriots of an earlier day: "perfect equality between the States of the Union is the corner stone . . . of American liberty," a group of citizens in Virginia intoned in 1850. More purposefully, southerners recalled the experience of their illustrious forebears to illuminate the seriousness of contemporary problems. Analogies with the American Revolution, more specifically with how the changing nature of the British Empire after 1763 altered the delicate balance between colony and mother country, were widespread. Like the American colonies, antebellum southerners sought "to maintain things as they are; not the Union of the vulture and the lamb—but a league between equals."

All around them, southerners sought and found new evidence for their minority status and impending subjugation. This is not to say that the economic indicators should have given the South little concern or that the increasing presence of the federal government in the national economy should have stirred little comment. Given the legacy of history—a history that southerners read perhaps too well—and given the importance attached to urban and regional economic growth and to the concept of equality, it is understandable to find southerners putting the darkest interpretations on virtually every event occurring in the 1850s. It is pointless to cite statistics revealing how many seats southerners held on key committees, or how they controlled the Supreme Court, or even how many appropriations they received for regional river and harbor improvements. The daily operations of the national economy and the southerners' perception of increasing national government complicity in that economy were sufficient to convince southerners that the trend, if not the reality, was in favor of their subjugation.

In this intellectual and economic climate, the atmospheric pyrotechnics caused by the shower of Republican votes in the North after 1856 raised severe storm warnings in the South. As historians have pointed out, the Republicans were less an antislavery party than an antisouthern party—and openly so. In the 1858 congressional elections, Republicans campaigned throughout the North on a platform of economic nationalism. They advocated tariff revision, increased railroad land grants, and additional funding for river and harbor improvements. Reciting this list, they also blamed Democrats, particularly southerners, for thwarting these programs in the past. The Republicans believed in what one historian termed the "genial broker" theory of government: a government dispensing "the good things with neither regulation nor restraint." Southerners obviously had serious doubts about how genial government would be toward them in Republican hands.

The alarm that rang throughout the South in 1860 when Republicans captured the national government was not surprising. After decades of battling federal aggrandizement and after nearly fifteen years of struggling to attain economic parity—a parity made equivalent with their own freedom—southerners concluded that the Republican ascendancy demanded an immediate response. The debate during the secession months of 1860–1861 really revolved around the issue of whether a Republican government meant that the South would be relegated to a permanent minority condition or whether that status was temporary. On a more specific level, the concern was how and to what extent the Republicans would manipulate the national economy. The South was divided on these issues because, like the British Empire, the national economy had its benefits and securities. The votes

across the urban South in November and through the following March reflected this ambivalence.

Analyzing those votes, however, presents a problem. The 1860 presiden-
tial election was not a referendum on secession, and local issues and personalities could have been responsible for certain results. The composition of
secession conventions is not an accurate guide, either, because some of these
bodies were not popularly elected and few candidates ran under banners as
neatly explanatory as "Unionist" or "Secessionist." Nevertheless, in general
terms, urban southerners (and their rural partners for that matter) opposed
or were merely lukewarm toward secession, especially in the cotton South
where integration into the national economy was most marked. New Orleans, for example, was a hotbed of Unionist sentiment, and in Natchez,
deep in the Mississippi Delta, four out of every five residents opposed secession. On the other hand, secessionists were prominent in Charleston and in
Lynchburg. In the former city, South Carolina politics and economic stagnation encouraged anti-Union sentiment; in the latter city, economic ties to the
North were at most indirect. This did not mean that market orientation determined attitudes toward secession, but rather that those with fairly large
stakes in the national economy tended to view secession as bad business.

The debates during the conventions themselves offer a more accurate
rendering of ideas and motivations than can be made by a study of voting
patterns alone. The debates demonstrated both an appreciation of the South's
dependent position within the national economy and the importance of
southern cities in the coming struggle. The only uncertain variable was the
impact of a Republican-dominated government on the region and its cities.

For some Unionists, secession merely implied the exchange of a northern
master for a European master. New Orleans' James Robb urged that, rather
than exchanging dependencies, the South should change its habits and re-
double efforts to develop its own commerce and manufacturing. Industrialist William Gregg echoed Robb's analysis and pointed out that southern
manufacturing interests, as modest as they were in competition with northern industries, could be overcome by British industrial might. In that case,
the South would become even more agrarian and specialized.

Some Unionists feared the South more than they feared the Union. Fifteen years of intense effort to capture western trade, establish industries, ini-
tiate direct trade, and build cities in general had generated intense urban
rivalries within the South. In the Upper South, where specialization was less

pronounced than in the Lower South, there were concerns that obsessions with free trade would ruin industry in Richmond and Louisville, that rival rail lines and the development of New Orleans and Mobile, rather than of Norfolk or Richmond, would plunge the latter cities into greater eclipse than if they remained in the Union; and that valuable slave labor would be drained off either through escape or through the expansive needs of cotton cultivation. The mechanisms of the national economy that had helped to awaken southern nationalism also produced economic and urban sectionalism within the South.

Southern businessmen were generally a conservative group. They had absorbed and even initiated the rhetoric of sectional dependence and northern economic dominance. Though their options, especially for expansion, were limited, the national economic framework provided convenience, some profits, and security. For some, it was a matter of convenience to cloak their actions in southern patriotism; for others, the patriotism was doubtless genuine but not something that weighed heavily day in and day out on the entrepreneurs' conscience. There were frustrations, to be sure: faltering railroads, sputtering factories, shortages of capital and labor, and unfulfilled hopes for trade empires. It was easy to blame the northern dominance of the national economy for these obstacles, even though that was really only part of a much larger story. But inequality may not be sufficient cause to dissolve a relationship, especially if the alternatives could be worse.

Secessionists, or at least those who were convinced that a Republican regime would be ruinous to the South, depicted a brighter economic future for the urban South and for the region generally in a southern confederacy. John Forsyth, a Mobile entrepreneur, reflected the opinions of a number of his colleagues who viewed the southern confederacy as a glorious economic adventure that would at last result in the fulfillment of objectives sought since the 1840s. Forsyth predicted that "the Union broken, we should have what has been so long the dream of the South—direct trade and commercial independence. Then, our southern cities that have so long languished in the shade, while the grand emporia of the North have fattened upon favoring navigation laws, partial legislation by Congress, and the monopoly of the public expenditure, will spring into life and energy, and become the entrepôts of a great commerce."

Over on the South Atlantic coast, the prospect of a new era for southern cities was invigorating, especially in Charleston. The Charleston *Mercury* observed that "there are no people in the Southern States who will gain so certainly by a dissolution of the Union as the merchants and mechanics of our cities. At present, Norfolk, Charleston, Savannah, and Mobile are but suburbs of New York, Philadelphia, and Boston. . . . Break up our union with the North—let Southern cities resume their natural commerce—and what a mighty change will come over the prospects of our cities." Dissolution of the Union, the *Mercury* hoped, would dissolve the national economy, extricate southern cities from its grasp, and enable those cities to attain their true potential unfettered by northern and federal dominance. Up in Richmond, political leader George W. Munford was equally sanguine of the region's economic and urban successes once the South separated from the northern oppressor. Munford looked forward to winning the West from the North and "then we shall be able to build up our cities, to erect our own manufactories . . . to carry our own commerce in our own ships." The southern city became at once the embodiment of present failures and the locus of future successes.

The secessionists' argument implied that this grand urban future could never be realized in a Republican-governed Union. The history of federal intercession in the economy and the well-known antisouthern and economic nationalist positions of the Republican party were sufficient to reach conclusions about the inherently perverse nature of a Republican government. The immense patronage power of the national government, the $80 million that government dispersed annually, and indications that both would increase in the future were uncomfortable thoughts for southerners. There were few who felt that such federal perquisites would be distributed evenly. A Danville, Virginia, attorney asserted during the secession debates that "politicians of the North do not care so much about your slaves as they do about riding to power on the strength of the agitation of the slavery question and clutching the spoils of office." What the "spoils" entailed specifically were navigation laws "benefitting the ship-owners of the Northern States"; "patronage and power . . . to prevent the attainment of either direct trade or the completion of the James River and Ohio Canal"; a Pacific railroad along a northern route; and a discriminatory tax structure featuring a prohibitive tariff. By the new year, the prophesied tariff had become reality. The Morrill Tariff created consternation in the South, and observers declared it "a bill by which it is intended to plunder the South."

These undoubtedly were some of the specifics that St. George Paxton would have laid before Dennis Leatherbury if Paxton had felt that his guest needed educating. But Paxton was not a secessionist. In his understanding of the national economy, "the North needs the South's subservience for their complete financial success, and they won't allow us to withdraw." For Paxton and for numerous southerners, this was indeed a Hobson's choice: to accept colonial status or face a potentially ruinous war.

For other southerners, of course, the choice was much simpler: subjugation or freedom. In the turbulent years preceding the Civil War, it was easy for both sections to reduce their frustrations to slogans and patriotic rhetoric. But the limits of southern development were evident long before the national economy and Republican ascendancy took root. And the city was the clearest manifestation of those limitations. When De Bow charged into economic battle with southern cities as the points of his spears, he was already fighting with blunted weapons.

By 1861, the urban South had come full cycle. Staple agriculture reinforced a biracial society, and both structured the southern urban system. The national economy reinforced the character of this urban system and simultaneously encouraged the expansion of staple agriculture and, by implication, biracialism. And a stronger staple agriculture and a more insidious biracial society in turn strangled southern urbanization. It was a vicious cycle. The next four bloody years would settle many things in American society, but this cycle would remain unbroken. And the Old South would melt into the New.

III ❦ The Old South Under New Conditions
1861–1920

The Winter Cities

April in Richmond. The bright blue mornings are framed in memories as fresh as the new leaves on the trees and as sweet as the linden blossoms. It was such a morning in Virginia when Nature's brush painted in bold strokes the yellow tulips, the light green ivy, and the blue waters of the James rushing and invigorated by this spring awakening. Everything was new—reborn to begin life unsullied by previous hardships, stretching forward toward the sun, toward the future. On such a morning, St. George Paxton went for a walk "past the old houses on Clay Street, their gardens drooped and faded, and thought of all his friends who had once sipped their brandies on the rear balconies. Now they were scattered, the men dead, the women forced out by poverty." The harsh light of reality had overcome the April sunlight, and instead of spring and the future, there were only winter thoughts and the past.

Southern cities, like southern men and women, took the war in different ways. Some put on a brave face and managed; others were crumbled and broken. Some would never be the same, yet all would recover and resume their lives as before. Things had changed, but somehow they were still the same.

Cities had an involuntary growth as refugees poured in from the countryside. Richmond, bloated unnaturally by new government bureaucracy, refugees, and profiteers of various sorts, swelled to six times its normal size. War created its own urban hierarchy, but it was all temporary, a product of emergency, not of development. After the war, these cities would resume their agrarian life cycle.

Merchants in all cities were concerned about the economic disruptions that inevitably attended war. Many of these businessmen, except those in Charleston perhaps, had little sympathy with the secessionists and supported the Confederate cause half-heartedly. In New Orleans, the metropolis of the South, merchants attempted to pursue business as usual, northern connections and all, but the Union naval blockade brought business to a standstill in the Crescent City by the end of 1861. "Merchants tell me that such times have never been seen here," one editor reported. "A great many houses have already suspended and if times don't get better pretty soon, others will have to follow." Even the Mardi Gras in February, 1862, "passed off with a quietness never before known in New Orleans."

When the city capitulated a few months later, merchants felt more relieved than humiliated and business soon began to reach its normal rhythms. Union soldiers injected much-needed Federal money into the economy, and the regular patterns of trade resumed. Even the social life assumed a gaiety one would hardly have thought possible given the Union occupation. Theaters, balls, gambling, and prostitution—the usual social activities of New Orleans—flourished. There were a few notes of discord that accompanied these revelries. One minister complained, for example: "There is a soirée here to-night and the young girls seem to have forgotten everything else— They dance beneath the very flag that has been the death of their friends and relatives."

Death was a constant intrusion into life, and for life to go on thoughts of death must be pushed far away. This seemed to be the psychological character of those southern cities like New Orleans that were spared from advancing armies. Business as usual was not only a way of balancing ledgers but also of keeping the war from the mind, even if it was as close as a neighbor's doorstep. Memphis businessmen learned to live with the war in relative comfort as the city became a center for illicit trade between North and South. In Nashville, local leaders quickly surrendered to Union troops after the Confederates evacuated in February, 1862. Like New Orleans, Nashville was lost to the South early and managed to profit from Union occupation. The city did, however, aid the Confederate cause indirectly by quickly becoming "the clap capital of the universe." Bradwell Tolliver, the main character in Robert Penn Warren's *Flood*, insisted that Nashville's unheralded

"VD Brigade" was more effective against the enemy than the cavalry of Nathan Bedford Forrest. Tolliver suggested that the earnest women of the United Daughters of the Confederacy would do well to erect a monument inscribed "to those gallant girls . . . who gave their all to all."

Some cities did more than scratch out a living off Union soldiers or illicit trade; they became veritable industrial boom towns. It was "almost incredible," historian Raimondo Luraghi exclaimed, what some capital, demand, and organization could do for traditionally ineffectual southern industry. The results of the war years supported those secessionists who predicted that the South would become an industrial power once removed from the national economy. A catalog of southern urban industrial accomplishments is impressive. Augusta, Georgia, a languishing textile-mill city in the 1850s, had the largest and best powderworks in the country during the Civil War. Charlotte, North Carolina, even less of an industrial factor in the antebellum period, housed the Marine Engineering Works, which helped to build the southern navy literally from the bottom up. Petersburg, Virginia, and Columbia, South Carolina, manufactured twenty thousand pounds of powder a month—impressive even by northern standards. Little Selma, Alabama, a lazy cotton-market town like so many in the Alabama black belt, received a cannon foundry, which cast the big Brooke guns, "almost the best in the world." All of these plants were run by the Confederate government and represented an "incredible process of organization."

If war brought the main chance to some cities, it also brought some startling physical and political improvements. Southern military government in Atlanta and Union armies in New Orleans and Memphis launched a series of public works projects that advanced the health, water supply, and street systems. Military leaders were particularly attentive to public health needs because disease could wreak considerably more havoc than opposing armies. Atlanta, under the guidance of Confederate general Braxton Bragg, benefited from a sewer system and organized waste removal. Union generals Benjamin F. Butler and Nathaniel P. Banks gave New Orleans its first major cleaning perhaps ever. Over objections of local merchants, they installed a vigorous quarantine and attempted to deal with the city's massive drainage problems. Once Federal troops (and Federal funds) were withdrawn, however, the city soon lapsed into its slovenly ways.

For other cities, the clouds of war cast a longer shadow. There were perhaps some initial profits and improvements, but in the end only chaos and destruction. The terrible swift sword of war sundered these cities, and with

Leading Southern Cities, 1920

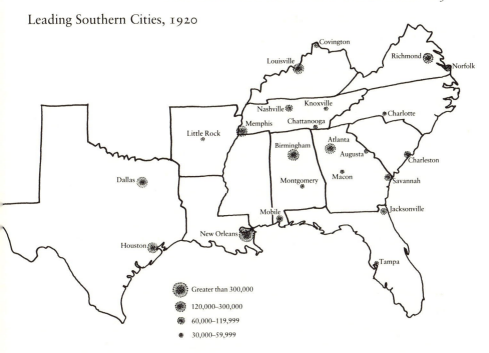

Louisville

Covington

Richmond

Norfolk

Nashville   Knoxville

Memphis   Chattanooga

Little Rock

Charlotte

Birmingham   Atlanta

Augusta

Charleston

Dallas

Montgomery   Macon

Savannah

Mobile

Jacksonville

New Orleans

Houston

Tampa

⬤ Greater than 300,000

⬤ 120,000–300,000

⬤ 60,000–119,999

⬤ 30,000–59,999

them fell the South. Before destruction, there was want. Inflation, scarcity, and profiteering weakened bodies and broke spirits. The decline in the Confederacy's fortunes on the battlefield was reflected in the empty plates and pockets of urban residents. By the end of 1863, the slow cancer of despair and deprivation had set in. Wooden shoes replaced leather ones; homeless civilians, wounded soldiers, and government workers crowded into already-burdened cities like Augusta and Richmond. By the first month of 1865, law and order had deteriorated and the usually ineffective police forces were even more so. Stealing became commonplace; even some churches were looted. Shootings, stabbings, fights, and fires occurred almost daily. By this time, citizens in affected cities resorted to barter because most merchants refused to accept Confederate currency. In any case, there was simply not enough money to purchase inflated goods. In Augusta, a bushel of salt sold for $150, wood close to $200 a cord, and a boy's wool hat for $125. Urban editors daily put forth plans for peace in their columns, but the war raged on.

And then it rained thunderbolts, and the winter of despair gave way to the spring of fire. The scene at the Atlanta railroad depot in the summer of 1864, with wounded and dying Confederates framed by a ruined city, is familiar as depicted by Margaret Mitchell. Though Atlanta in reality never approached the degree of devastation claimed by Mitchell, General William T. Sherman knew quite well where to concentrate his incendiary activities. The economic heart of the city—the central business district—was destroyed, and scarcely a building remained standing. "A dirty, dusty ruin it is," sighed one merchant almost one year after the attack.

The destruction was greater in Richmond, but there the fleeing Confederate troops were the culprits when a fire they set to destroy supplies, ammunition, and weapons before the onrushing Union army predictably raged out of control and destroyed most of downtown and parts of adjacent areas as well. The Confederates' scorched earth policy backfired, so to speak, again in Columbia, South Carolina, and in Montgomery, Alabama. General Sherman completed the destruction in the latter city by razing all of the public buildings.

Shortly after the war, northern newspaper correspondent John T. Trowbridge visited Charleston, South Carolina—the most hated of Confederate citadels. The proud port city that had inaugurated the war with banners flying and cannon booming now lay sullen and silent. "Since those recent days of pride and prosperity," Trowbridge wrote, "it has been woefully battered and desolated. . . . The gardens and broken walls of many of its fine residences remain to attest their former elegance. Broad semi-circular flights of marble steps, leading up to once proud doorways, now conduct you over cracked and calcined slabs to the level of high foundations swept of everything but the crushed fragments of superstructures." Over the hollow city that once swayed to the music from balls and cotillions it was still possible to hear another refrain—the echo of General Sherman's troops as they marched through the deathly silent streets singing "Mine eyes have seen the glory of the coming of the Lord."

But through defeat and destruction the urban South remained perhaps more "southern" than ever. Agriculture, blacks, and the Yankees—the three regional furies—remained, changed to some degree, of course, but still present to direct the course of southern urbanization in much the same manner as before. It was understandable, seeing the human and physical litter of war strewn randomly about shattered cities, to believe that an era had ended, that the future must be different from the past.

The spring blossomed into summer and the travelers began noticing other things. "The most beautiful city" were common appraisals of Montgomery and Richmond. Even in desolate Charleston, Trowbridge admitted that "its ruins are the most picturesque of any I saw." There was the southern city, emerging from war like the proverbial southern belle: beautiful, vulnerable, and dependent.

Cotton Grew Up to Our Front Door

> Mama never had a flower garden;
> Cotton grew up to our front door.
> —Billy Sherrill, "The South Is Gonna' Rise Again"

The rebuilding process went on quickly enough. Some physical scars remained through the 1870s, but for the most part the recovery of the urban infrastructure in many cities was complete by 1870. The most remarkable resurrection occurred in Atlanta. Immediately after the war, a startled visitor stepped into the whirl of activity and reported that "from all this ruin and devastation a new city is springing up with marvellous rapidity." The city seemed to be "running on wheels." By early 1867, the gutted central business district was rebuilt and Mayor James E. Williams christened it with these words: "A little over one year has passed, and how changed the scene. The city has been rebuilt and our thronged streets and active mechanics and businessmen indicate that Atlanta fresh from her smouldering ruins of the past . . . is again on the way to prosperity." The phrase "Atlanta Spirit" became a synonym for the progress of the urban South in the decades after Appomattox. And progress there was. After a tour of southern cities in 1869, one foreign visitor remarked that it was "marvelous how quickly towns are rebuilt in America. It is . . . still more surprising . . . in a ruined country."

But the urban renaissance was deceiving. A "ruined country" could perhaps support a rebuilding program, but southern cities would face a more serious challenge in going from physical to economic rehabilitation. The agricultural economy on which southern urbanization depended was indeed in ruins, and cotton production did not attain its prewar levels until 1880. In addition, the status of an entire labor force had changed virtually overnight, casting doubts on whether labor-intensive southern agriculture could ever attain profitable production levels. Finally, since agriculture was the region's primary capital-generating activity, it was not clear whether investments necessary to resume and sustain cultivation could be made.

Southern planters evolved two solutions to these problems of capital and labor. Since staple agriculture had traditionally provided the southern economy with needed capital, that type of cultivation would be emphasized even more than before now that capital requirements were greater. The emancipation of slaves ironically reinforced the resolve toward more intensive staple production, since planters no longer needed a diversified agriculture to fill out the work year for slaves.

The second solution involved the creation of mechanisms designed to ensure a more or less stable labor force. Through an elaborate, if not byzantine, system of sharecropping, crop lien, debt peonage, country stores, and tenancy, the planter assured himself of both production and labor. Since the entire system depended on the quantity of staple production, and since such production provided the economic leverage for both planter and laborer, one-crop cultivation became even more preeminent in the southern economy.

The development of the southern urban system following the Civil War reflected the South's increased dependence on staple agriculture. During the period of agricultural recovery to 1880, urbanization came to a virtual halt. The percentage of the South's population residing in cities increased from 9.6 percent in 1860 to only 12.2 percent by 1880, whereas in the highly urbanized Northeast those figures were 35.7 percent and 50.8 percent respectively. The ground lost by the laggard pace of southern urbanization just prior to the Civil War would never be recovered, even after staple agriculture achieved a modicum of prosperity during the 1880s. In 1830, five southern cities were among the nation's twenty leading cities; in 1900, only one (New Orleans) remained, and only six southern cities were among the fifty major cities.

Staple-crop cultivation was in part responsible for both the pace and the character of southern urbanization through the early twentieth century. Changes in both the marketing and the processing of cotton led to the even greater prevalence of smaller urban places in the southern urban system than had existed in the antebellum period. The appearance of country stores, storehouses, and taverns around rural railroad stations signified a localization of cotton marketing. Normally, this system should have benefited the southern port cities that could be expected to supply these merchants' crossroads settlements. However, the extent of the national railroad network enabled these storekeepers to bypass southern cities in favor of connections with northern cities. In this way, the country merchant (frequently a planter as well) could market the local cotton crop in exchange for goods without requiring any contact with southern ports.

The country store became a major business enterprise, some merchants selling over $200,000 in provisions a year. In the cash-poor economy of the postwar South, cotton became currency and paid for those provisions. This, of course, required the continued and expanded cultivation of the staple. The merchants, in turn, supplied everything from farm implements to cologne; they were also bankers, postmasters, and occasionally undertakers. The facility of long-distance railroad communications enabled them to keep their shelves stocked with a variety of the latest equipment and notions from northern emporiums. The country merchant-planter was replacing the urban port merchant as the middleman in the link between plantation and northern market.

The precipitous decline of New Orleans reflected the new marketing arrangements. New Orleans remained the major southern cotton port, but only because the lower Mississippi provided easier transportation for some planters than the railroads running eastward and westward. It seemed that one reverse after another afflicted the Crescent City during the 1860s and 1870s: a broken financial structure resulting from accepting credits in worthless Confederate currency; a devastating hurricane in 1867 that not only damaged the city but the cotton crop as well; a series of yellow fever epidemics in the 1870s that diminished business activity; and of course the change in the marketing system. It was only in 1883 that cotton receipts at the port attained prewar levels. Population melted away with commerce. In 1860, New Orleans was the sixth largest city in the nation; by 1900, the city had slipped to fifteenth and was on a downward spiral. Other southern ports experienced the same economic doldrums as New Orleans.

During the 1850s, the cotton revival precipitated a renewal of growth in such stagnant cities as Mobile, Savannah, and Charleston. With the decline in cotton production after the Civil War and the subsequent alterations in marketing patterns, these cities suffered economic relapses. Mobile, like New Orleans, depended on its river connections with black belt plantations, but the ubiquitous country store and its direct access to rail lines superseded the Gulf seaport. The national railroad network that led first to Atlanta and then northward doomed Savannah and Charleston, neither of which possessed direct rail connections to the North. The condition of these port cities in the fifteen years following defeat belied the exuberant descriptions of travelers. Charleston's center, as late as 1879, remained a charred and ruined reminder of the Lost Cause. New Orleans, whatever signs of recovery it demonstrated by 1880, was falling into disrepair. Mobile was "dilapidated and hopeless," and Norfolk lay "asleep by her magnificent harbor."

In addition to marketing changes, the improvement of processing techniques in the late-nineteenth-century South induced further decline in the region's major ports. Technological innovations that enabled cotton gins to process more cotton encouraged the removal of ginning from individual plantations to nearby towns along rail routes where cotton could be cleaned more cheaply in greater volume. By the 1880s, two new processing techniques had appeared: cotton compressing, which reduced the size of bales, and cottonseed oil mills, which extracted oil from crushed cottonseeds. Both of these techniques required relatively sophisticated machinery that could handle the product of roughly thirty cotton gins at one time. Such industries, therefore, commanded a wider market area than the ginning enterprises and consequently produced urban growth. Until 1930, those communities that were able to secure all three processing services were the fastest growing cities in the cotton belt. These additional services left the planter even less reason to patronize the once-flourishing seaports.

Although the processing communities were major beneficiaries of cotton belt urban growth, they attained the limits of their expansion relatively quickly. By 1900, these towns, which were scattered remarkably evenly throughout the area of cotton cultivation from Texas to southern Georgia, had reached a population of five to ten thousand inhabitants and rarely grew beyond that. The market area required by the new procedures remained relatively stationary and, since the processed cotton was immediately transshipped by rail to a major rail center like Dallas, Atlanta, or a northern city, there was little need for the development of higher functions. Mark Twain described one of the towns possessed of a "fine big mill for the manufacture of cottonseed oil" in the mid-1880s—a town that must have been typical of the numerous settlements that blossomed to urban status with the arrival of the railroad and the new processing techniques: "There were several rows and clusters of shabby farmhouses, and a supply of mud sufficient to insure the town against a famine in that article for a hundred years. . . . There were stagnant ponds in the streets . . . and a dozen rude scows were scattered about. . . . Still, it is a thriving place."

Actually, those cities that were outside the cotton belt or had very little contact with the staple were most successful in generating large-scale urban growth. Cotton cultivation, as in the antebellum era, could produce a significant number of urban places, but their size was severely restricted by the limits of the marketing and processing activities imposed by the crop. And as staple cultivation came to characterize the postwar South to an even greater extent than in the antebellum era, the small city became even more characteristic of southern urban settlement as well. In 1850, the South had 68.7 percent of its urban population in cities over 25,000 inhabitants. By 1900 this figure had declined to 48.1 percent, even though more southerners lived in cities by the latter date.

There were indications, however, that cities which could either serve as major transshipment points for cotton or which had little direct contact with the staple would become the region's new growth centers. Among the South's five most populous cities in 1920, Atlanta possessed only a few hundred citizens in 1850, and Birmingham did not exist at all at that date. Atlanta, child of the railroad, became the region's major cotton transshipment center as a result of its rail connections. For miles around this northwestern Georgia metropolis, scarcely a cotton plant was cultivated. There were abundant cotton fields south of Birmingham, of course, but the city hewed out of the northern Alabama woods and mountains rarely saw a bale. Its growth was due primarily to the iron and steel industry.

Atlanta and Birmingham were only the most prominent examples of urbanization beyond simple staple marketing and processing. The growth of cities like Durham, Charlotte, and Greenville in the Carolina Piedmont reflected a more complex industrial base than basic processing. The rise of Florida's cities, such as Jacksonville and Tampa, which grew from a diversified commerce and industry, and the growth of Chattanooga, Knoxville, and Nashville from various railroad, industrial, and educational and cultural enterprises—all within the last two decades of the nineteenth century—indicated urban economies serving other masters besides or excluding King Cotton.

These new urban centers, together with the proliferating cotton marketing and processing towns, represented a shift from the antebellum pattern of one primary city—New Orleans—a few secondary seaports, and a host of small urban communities. Urban settlements were now strung out like baubles along the railroad tracks, much as their antebellum predecessors hugged the coasts. The shift, however, did not signify a change in the nature of

southern urbanization but merely a change in geography. Up to World War
I, urbanization in the South was, as C. Vann Woodward stated, "compara-
tively unimportant." When the urban "boom" generated by new industries
and railroad connections in the 1880s subsided in 1900, the South Atlantic
states showed an urban population of 17 percent compared with 58.6 percent for the North Atlantic states. In North Carolina, where Piedmont urbanization was one of the major urban trends of the late nineteenth century,
no city exceeded 25,000 inhabitants in 1900 and only six possessed more
than 10,000 people.

Essentially, cities in the New South performed the same agricultural
functions as they had in the Old South: they were primarily agricultural
marketplaces, "mere adjuncts to the countryside," as one historian put it.
Even in the region's few larger cities, the economic dominance of agriculture
persisted. By the early twentieth century, the country store began to fade in
certain areas of the cotton district as merchants in larger cities, armed with
more attractive credit and marketing arrangements, combined with planters
to squeeze out the country storekeepers. This development was not helpful
to the seacoast cities, but rather benefited interior depots like Memphis and
Atlanta with superior rail connections to the North.

In Memphis, the cotton factor directed the cotton traffic. He was, according to historian William D. Miller, "the prime mover of the whole cotton cycle." By 1920, the cotton factor, like the country merchant before
him, was giving way to another cotton functionary—the "spot" broker who
moved cotton from farm to mill. Regardless of the personnel, however, the
common denominator was the quantity of staple-crop production. The fortunes of Memphis lay in the cotton fields. "Cotton made Memphis a city," a
visitor noted emphatically in 1898—and, he might have added, many other
cities as well.

The identity of economic and political ideals between planter and urban
merchant followed the close commercial arrangements between city and
country. Typically, the best spokesmen for planters were the editors of the
urban press. In Alabama, for example, the Montgomery *Advertiser* and the
Mobile *Register* were planter organs that helped the cotton growers loosen
the economic grip of country merchants. They frequently extolled the virtues of staple agriculture and occasionally even denigrated their own prospects in favor of agrarian pursuits. The Montgomery *Advertiser* advised
young farm boys to "keep away from the cities . . . and call upon mother

earth for employment. She will welcome you." In Atlanta, the capital of New South boosterism, the cotton connection was worn proudly on the chests of merchants boosting an automobile exposition in 1909. The symbol for the fair, as displayed by lapel buttons, was a bale of cotton framed in an auto wheel. It was a less-than-subtle reminder to visitors, especially those from the North, that though Atlanta welcomed the opportunity to become the region's automobile market, the success of the new technology depended more on that bale of cotton than on any other factor.

At the 1896 Democratic party convention in Chicago, William Jennings Bryan, the "boy orator" from Nebraska, presented an agrarian homily that electrified the convention and found an especially warm response among southern delegates. Bryan reminded the delegates that cities, once destroyed, would magically arise and prosper, but that if farms were obliterated, grass would grow in the streets of every city. For southerners, the experience of war, destruction, and defeat was not yet so far off. Their own encounters with the remarkable resurrection of Atlanta and Richmond confirmed Bryan's assertion, as did his stress on agriculture as the economic if not philosophical foundation of a society. Two decades earlier, the Birmingham *Iron Age*, an industrialist organ in a city with relatively minor connections with staple production, revealed the grip of agriculture on the regional mind by offering a remedy for Alabama's chronic capital anemia: "It would be better for the state that our mountains of iron and coal should remain untouched than they should be developed for the purpose of building up other sections . . . the best way to get capital, such as we want, is to build up our agricultural interest." The *Iron Age* went on to observe that, although Birmingham and other southern cities seemed to be growing and prosperous, "the population of towns in the South is by no means the index of prosperity. . . . Now they are entirely too prosperous. . . . When the country begins once again to be attractive *then* the towns will prosper."

The agrarian logic as practiced by the southern urban press reflected not only the economic bonds between city and country, but also the fact that, as editors rattled off their cotton philosophy, they were looking from their windows onto what was in many respects a rural environment. Southern cities still maintained a rural casualness about their physical appearance. When New Orleans merchants wanted to show off their city to visitors during their World's Industrial and Cotton Centennnial Exposition in 1884, they were apparently oblivious to the muddy, unpaved streets and to the flimsy, rotting wharves. Some parts of the city were positively wilderness, and a guidebook of the time recommended fishing and duck-hunting in the city's ninth ward, a district "which has never been visited by man, and as unknown as the centre of Africa." In Atlanta, "mud was everywhere," and in Memphis ravines and wildflowers punctuated the landscape.

Local leaders seemed unperturbed by the physical condition of their cities beyond the central business districts. If anything, their attitudes toward public services revealed an even stricter definition of "benefit to business" than had existed in the antebellum period. Streets were terrible, as the above descriptions implied. In theory, street paving continued to be the responsibility of private property owners, but in practice, city funds were applied to streets in the downtown and fashionable residential areas. Occasionally a local official might be sufficiently embarrassed by the contrast in street quality between different parts of the city to acknowledge, as Atlanta mayor William Ezzard did in 1870, that "while it is important to keep in good order the main streets in the business parts of the city . . . those in other parts of the city should not be neglected."

But these were suggestions, not plans for action. Southern urban streets remained the worst in the country through the early twentieth century. More than a generation after Mayor Ezzard ventured his opinion, 68 percent of Atlanta's streets were still unpaved. By comparison with other southern cities, though, Atlanta's streets were in good order. Over 70 percent of Birmingham's streets, 85 percent of Memphis' streets, and 92 percent of the thoroughfares in Dallas were unpaved in 1903. This performance contrasted with the record of New York (never particularly conscientious in the provision of public services), where 29 percent of the streets were unpaved, and of Boston, where only 1 percent of the streets were unpaved. In some southern cities, notably Memphis, wagons had given up the streets and were challenging the electric trolleys for the use of their tracks by the turn of the century.

The rough character of southern urban streets was matched by the rough character of other public services. Gas and later electric street lighting were selectively applied as well. The more dangerous (usually the poorest) sections of a city were invariably in the dark. One Atlantan complained that "after one gets off the main streets near the centre of the city, the scarcity of gas lights affords many convenient dark corners where almost any kind of evil deed [can] be perpetrated." And there were a considerable number of "evil deeds" in southern cities, since the police scarcely improved over their antebellum performances. New Orleans continued the least effective and most colorful police services in the region. The police in the Crescent City often refused to answer calls to break up the frequent brawls that occurred in the poorer districts. The corruption of the court system rarely led to convictions, and this, combined with low salaries, were hardly incentives to diligent police work.

New Orleans provided one of the more spectacular police dramas of the late nineteenth century, an incident that reflected the city's loose system of criminal justice. David C. Hennessy, one of the city's few able police officers, had successfully exposed organized crime among a portion of the Italian immigrant population during the 1880s. His zeal earned him a gangland-style execution in October, 1890. The police rounded up nineteen Italians, and the prosecutor eventually compiled seemingly strong cases against seven. The jury, however, acquitted six of the seven defendants and was unable to reach a decision on the seventh. Rumors of jury-fixing circulating about the city inflamed public opinion, and a notice appeared in the city's newspapers calling on citizens to participate in a meeting to take "steps to remedy the failure of justice in the HENNESSY CASE." Several hundred people assembled and quickly pronounced guilty verdicts on eleven of the alleged conspirators, some of whom had not yet been brought to trial. Armed with weapons and the verdict, the mob marched to the prison, removed the eleven men, hanged two and shot the rest.

Lynching, of course, was not strictly a New Orleans phenomenon. Although cities in the South were less likely to indulge in the regional lynching hysteria that grew during the 1890s, it is possible that the malleable urban press suppressed stories about such occurrences or that, in a poorly policed urban milieu, such crimes went undetected. There was sufficient violence in the southern city to suggest that lynching was more prevalent than the statistics show. The statistics indicated that urban southerners lived in a more violent environment than their urban colleagues in other regions. Specifically, urban murder was decidedly a southern urban phenomenon. During the early 1900s, the national homicide rate per one hundred thousand inhabitants was 7.2. Every southern city over 25,000 exceeded that rate. Memphis was far and away the nation's murder capital with a rate of 47.1; Charleston was a distant second at 27.7, with the other cities ranging from

13.6 in Nashville to 25.6 in Savannah. High murder rates were only one indication of a consistent pattern of southern urban violence.

Ineffective police service explained a part of the almost frontierlike conditions that existed in some southern cities, but the nature of the residents themselves caused much of the turbulence experienced in these communities. As in the antebellum period, and usually more so, the roots of the southern urban population were sunk deep in rural soil. Nearly three million black and white rural migrants entered southern cities between 1870 and 1930. Those who remained there added to the overwhelmingly rural character of the population. The migration to the city was particularly intense after Appomattox. As early as 1868, one-half of Atlanta's population had arrived from the countryside since the end of the war. Rural migration receded, especially with the return of staple prosperity in the 1880s, but a steady rural stream flowed into southern cities for the remainder of the century. Memphis, one of the region's few prosperous larger cities, was also the most rural. By 1900, 80 percent of the city's residents were from the adjacent Mississippi or Tennessee countryside. Similar percentages prevailed for Jacksonville, Birmingham, and Atlanta. While rural proportions increased, the immigrant population usually declined. In Memphis, for example, 37 percent of the population was foreign-born in 1860; by 1900, that figure had declined to 15 percent. Southern cities were becoming more rural and less diverse, just as their region was becoming more oriented toward staple agriculture.

The predominantly rural character of the southern urban population and of the cities themselves necessitated few value or life-style adjustments among rural newcomers. Rural southerners, according to historian Gerald Capers, "were addicted to violence, carried guns, and believed in the right of private vengeance." Chiseled on gravestones throughout the southern countryside, words like *fidelity, honor,* and *integrity* reflected the code that sent these unfortunate victims to a violent death. The southern woman—the "shield-bearing Athena gleaming whitely in the clouds," as W. J. Cash noted with some sarcasm—was frequently the excuse for resorting to violence in the countryside. The rigidity of these values, as well as their primitiveness, survived in an urban environment where they became more dangerous as a result of physical proximity created by the urban setting. These beliefs transcended race and tended to define law and legality in extremely personal terms.

Evangelical Protestantism, perhaps the region's dominant postwar cultural influence, saturated the regional psyche. The pain and martyrdom evoked by the Lost Cause blended well with a religion obsessed with suffering and salvation. For a poverty-stricken region wrapped in grief and defeat, evangelical ritual, liturgy, and promise filled a deep spiritual need. The migrants carried this heavy emotional burden with them to the cities. Some rural churches, in fact, were transplanted whole to the town center. Edgar Thompson remarked of this era that "southern town and even city churches generally might almost be described as transplanted rural institutions." By 1885, a southern minister declared that "the controlling sentiment of the Southern people in city and hamlet, in camp and field, among the white and the black, has been religious." Between 1890 and 1906—the period of greatest religious revival in southern city and countryside—white church membership in the evangelical sects increased by 51 percent to over nine million communicants.

Evangelical religion was thus a major force in southern urban life. It was a conservative agency that countenanced official neglect of the migrants' generally low living standards and supported the biracial society. Church doctrines preached that "the Christian is merely a sojourner in this world, evils have to be endured, and the evangelical gospel makes them endurable." Such notions as the Social Gospel, which informed northern urban Protestantism during the late nineteenth and early twentieth centuries, were inconsequential in southern evangelical sects. The reform impulse of southern urban churches in the early 1900s was generally expended on prohibition and blue laws.

So the migrants lived undisturbed among filth, disease, and poverty. During the late nineteenth and early twentieth centuries, New Orleans consistently was the nation's most unhealthy city as measured by death rates per thousand population. Yellow fever was almost a yearly visitor to the port, yet the city's business leaders succeeded in forcing a loophole into the quarantine legislation that enabled vessels to slip through quarantine if the less-than-thorough port officials found no disease on board and fumigated the ship with carbolic acid. The devastating yellow fever epidemic of 1878 probably resulted from this ineffective inspection system. The city's general neglect of health matters finally led, in 1898, to the establishment of a state-ordered board of health for New Orleans that operated independent of all city agencies.

The 1878 yellow fever epidemic that struck New Orleans also laid Memphis to waste. The city went bankrupt and surrendered its charter to the state of Tennessee; it would take another decade for the city to replace the population it lost through death and desertion, and as late as 1920 eastern states prohibited insurance companies from investing in the city's bonds. A United States Surgeon General's report termed health conditions in Memphis "shameful and a disgrace," especially in view of the official ignorance about modern sanitary engineering techniques that might have thwarted the epidemic. Local leaders further exacerbated the deteriorating health of the city by ignoring the contamination of cisterns and wells that supplied water for most residents.

Water contamination, in fact, was a problem in many southern cities where officials eschewed investments in sanitary systems until early in the twentieth century. It was still unsafe to drink New Orleans water, which reputedly rivaled the Mississippi River for color, in the 1920s. In Atlanta, where the city's elevation should have spared its residents some of the destruction of disease, the fact that public sewers served only one-third of the city's water closets counteracted altitude. The problem in Atlanta, and in many other southern cities, lay with a weak board of health that was dependent upon municipal authorities for its existence. The powers of these boards were primarily advisory, and only when the state (as Louisiana did in 1898) took control of the city's health affairs did a general housecleaning occur.

Disease and poverty were usually in tandem in southern cities, and local leaders ignored both. The rural migrants were generally poor and soon strained the efforts of private charities. While Danish immigrant Jacob Riis exposed how "the other half" lived in desperate poverty in New York, the extensive misery of the southern white and black urban poor rarely surfaced in print, much less in the consciousness of local leaders. Grinding poverty was a way of life in the southern countryside. Why should it be any different in the southern city? The relatively low density of southern cities—another dimension of their agrarian aspect—and the relative residential separation of the poor facilitated the neglect of poverty. New Orleans, probably the region's densest city in 1890, counted 10.2 people per acre, compared with New York's 58.87 people per acre, and most southern cities were considerably less dense. While low density seemed to lessen poverty's impact, the experience of urban residents made it the normal human condition. The visual spectacle of thousands packed into dense tenements—a display that moved councils and legislatures in the North—was rarely found in southern cities.

The dislocations of war, of course, generated hardships beyond local government's fiscal abilities to relieve them. In Atlanta during the immediate postwar years, temporary shelters became permanent homes for rural refugees. Some carved out homes in pits or in Confederate breastworks. A visitor to one of these camps in 1866 reported "hundreds of the inhabitants, white and black . . . living in wretched hovels." The camps were gone by the 1870s, but the poverty remained in Atlanta, the New South's showcase city. The peripheral areas that were the sites of these flimsy settlements had become permanent pockets of poverty, and the residents became victims of flood, fire, and disease. They bore the price of poverty by themselves. The press charged that local Atlanta officials were "extravagant" in donating funds for poor relief and suggested investigations for "graft." The poorhouse, supported at city expense, consisted of two-room wooden "cottages" without ceilings or heat. In the middle of winter, children dressed "in rags and tatters." Yet few Atlantans disagreed with Mayor John H. James, a banker, when he lectured: "Idleness is a great source of evil. We should not encourage it in our institutions of charity."

Conditions were equally bad, if not worse, in Memphis and New Orleans. The rooming-house district along Gayoso Street in Memphis was usually the final stop in a life of poverty and despair. There the poor played out their lives with alcoholism, gambling, and violence. The area produced one of the highest suicide rates in the nation. In New Orleans, the poverty and neglect were greater than in any other southern city. The city noted for its gaiety was a bittersweet encounter for those who traveled through all of its diverse parts. The city's poorhouse was administered by the head of the waterworks, and the city's charity was on the same level of quality as its water supply. The Irish-dominated Catholic Church provided the only consistent poor relief in the city.

Southern cities were not, of course, the only cities with a poverty problem; they just did less about it—much less. The same local governments that left streets unpaved and disease unconquered allowed poverty to go untended. Per capita expenditures of southern urban governments were well below national averages. In 1880, New Orleans spent $8.70 per inhabitant, compared with $50 in Boston. Only Louisville spent less per capita on sanitary measures than New Orleans, the most infected city in the country. Despite such budgeting, cities such as Memphis and Savannah went bankrupt, and others after the experience with railroad extravagances in the 1850s barely paid off their debts and resolved not to contract any others. The regional economic depression after the war exacerbated urban financial problems. Following the Panic of 1873, revised charters and self-imposed restrictions circumscribed the fiscal role of local governments to an even greater extent. Southern cities were not sound financial operations for several years after the Civil War, but it is also true that tax burdens on citizens were relatively lower in southern cities than in other regions. The penny-pinching of the antebellum era had become miserliness. The connection, if not identity, between business and government remained the same.

As the population of the southern city became more rural and poorer, the power of the local elite increased. The leadership had a great advantage over much of the urban population in that it remained a relatively stable and uniform group into the twentieth century, though policy disagreements occurred occasionally. In Atlanta, political analyst Floyd Hunter's characterization of the elite in 1950 was applicable to the leadership in 1900, and probably in 1850 as well: they were men drawn from the commercial and professional ranks, southern-born, from well-placed families, and relative old-timers in terms of residence. In the late nineteenth century, Atlanta's political leaders went through what historian Eugene Watts described as a "social filter." The political system filtered workers, blacks, and newcomers out of the leadership selection process. Throughout the late nineteenth and early twentieth centuries, merchants and lawyers continued to dominate the city's leadership. If anything, the group became more exclusive in terms of wealth and social standing as time passed.

The maintenance and cross-fertilization of economic and political elites was much less common in northern cities by 1900. In the urban South, the unsophisticated and politically inactive rural migrants who requested very little from government did not challenge the leadership. Industrial workers frequently lived on the periphery, outside city limits, or in rural communities quite apart from the cities. The blacks, by the 1890s, were political nonentities. Finally, in a region that abhorred change, it seemed natural for continuity to predominate in southern urban leadership patterns. The relentless expansion of staple agriculture maintained its urban beneficiaries in positions of economic and political power.

Occasionally, as a city's economic base was diversified by the addition of industry, manufacturers entered leadership circles. This did not alter the exclusive character of the leadership, however. Industrialists usually possessed the same values as the merchants (frequently they were former merchants), especially if they engaged in some aspect of staple-crop processing. Despite some policy disagreements, the basic philosophy of urban government as an engine for economic growth remained unchanged.

The belief persisted, long after it was challenged in northern cities, that the interests of a narrow economic elite defined the interests of the community as a whole. The extent and selective application of public services was one indication of this attitude; the vigorous pursuit of land speculation as reflected in the close connections between transportation franchises and local officials was another. In Richmond during the early 1900s, the streetcar companies directed the city's peripheral development and created substantial suburban empires. Following the antebellum precept that growth meant progress, southern urban leaders made up in territory what they lacked in economic and population growth. The work of the streetcar companies in Richmond led to a massive annexation in 1914 that doubled the city's size. Nashville leaders also pursued a vigorous annexation policy. Their justification typified the "bigger-is-better" philosophy that pervaded the rhetoric and actions of the southern urban elite. A local editor reminded critics of annexation in 1880 that "the census report of 1880 will have much to do for or against the prosperity of Nashville in the future." If the city could not attract population, at least it could go out and capture it.

The booster philosophy of annexation ignored the realities of providing services for the new areas, and the already-thin service expenditures had to be stretched even further. When annexation involved wealthy suburbs, such as Edgefield outside of Nashville, these districts received service priority as older sections of the inner city suffered. Yet growth had an attraction of its own that seemed to transcend fiscal conservatism much as railroad fever did in the antebellum era. From the late 1890s into the 1920s, Memphis leaders timed their annexations to occur just prior to the decennial census count. The census became such an important indicator of progress that Memphis political boss Edward H. Crump fired off a letter to Washington suggesting that the government undertake the count every five years. When the 1900 census revealed that recent annexation had resulted in a 58.6 percent population increase since 1890, Memphis officials ordered a parade and bonfires to celebrate the census announcement. At the time, Memphis possessed no parks, zoos, or public cultural institutions.

That local leaders pored over census figures while many of their fellow citizens resided in filth and poverty reflected in part the relative absence of opposition to government by business. When workers in Atlanta began to demand a voice in government during the late 1870s, the elite succeeded in evolving a compromise where workers would receive certain offices—minor ones, to be sure—in the city bureaucracy. If workers became too vociferous, the race issue was always available to promote white solidarity and diminish dissent.

The uniformity of leadership in southern cities should not imply that local politics was necessarily uneventful. Though officials probably had less budgetary discretion than they possessed in antebellum days, government carried sufficient fiscal and patronage attractions to generate vigorous contests among the elite. Predictably, New Orleans furnished some of the region's most interesting political shows during the late nineteenth and early twentieth centuries, since the diversity of the city encouraged a more open political system than existed in other southern cities. During the 1880s, the "Ring," a group primarily from the working class, and the "Reformers," a "silk-stocking" organization whose major reform was to throw the Ring out of office, battled for political power. The differences between the two factions were much less than their origins imply; they both operated government for the benefit of business interests, though the Ring was more generous in its patronage rewards. Corruption proved the Ring's undoing. By 1896, thirty councilmen had been indicted on various charges of misusing public funds. A new ring emerged from that wreckage and, under the leadership of Martin Behrman, a genuine political boss, dominated New Orleans politics for the next quarter century. Ultimately, the new Ring proved the more reformist of the two groups as it launched the city's first major public works program in the years after 1900. The huge debt generated by these programs led to a return of "business efficiency" by the 1920s, however.

Memphis had its own version of a machine in the person of Edward H. Crump, a rural immigrant from Holly Springs, Mississippi. But Crump was not as generous as the New Orleans Ring, though he frequently sounded like a Populist. More characteristic was his dictum that "Memphis should be conducted as a great business corporation." He maintained a low tax structure and a corresponding low service level. Aside from his own personal dominance, Crump's regime differed little from the more anonymous but equally business-oriented governments in Atlanta, Birmingham, or Nashville.

The southern version of the national reform movement known as Progressivism generally avoided the social improvement aspects of the movement but participated in political reform efforts. In fact, some southern cities pioneered such Progressive government experiments as the commission plan, which premiered in Galveston in 1900, and the city-manager form of political administration, which first appeared in Staunton, Virginia, in 1908 and Sumter, South Carolina, in 1911 before spreading throughout the country. The basic thrust of these administrative adjustments was to increase government efficiency, reduce financial waste, and upgrade service quality and quantity. On the latter front, southern urban governments in general improved their records between 1900 and 1910, paving streets with unprecedented vigor (though selectively), improving wretched school systems, and introducing concepts of modern city planning.

The Progressive reforms were hardly revolutionary and fit into the conservative urban political scheme quite well. Crump was a forceful advocate for commission government, for example. In Greensboro, North Carolina, proponents for the commission system promised "a businesslike, nonpartisan, economical, efficient government." Of course, this was the prevailing municipal government philosophy in the South, anyway; the reforms merely institutionalized such views in a permanent bureaucratic framework, relatively safe from the electorate.

City planning was among the more popular Progressive devices adopted by southern urban governments. Its implementation underscores how reform served traditional southern values. The somewhat chaotic, rustic environment that characterized southern cities concerned image-conscious leaders, though they did little beyond tidying up the central business districts. The rural quietude and charm that marked the southern city in the antebellum era seemed to be disappearing. Even lovely Natchez was a rotting relic of the past. In newer cities like Atlanta, parks and open spaces were rare, if they existed at all. A visitor to Atlanta in 1879 observed the priorities: "the city has not parks but an abundance of substantial business edifices." It was not surprising, then, that under the rubric of "planning," projects emerged to spruce up southern cities.

Much of the impetus for southern "city beautiful" campaigns came from women's clubs. The activities of such groups throughout urban North Carolina from 1902 to 1915 were typical of efforts elsewhere in the South. The Charlotte Woman's Club presented awards for the best gardens along the street, and a similar group in Wilmington donated prizes to residents who chose a special flower for their particular street. Occasionally, businessmen joined the ladies, as in Greensboro where they presented awards for the cleanest backyard and the neatest lawn. But when the Woman's Club of Raleigh hired city planner Charles Mulford Robinson in 1912 to draft a comprehensive plan for the city, official support faded. The message was clear: occasional shrubs, "comely" waste receptacles, and flower beds would receive praise and even a few dollars, but Robinson's suggestions—which involved groupings of civic buildings, formal plantings and statues, and a major thoroughfare designed as a "triumphal way lined with groups of sculpture and gay with banners and the splash of fountains"—were a bit too grandiose for conservative businessmen. Anyway, their implementation would have little effect on providing necessary public services to all citizens.

Local leaders expressed some interest in the broader questions of planning as their cities continued to expand geographically, but much of this interest was in the nature of encouraging private developers to acquire land and design attractive suburban communities for the more affluent urban residents. Atlanta entrepreneur and transit magnate Joel Hurt hired John C. Olmsted, stepson of the famous landscape architect, to design fashionable Druid Hills. The curvilinear road system and the chain of parks running through this community gave it a garden quality. The large lots, which, in Olmsted's words, mitigated against "the likelihood of poor purchasers," became sites for magnificent homes, most with the inevitable classical porticos of the antebellum plantations. Another Joel Hurt venture, Inman Park, failed to become a wealthy garden suburb—there were not enough people in Atlanta with sufficient wealth to support two affluent developments. The only exclusive feature of this suburb and of similar residential suburbs emerging on the outskirts of other southern cities during the early 1900s was their racial homogeneity. Deed covenants and restrictions ensured that the suburbs would, like the better residential neighborhoods of the city, maintain the color line.

The elite did not generally desert southern cities for the suburbs. There was really no need to do so, because their cities, in terms of segregation and density, were not too different from the suburban spatial arrangements. Consequently, the urban elites continued to control most aspects of city life, and their business interests, specifically the maintenance and extension of ties with rural customers and partners, remained their primary concern. The exchanges, fairs, and expositions designed to solidify the city-country relationship were the major institutions and events of an urban life dedicated to staple agriculture. Rhythms, it is true, varied from city to city. In Atlanta, life advanced at a quicker pace; in Charleston, it moved backward; and in New Orleans, it was syncopated, like the new music that drifted out of the Storyville bordellos. But jazz was a rural beat, too, and in all cities, regardless of pace, agriculture called the tune. In 1895, the *Atlantic Monthly* summarized urbanization in the New South era: "In the Southern States the rate of urban growth is not very rapid. The people are still predominantly agricultural." And, the magazine might have added, so were the cities.

New South spokesmen liked to point to Atlanta as a regional symbol of growth and prosperity. Actually, the city was little more than a large country town in 1900. Its area, depite annexations, was four times less than Boston and thirty times less than New York. It was still a walking city—that is, if you could negotiate the ravines and ditches. Despite its role as a cotton nexus, the city's bank clearings were at least seven times smaller than those of the major northern cities. In most statistical and physical aspects, Atlanta was still an antebellum city.

The South itself was, in many ways, still an antebellum region. Staple-crop agriculture continued to dominate the region's economy and life-style. Its vagaries gave shape and character to southern cities and to the southern urban system. Above all, it carried into the New South the legacy of a biracial society.

The Negro's Chance

In 1908, black leader W. E. B. Du Bois asserted that the "country was peculiarly the seat of slavery, and its blight still rests . . . heavily on the land . . . but in the cities . . . the Negro has had his chance." Indeed, southern blacks had been acting on similar beliefs for decades before Du Bois made his claim. For numerous former slaves, the first act of freedom was to leave the farm and move to the city. It was not only to test their freedom but also, as Du Bois implied, to take advantage of the benefits of urban life—the increased economic opportunities, the decreased surveillance, and the greater possibilities to read, write, and learn a trade. And they came to southern cities in unprecedented numbers following the Civil War. By 1870, black populations of southern cities containing more than 4,000 inhabitants had swelled by 80 percent, while the corresponding increase for whites was only 13 percent. Montgomery and Raleigh became predominantly black cities during this period; Richmond, Atlanta, and Nashville, nearly so. The great majority of these migrants came from rural counties surrounding southern cities or from Freedman's Bureau and Union Army camps established on the outskirts of cities at the end of the war. It was thus possible for whole families to migrate the relatively short distances—a luxury rarely permissible in antebellum days. By 1890, 15 percent of the region's blacks lived in southern cities, accounting for one-third of the South's urban population and 70 percent of the nation's black urban residents.

The very visible influx of blacks into southern cities alarmed whites who had nourished grave doubts about the wisdom of urban residences for blacks since the antebellum era. The advantages that blacks sought in city living were precisely those that made whites uneasy. It was a characteristic of the biracial society, especially in the cities, that the basic American values of ambition, education, and mobility were inverted when applied to blacks. The Freedman's Bureau and the Union Army were among the first organizations to persuade blacks to return to their rural homes, and the urban press kept up a steady campaign to convince blacks that a rural life was the best life for them. The Montgomery *Daily Ledger*, in a typical editorial during the fall of 1865, argued that blacks should "cultivate the soil, the employment God designed them for. . . . The city is no place for them; it was intended for white people." The blacks were evidently unmoved to resume their divine calling, since they continued to come into Montgomery over the next four years. None of these early efforts was successful in discouraging black migration to the city.

The *Daily Ledger* was undoubtedly reacting to general fears about the presence of large numbers of blacks in the relatively small confines of southern cities, but there was another equally serious concern. The southern economy was more dependent than ever on staple production, despite the prattling of New South boosters. A mobile labor force that viewed agricultural labor as a mark of its former enslavement and found urban opportunities more attractive threatened staple production and, as a consequence, the southern economy. For white southerners, there was the additional problem of coping with new relationships within the biracial society—that of employer-employee, instead of master-slave, for one major example. The status of the black, at least legally, had obviously changed, but between "slavery" and "freedom" there were many degrees of behavior to govern relationships.

The agricultural labor systems that evolved after the Civil War, especially after 1870, were complex and varied within the South. Some historians have called the systems slavery under another guise, but our vocabulary is more suited to describing what the systems involved rather than what they should be called. Peonage was one labor device utilized to secure long-term service from blacks after the Civil War. By this system, merchants and planters kept laborers in debt from year to year, coercing them to work off their debt only to confront them with another debit in their accounts at the end of the year. When the laborer had paid his debt, he was of course free to go. If he decided voluntarily to remain, he no longer was a peon, but, as historian Pete Daniel has noted, "when any element of coercion entered he became a peon. The line was that thin."

Sharecropping was not in itself a coercive labor system but a method to rationalize staple production and to accommodate the new realities of southern labor. However, it forced the sharecropper, black or white, to produce staple crops almost exclusively, thereby increasing his dependence for everything else—from food to clothing—on the merchant and/or planter. A poor crop year or inflated prices at the store could force the cropper into debt. Since cropping was covered by contract law, failure to work off the debt was a crime, and the punishment frequently was a term on the nefarious chain gang. The coercive labor systems involving blacks and an increasing number of whites set the South apart from the rest of the nation after the Civil War. The systems fulfilled the objectives of limiting mobility, evolving a new (and acceptable to whites) pattern of race relations, and achieving an economic order and stability geared to the production of a staple crop.

The relative decline in black migration to southern cities reflected the effectiveness of the new labor arrangements. After 1870, black urban population increased barely as fast as the white urban population. During the agricultural revival of the 1880s, black migration slowed to an even greater extent, and migration to other regions declined as well. Between 1870 and 1910, blacks comprised only one-third of the net migration from the Southeast. The familiar antebellum pattern was re-emerging: fluctuations in staple-crop agriculture determined the urban population of blacks, especially of black labor.

In the competition between city and farm for labor, the city would always lose. Throughout the late nineteenth and early twentieth centuries, three-quarters of the southern work force remained in agriculture. Since the region's economy depended on staple production, this priority was understandable. Moreover, the rules of biracialism prohibited urban entrepreneurs from openly coveting black labor, given the preeminence of agriculture and the widespread prejudices against blacks in cities. In the antebellum era, urban leaders had tried to attract immigrants as labor substitutes, and as immigration declined in the postwar era, southern entrepreneurs renewed their efforts to secure this more acceptable labor force.

In that rhetorical collection of propaganda, myth, and reverie known as the New South Creed, attracting European immigrants, especially those with skills, received a high priority. A Norfolk editor in an appropriate agricultural metaphor likened European immigration to "a human Nile. Wherever its waves flow fertility is established." In Atlanta, boosters issued this greeting: "Come whatever your political and religious creed; visit us, live with us." The city formed an immigration committee and sent representatives to Europe.

Atlanta managed to attract some Russian Jews and Greeks between 1890 and 1920, though the total Jewish population at that latter date was only 3 percent and the Greeks only .3 percent. The Jews were markedly successful in Atlanta, proving at least one claim of the city's boosters. In terms of property accumulation and occupational mobility, they outdistanced their northern brethren, and they were the most stable population element. There was, of course, some self-selection among Jews arriving in Atlanta or in any southern city. They already possessed some residential experience in America; they frequently arrived with capital and marketable skills; and they had less need for a relatively large community of coreligionists to provide support.

In most southern cities, despite the relative success of immigrants, their proportion of the population declined through the late nineteenth and early twentieth centuries. This was true even in port cities like Houston and New Orleans. In the former city, the immigrant portion of the population declined from 16 percent in 1870 to 10.4 percent in 1900; in New Orleans, there was an absolute decline in the number of foreign-born Germans as that population fell to half of what it was in 1860, and the Irish population increased by only one-fifth.

Immigrants generally found the South and the southern city even less attractive and convenient in the postwar era than in the antebellum period. Since immigration followed the same lines as commercial shipping, the continued decline of direct imports to southern ports indicated fewer possibilities for immigrants to enter those ports. In addition, staple agriculture was an even more dominant aspect of the southern economy in the postwar years, whereas the so-called "new" immigration that began during the 1880s was attracted most by urban-industrial opportunities. Working on southern farms as tenants and sharecroppers would not be much different from the agricultural tenure systems of their homelands. There were, of course, greater economic opportunities in northern cities, especially those in which industry was becoming a major economic force. Not only was it easier to migrate to these cities, but the presence of established ethnic communities, many dating from the antebellum days, made the transition to American life easier for the new arrivals. In southern cities, the antebellum ethnic communities were small and, by the late nineteenth century, relatively assimilated into the larger southern urban society.

The prevalence of the biracial society had some impact on the reluctance of immigrants to travel South. Rumors persisted that the large presence of black labor—90 percent of the nation's blacks still resided in the South as late as the 1890s—depressed wages for all workers. There was also a reluctance to compete with black labor, both from fear of racial conflict and from a concern that such competition could only result in the same miserable living conditions for the immigrant. In 1906, Jewish philanthropist Jacob Schiff devised a plan for diverting Jewish immigrants from northern ports and dispersing them more evenly throughout the country. He was concerned that concentration in the industrial northeast would generate prejudice and decreasing economic and housing opportunities for Russian Jews. Dispersion would also help to repair the growing split between the well-established German Jewish community and the newer arrivals from Russia. His plan included the diversion of immigrant ships to Galveston—a plan that should have resulted in some Jewish migration to nearby southern cities. Schiff, however, opposed southern settlement for these Jewish newcomers: "I am afraid Jewish immigration into the South would to a very large extent be used to place it in competition with Negro labor, and to attempt . . . to diminish the black predominance." Schiff believed that this scenario would ultimately work to the economic disadvantage of the Jews. His scheme for "immigrant deflection" achieved only meager results, but the avoidance of southern cities by Jewish newcomers in general indicated that other Jewish community leaders shared Schiff's concern about the economic impact of pitting Jews and blacks against each other.

It is probable that reports filtered back to northern immigrant communities indicating that, despite the expressed welcome for immigrants, hostility lay beneath the smiles and handshakes of southern urban boosters. White solidarity was crucial in a biracial society, and the introduction of diverse groups into a culturally homogeneous environment increased the threat of dissent. Though immigrants in southern cities generally supported Confederate efforts, most of them professed Unionist sentiments at the outset and were hardly bitter at the peace. The same Atlanta booster who invited immigrants to "live with us" also issued an italicized warning that would scarcely warm immigrant hearts toward southern cities: "*mind your own business*, and have no fear of G.A.R.'s, K.K.'s, or anything else." In addition, the "new" immigration of the 1880s—southern and eastern European Catholics and Jews—could not have diverged more from the fiercely Protestant rural migrants who comprised the majority of the white southern urban population. New South publicist Richard H. Edmonds reiterated his hope for European immigration to southern cities but at the same time complained that the immigrants of the 1880s were "not composed of the character of people desired by the South."

Occasionally, these sentiments flared into more overt expressions of nativism. Not only the Italians in New Orleans but all immigrant groups in that city received coarse treatment from the press in the form of derogatory remarks and denigrating cartoons, especially during the 1890s. The Italians were confined to the worst sections of the city, even more wretched than some of the black quarters. One magazine writer reported after a tour in 1898 that he found "a ten-roomed, leaky-roofed tenement house where fifty families eat, sleep, and have their being; old hags, drunken men, pale-faced young mothers and ghastly, bold-eyed children huddled together in penury and filth. . . . A dozen rickety stairways lead up to as many unwholesome rooms, about whose upper galleries, out of reach of molding damp and hungry children, hang festoons of macaroni, peppers and garlic." Considering the alternatives available to immigrants of all nationalities, the southern city in the midst of an overwhelmingly agrarian region held little attraction.

The failure to attract immigrants placed burdens on the urban black population, and their condition in cities deteriorated after the mid-1870s.

Since entrepreneurs had few labor options—immigrants were scarce, rural white women worked in rural textile mills, and everyone seemed to be tied to the farm in one manner or another—they had to ensure the reliability and availability of the black labor source, consistent with the demands of the biracial society, of course. The restrictions the white leaders devised made the city less attractive to blacks, even if they could extricate themselves from the agricultural labor system.

Vagrancy laws became the primary measures for controlling black labor and behavior in the city. Though the laws themselves never mentioned race, many more blacks than whites were arrested under these statutes. White employers invariably paid the fines of their convicted black employees, who were in turn legally obligated to work off the debt. If the black was unemployed, the court had no difficulty in securing a willing employer to post bail or pay the fine. Thus peonage, a predominantly rural method of race and labor control, had an urban variant as well. Actually, vagrancy was but one of a number of petty offenses that resulted in high black arrest ratios. In some instances, courts would set extremely high fines for light offenses in order to supply the local chain gang with labor. In Montgomery during the 1880s, roughly 90 percent of the cases before the city court involved blacks arrested for petty offenses and for whom punishment was forced labor on the chain gang.

Black labor and biracialism were valued enough institutions to encourage southern urban leaders to erect these cynical legal mechanisms to control both. Other devices, less formal and supported more by custom than by law, kept the urban black in his place. Emancipation had the ironic effect of depressing the economic situation of the free blacks. Though the distinctions between slave and free black were relatively minor in antebellum white opinion, there were examples of a free black elite, especially in some cities of the Lower South. After the Civil War, however, "nigger work" was tightly defined and occupational advancement became extremely difficult.

Urban blacks were usually employed either as domestics or as unskilled laborers. Occasionally they supplied labor as bricklayers and cement masons, but these were occupations dominated by slaves in antebellum southern cities. Even in Atlanta, where diverse economic opportunities existed and where the antebellum legacy was relatively weak, 90 percent of black workers were manual laborers. Black occupational status did not improve as time passed; in fact, there was some erosion in the skilled trades that blacks had monopolized since the antebellum era. In 1865, roughly 80 percent of the artisans in southern cities were black; by 1890, according to C. Vann Woodward, "they made up only a small proportion of the labor force in most crafts." It was rare by this time to find an urban black who was not a laundress, domestic, or unskilled laborer. As new trades appeared during that nadir of black fortunes, whites systematically excluded blacks from them. New techniques in plumbing, carpentry, and the assorted jobs associated with electrical work were closed to blacks, who were denied opportunities to learn or work at these skills. Mechanization forced blacks out of their traditional work in the tobacco factories, and the increasing preference for white women and children in southern industry reduced black employment opportunities even further. Nor were the traditional service occupations safe for black workers. White rural migration enabled middle-class families to hire white women in domestic work. A New Orleans resident boasted in 1904 that "it is possible now to live in New Orleans as free from any dependence on the services of negroes as one could be in New York or Boston."

Race was the fundamental factor in determining occupational mobility in the southern city. White rural and European newcomers fared reasonably well in moving up the status ladder. In fact, ethnicity was not a significant factor in determining urban occupational success; race was. In Atlanta between 1870 and 1896, 91 percent of the black work force remained in the same occupational rank, as compared with a 29 percent and a 26 percent upward mobility rate among native whites and immigrants respectively. True, there was little downward mobility among blacks, but they were already starting from the lowest positions. Blacks clearly functioned as "surrogate immigrants" in the southern urban labor force. In the North, immigrants generally held the lowest occupations. The important difference was that neither coercion nor permanence were among the handicaps confronting immigrants in northern cities.

Just as some unusual slaves managed to "beat the system" during the antebellum period and achieve economic success and even freedom, there were some unusual blacks after the war who hurdled the numerous obstacles and secured economic advancement. Blacks, discouraged from trades, occasionally began their own businesses, though many of these were small groceries catering to an impoverished clientele and most of them provided little employment or capital for the black community. Life insurance and banking were enterprises of larger scale, but the limited financial resources of the black community made these activities appear very modest when compared with white-owned counterparts. Undertakers were among the most affluent businessmen, and barbering was a black preserve until the late 1890s. In fact, one of the more prominent black entrepreneurs of the time was an Atlanta barber, Alonzo Herndon. Born a slave in rural Georgia, he migrated to Atlanta at the age of twenty-four in 1882. Working his way as a barber for white clientele, he eventually opened a shop of his own in 1896. Herndon went on to establish two more barber shops and found the Atlanta Life Insurance Company, the largest black stock company in the world. But Herndon was one of the few postwar black success stories, and his uniqueness underscored the limits of black opportunities in the urban South.

The economic color line was one of the most frustrating aspects of urban life for ambitious blacks, but the black found himself set apart from the white urban society in other ways as well. The biracial society insisted on an inferior role for blacks in all areas of urban life. With the demise of slavery, the distinction between black and white was strictly one of color, so color became the decisive factor in maintaining the distinction of the races. As in the old master-slave relationship, the new one would inevitably cast blacks in the inferior role. "Separate" and "unequal" were the watchwords of the biracial society.

Segregation had antebellum antecedents, but federal authorities adopted it as official policy toward blacks immediately after the war. As early as 1873, according to historian Howard N. Rabinowitz, "the urban landscape for blacks was dominated by segregation." Northerners viewed segregation as a partial reform, since the practice at least entitled blacks to their own schools, orphanages, and hospitals, whereas formerly they had none of these facilities at all. The removal of federal supervision left these institutions in the charge of native whites. Since most of these facilities for whites were of mediocre quality, those available for black clients were dismal, especially after the financial retrenchments following the Panic of 1873. Public service expenditures for separate black and white institutions reflected the unequal quality of these facilities. In Richmond in 1900, for example, city contributions to black charities amounted to $550; to white charities, appropriations amounted to $7,722, despite the greater prevalence of poverty in the black community.

The most serious inequalities related to black residence. Some residential dispersion existed in the antebellum era owing to the necessities of slavery, but, as in most other facets of southern urban life, the lines dividing black and white residential communities hardened and were more clearly defined by the 1890s. Identifiable black ghettos emerged, such as Richmond's Jackson Ward, which was only one of several Negro clusters in the prewar era. Moreover, residential segregation increased toward the twentieth century. If the cluster pattern prevailed in some cities, it was not a function of white liberalism but rather of the scattered nature of undesirable housing sites. In 1877, the Nashville Board of Health reported that the city's blacks "reside mainly in old stables, situated upon alleys in the midst of privy vaults, or in wooden shanties a remnant of war times, or in huts closely crowded together on the outskirts." By the 1890s, in cities like Atlanta, Richmond, and Durham, some of the clusters began to merge to form the nucleus of future ghettos. Frequently, the worst sites experienced the greatest growth, such as the "Hayti" cluster in Durham, a poorly drained area on the outskirts of the city.

Life in these communities was miserable for most blacks, given the inherent unsanitary conditions of the sites and the almost total absence of city services. The neighborhoods, especially those on the outskirts, presented the same rural appearance as they had in the 1850s: dirt roads, outdoor facilities, poor drainage, and frame "double-pen" houses or "shotgun shacks" that differed little from sharecroppers' dwellings. Statistics pointed out these neighborhoods quite well: the greatest illiteracy, the highest death rates, and the highest infant mortality.

Perhaps the most remarkable feature about black life in these neighborhoods was that a culture and a society evolved there and survived. The bitter disappointments of black freedom in a biracial society were not sufficient to extinguish some black spirits. Since many black neighborhoods were first-occupancy areas, especially those on the urban periphery, they controlled their neighborhood economy, meager as it was, and the small shops and groceries provided opportunities for entrepreneurship not available in other areas of the city. Through personal policies of "ruthless underconsumption" similar to those practiced by many immigrant groups in the North, blacks were able to accumulate property from their small profits and wages. In 1869, Atlanta blacks, for example, owned $37,000 worth of real estate; by 1890, the figure was $855,561. Most of the holdings were in small parcels, indicating the savings of families and individuals.

The church was the center of black community life, as it had been before the war, and the relative autonomy from white churches achieved in the 1840s and 1850s allowed black urban congregations to begin the new era with a firm foundation of leadership and tradition. The church was the pride of the black community. In Nashville, blacks collected $25,000, mostly in small donations, to erect a new brick and stone building for the First Colored Baptist Church. The quality of black churches in Macon and Atlanta led one traveler to remark in 1870 that "the Freedmen give more liberally for church purposes than even towards the support of their schools." The church transcended the religious purpose to become an all-purpose institution for southern urban blacks. As Du Bois asserted, "the church became the center of economic activity as well as of amusement, education and social intercourse." The dissolution of integrated churches and the disappearance of white ministers from black churches by the 1890s reinforced the position of the black church as the major indigenous institution by and for urban blacks.

It is not surprising to find ministers among the black leadership in postwar southern cities, but the development of a separate black society brought other leaders forward. Professional men trained at the prominent black urban universities, such as Fisk in Nashville, Meharry Medical College in the same city, and Atlanta University, began to make contributions to black urban life during the 1880s. The career of Nashville lawyer and businessman J. C. Napier indicated the institutional diversity of black communities by the 1890s. Napier was a prominent layman in the First Colored Baptist Church, one of the few black municipal officeholders, president of the black YMCA, and a member of various temperance and fraternal organizations.

Napier's activities heralded the emergence of an urban black middle class composed of teachers, lawyers, doctors, dentists, pharmacists, and businessmen nurtured in black institutions and frequently relying on an all-black clientele. In Savannah and Atlanta, skilled black workers in trades and service occupations assumed leadership roles. But the gap that existed between this "talented tenth" and the rest of the urban black population was enormous. Modest wealth, education, and life-style also placed the leaders apart. Social clubs and literary societies were unknown worlds to blacks who spent their recreation gambling, drinking, playing numbers, or more usually merely trying to survive until tomorrow. To the leaders, some of their lower-class brethren were embarrassments, and class divisions subverted whatever collective energy could have been generated to improve general conditions. Many of these black leaders had made their own peace with the biracial society; they accepted the rigid realities of segregation and attempted to follow the precepts of black leader Booker T. Washington, whose emphasis on self-help, strengthening community institutions, and industrial education reinforced what southern urban blacks had been practicing since the 1870s.

The construction of a black community—institutions, leadership, and business—did not imply a withdrawal from urban society but rather a temporary accommodation to that society. Although some blacks counseled strict compliance with the custom of segregation and urged fellow blacks not "to make themselves obnoxious" by agitating for their civil rights, others, including Booker T. Washington, fought the biracial society. In response to segregated streetcars, for example, blacks in cities across the South from 1900 to 1906 organized boycotts, formed their own transit companies, or walked in protest. Streetcars were one of the last urban facilities to remain integrated by 1900, primarily because the companies objected to the expense involved in establishing segregated accommodations. As the last bastion of integration, the streetcars were symbolically important to blacks who had seen whatever privileges they possessed, from voting to employment opportunities, erode during the 1890s. When southern cities began to pass general segregation ordinances to codify custom or to consolidate existing legislation, blacks initiated a boycott. The protests were successful in Jacksonville and Savannah, though they failed elsewhere because the black community lacked the economic power to force submission from the companies and city officials. Nevertheless, the boycotts indicated a degree of solidarity in the developing black community and a resistance to the strictures of the biracial urban society.

The growth of black militancy usually aroused hostility rather than conciliation in the white community. Protests against violations of the 1875 Civil Rights Act in southern cities led to the dismissal of complaining blacks. Economic pressure was an efficient instrument in stifling dissent in a black community that still depended on whites for employment. During the 1880s, growing black demands for improved services and representation in Atlanta city government launched successful white efforts to establish the white primary and effectively to exclude blacks from political participation. Finally, the codification of segregation during the 1890s, after a generation of controlling the biracial society through the force of custom, was primarily a reaction to increasing black protest against customary segregation. The emergence of a black middle class and of a generation grown up in freedom, and the awareness of the indignities and broken promises of an allegedly free society, had helped to raise black consciousness—and white reaction as well.

White reaction often went further than transforming custom into law. An acceleration in vagrancy arrests and chain gang recruitment were methods of expressing white displeasure at black pretensions. Blacks occasionally resisted arrest to avoid inevitable work impressment, and the police dealt harshly with these offenders. Sometimes police officers scarcely required an excuse to attack a suspect, and complaints against police violence were frequent from blacks in Atlanta, Nashville, and New Orleans. The legal system, however, offered scant protection for blacks and, in fact, encouraged the use of extralegal force by whites.

In 1900, Memphis saloonkeeper "Wild Bill" Latura walked into a black saloon and without provocation shot and killed six customers. Latura became an instant folk hero among Memphis whites. Although he was brought to trial, the court set him free. More widespread violence against urban blacks occurred periodically at ballot boxes, on the streets, and at work places where whites believed blacks were competing with them unfairly. White laborers in Memphis rampaged against the black community for two days in 1866, killing forty-four blacks and destroying a considerable amount of property; violence erupted between black and white strikers on the New Orleans docks in 1894 and again in 1900; and, finally, the Atlanta race riot of 1906, during which whites indiscriminately attacked unoffending blacks, were some examples of collective violence employed by whites who feared black assertiveness. These aggressions were not necessarily condoned by the general white population; they were just ignored.

It was extremely frustrating for blacks who strove for a better life in a biracial society to be confronted by the complicity of most whites, regardless of social class, in the suppression of the Negro race. The urban boosters of the New South might parade the lie of smooth race relations in front of potential northern investors, but in their actions in government and business they were vigorous supporters of the biracial society. Atlanta's Henry W. Grady, the embodiment of the New South, put it matter-of-factly: "the supremacy of the white race of the South must be maintained forever, and the domination of the negro race resisted at all points and at all hazards—because the white race is the superior race."

This was the pledge of allegiance to the flag of white supremacy. The flag cast its long shadow not only over blacks but over whites as well. The biracial society held within it the ironies of southern urban life: it restricted the very urban development that boosters sought to achieve by maintaining it, and it circumscribed the possibilities for white rural migrants who looked to it for liberation and self-respect. The requirement of white solidarity meant that some urban whites, usually the poorer residents, lost part of their liberties. In 1869, Atlanta's skilled white laborers formed a workingman's party to advance their interests in municipal government. The organization dissolved when local Democratic leaders warned workers that their party's challenge would result in "Negroes holding lucrative positions in your workshops, and acting as yardmasters over you." The New Orleans machine used similar arguments during the 1880s to beat white political opposition. Of course, such tactics were typical throughout the South during this period, as the southern Populists ruefully discovered. In the cities, raising the flag of white supremacy meant that a portion of the white population was effectively disfranchised. It was also one of the reasons why public services could remain limited without leaders fearing electoral reprisals.

The biracial society not only limited the political rights of the white working man but his economic rights as well. Since blacks worked for low wages, the general wage scale tended to be depressed, and southern cities consistently recorded the poorest wage levels among the nation's cities well into the twentieth century. Employers' use of blacks as strikebreakers turned the attention of white laborers away from their grievances against management. Shippers effectively played the race issue in New Orleans to defuse labor demands and maintain low wage scales.

If the biracial society restricted whites, it virtually eliminated blacks as contributors to urban development, although emancipation unleashed a vast potential of human energy and capital ready and anxious to serve the region and its cities. The South, traditionally an area rich in natural resources, now grew in human resources. Southerners acknowledged the human capital in their midst, but, like the soil that grew their cotton and tobacco, they squandered it. The black was foremost a source of labor, and a rather restricted type of labor at that. The tenets of the biracial society not only inhibited the formation of creative black economic responses but actively discouraged such initiatives. If blacks could not grow, however, neither could southern cities.

The purposely low wage scales hampered capital accumulation and reduced investment opportunities. Low consumer demand affected retail growth, industrial development, and generally the evolution of higher-level urban functions that could have generated an urban civilization beyond the market town. This was precisely the situation in the antebellum era. The biracial society was consistent: urban whites succeeded in re-creating not only some of the same racial relationships that prevailed before the war but similar economic debilities as well.

Blacks occasionally challenged the biracial society, but rarely with success. Instead, they turned their stifled creative energies toward developing their own communities and institutions, despite their overwhelming poverty. For urban blacks, the sense of fulfillment had to be sought in their own circumscribed society, but this restricted urban life was still better than what the countryside offered them. The cities took their initial racial cues from the countryside, to be sure: social separation and labor coercion were the central aspects of the biracial society both on the farm and in the city. In those states where rural race relations tended to be relatively mild within the biracial framework—in Tennessee and North Carolina, for examples— blacks built stronger and more prosperous communities in the cities within those states, such as in Nashville and Raleigh respectively. On the other hand, the severe rural repression in Alabama and Georgia carried into cities like Montgomery and Atlanta. Despite the similarities between city and country, however, the very nature of urban society, which threw blacks together in a common community, provided more opportunities for accomplishment.

Blacks were virtually sequestered away in their separate lives within the biracial urban society. This isolation allowed opportunities for self-help and institutional growth, but it was also a badge of degradation and a daily statement that their lives were not only separate but unequal. Two societies lived side by side, relatively speaking, in the southern city, yet their separation was complete in most aspects of urban life. As an Atlanta reporter confessed in 1881, "by far the largest proportion of Negroes are never really known to us. They are not employed in private homes nor in the business houses, but drift off to themselves, and are almost as far from the white people, so far as all practicable benefits of associations are concerned, as if the two races never met."

The separateness of the two societies—black and white—reflected the priority of maintaining the biracial society over investments in human capital. The returns to southern cities were consequently small, and this reinforced the dominance of the small southern city predicted by staple agriculture. It also helped to ensure that the urban South's old position as a colonial partner in the national economy would be retained in the New South era.

Southward the Star of Empire

The lessons of the Civil War were obvious to southern urban entrepreneurs: the North was victorious because it had more industry, larger cities, longer railroads, faster ships, and more people than the South. Collectively, these features of northern society first weakened, then conquered the South. Mayor John W. Daniel of Lynchburg, Virginia, summarized this view in 1877 when he lectured fellow citizens that the Union won because it "had cultivated the conquering ideas of the world. . . . It was because she had shown herself our superior in finance, . . . commerce, and manufactures. . . . These are the facts; thus it is that we are conquered." The remedies were as obvious as the causes; they involved the resurrection of the antebellum programs for commerce, manufacturing, and export trade built around urban development. Indeed, the New South spokesmen, many of whom came from urban mercantile backgrounds, freely acknowledged their philosophical debts to the Old South. In 1903, New South publicist Richard H. Edmonds looked back on a generation of economic hyperbole and asserted: "The South of today, the South of industrial and railroad activity, is not a new South, but a revival of the old South, whose broad commercial spirit, crushed by the war, is again seen in the development of every line of industry in which this section was bending its energies prior to 1860." Or, as Henry W. Grady frequently noted, "the new South is simply the old South under new conditions."

There was an important distinction, however, between the Old South and the "Renewed South," as one Georgian called the New South. The programs devised by antebellum urban entrepreneurs were designed to help their cities and their region obtain a measure of independence and a position of equality within the national economy. By 1860, it appeared that these hopes, if not dashed, would at least be some time in fulfillment, and the outcome of the Civil War made talk of economic independence and equality seem dated, if not futile. Southern entrepreneurs were convinced that if they could not beat their northern counterparts, they could at least join them and secure their measure of prosperity in the place allotted to them in the national economy. Edmonds admitted as much when he wrote at the turn of the century that his goal for the region was for the South "to regain the relative position held in 1860." And that position was as a colony—a prosperous one to be sure—in the national economy.

The federal government, the object of so much antebellum southern anxiety, scarcely appeared in New South rhetoric. Republican administrations did not prove particularly difficult to live with, especially after 1876, and the common objective of generating profits for private enterprise united rather than divided the former adversaries. Republican Congresses appropriated funds for southern river and harbor improvements in Mobile and Houston, and federal land grants helped to secure the route of the Southern Pacific Railroad system completed during the 1880s. Although it was true that federal regulatory agencies did not regulate—and this hurt southern cities beleaguered by inflated railroad freight rates—southern entrepreneurs rarely felt threatened by the government's benign presence in the national economy. It would seem that cooperation with Washington held more potential benefits than conflicts.

So sectional conciliation became the new theme, fitting alongside the familiar economic panaceas of the Old South. In this new partnership, southern urban leaders looked with obvious relish on the potential for growth, given the huge capital reserves built up in northern cities before and during the Civil War. It mattered little to these boosters that northern investments implied northern profits. In the new conciliatory spirit there would be enough profits to find their way into southern pockets as well. Southern entrepreneurs accordingly went out courting northerners and their capital in an unabashed desire to stimulate urban growth and their own bank accounts along the way.

Atlanta, the home of supreme New South booster Henry W. Grady, played the theme of sectional reconciliation most vigorously. Without much of an antebellum history, local businessmen could promote their city as truly the offspring of a new era. While some cities like Savannah and Mobile proudly shunned northerners, Atlantans promised "kindness and respect" to visiting northerners, especially "when they come on business, or for investment." Occasionally the Atlanta penchant for the northern dollar pushed conciliation to ridiculous proportions. In 1867, several boosters organized the "Lincoln Memorial Association of Atlanta" for the purpose of erecting a 145-foot tower constructed out of Georgia marble. The city council first supported the idea but changed its mind after a group of Confederate veterans understandably objected to such use of public funds. Instead, the council lavished food and drink upon Union general John D. Pope and the hero of Gettysburg, General George H. Meade.

These were not the last encounters between Atlanta boosters and their former adversaries. In a speech before the New England Society of New York in December, 1886, Henry W. Grady pointed to the guest of honor, General William T. Sherman, whose burning desire to destroy Atlanta had given Grady his life's work. After chiding Sherman for being "a kind of careless man about fire," Grady assured the general and, more important, the wealthy dinner guests that "from the ashes he left us in 1864 we have caught the sunshine in the bricks and mortar of our homes, and have builded therein not one ignoble prejudice or memory." For his efforts that evening, Grady received the title of "Pacificator."

The Great Pacificator spent much of his time attempting to attract the Great Northern Investor. In order to rebuild the South and its cities after the Civil War, capital from the North was essential. The region's major capital-generating activity—staple-crop production—struggled until the 1880s and consequently could generate little local capital. But northern capital was selective. Northerners invested in land and railroads but not usually in manufacturing or city-building enterprises. Nashville newspapers, for example, reported northerners investing in land outside the city, including some plantations. Northern investment was heaviest in railroads, a reversal of the antebellum trend when regional capital was primarily responsible for railroad construction. The huge debts contracted by local and state governments before the war discouraged a repetition of such investment activity following the war. In Virginia, where railroad debts were enormous, the new constitution of 1867 prohibited state investment in railroad stock. Mindful of the need for capital, however, the constitution doubled the interest rate to 12 percent as an attraction for investment capital. Northerners responded by securing control of Virginia railroads and forcing out local urban entrepreneurs like Norfolk's William Mahone. By 1890, the great Richmond Terminal Railroad Company had become a northern operation.

Yankee capital was curiously absent, though, during urban rebuilding efforts of the 1860s and 1870s. Atlanta, the South's most spectacular example of urban resurrection, achieved much of its rebirth from local capital—

an impressive achievement for a capital-poor region. Whitelaw Reid, a northern reporter traveling through the rebuilding city in 1866, marveled at the progress already made: "What is more remarkable, the men who were bringing a city out of this desert of shattered brick—raising warehouses from ruins, and hastily establishing stores in houses half-finished and un-roofed—were not Yankees, but pure southerners." The "pure southerners" were also found working hard in other cities rising from the ashes, such as Richmond and Columbia.

It can be argued that northerners were understandably wary about southern urban investments during the immediate postwar years. It was not yet possible to discern how southerners would handle defeat and the pres-ence of an occupation force, and reports of urban racial strife that filtered northward and stimulated congressional debates doubtless had a chilling effect on potential northern investments in rebuilding southern cities. The depression in the 1870s limited northern investments generally, and during the 1880s there were more attractive southern investments—railroads, for example—than the South's small urban marketplaces. It could also be ar-gued that northern capitalists had little interest in staking potential urban rivals to huge sums of money that would help them renew their antebellum quest for economic independence, New South rhetoric notwithstanding. Since railroads were more or less southern-owned northern highways in the antebellum period, postwar northern investment involved only a change in ownership, not in function. The pattern of northern investments in southern industry lends some support to the view that northern capitalists con-sciously sought out those southern investments that would inevitably lead to increasing dominance of northern cities in the national economy and avoided investments that could generate competitive rather than complementary development.

Industrial enterprise occupied a major role in the New South philosophy. The New South spokesmen agreed that this was one of the most glaring weaknesses of antebellum southern society in general and of southern cities in particular. And the same catalog of industrial deficiences that Albert Pike had listed in 1850 remained. Henry W. Grady updated the catalog for Atlan-tans after the war when he spoke of a fellow Georgian's burial:

> They buried him in the midst of a marble quarry; they cut through solid marble to make his grave; and yet a little tombstone they put above him was from Ver-mont. They buried him in the heart of a pine forest, and yet the pine coffin was imported from Cincinnati. They buried him within touch of an iron mine, and

yet the nails in his coffin and the iron in the shovel that dug his grave were imported from Pittsburgh. They buried him by the side of the best sheep-grazing country on the earth, and yet the wool in the coffin bands and the coffin bands themselves were brought from the North. The South did not furnish a thing on earth for that funeral but the corpse and the hole in the ground. There they put him away . . . in a New York coat and a Boston pair of shoes and a pair of breeches from Chicago and a shirt from Cincinnati, leaving him nothing to carry into the next world with him to remind him of the country in which he lived and for which he fought for four years, but the chill of blood in his veins and the marrow in his bones.

When misted eyes had cleared, the southern congregation lifted their voices in praise of southern industry. In 1867, veteran urban booster J. D. B. De Bow sang out: "We have got to go to manufacturing to save ourselves"— a variation on his antebellum theme that "no country that produces raw materials only can be prosperous." Other New South spokesmen picked up De Bow's refrain. Louisville journalist Henry Watterson declared that "smoky cities and blue overalls promise more for the South than white Grecian porticoes and Crinolines." The smokiest of New South cities, Birmingham, produced a great paean to manufacturing when an editor trilled that industry and industrialists "filled the earth with the most beneficent and utilitarian civilization it has ever witnessed, and strewed the shores of its oceans with mighty cities, reticulated its surface with steam roads, covered the wild seas with the white wings of commerce, and even invaded their unknown depths with the iron-shod pathways of lightning."

The chorus of excitement focused naturally on Birmingham, literally a child of the New South, where mountains of iron and coal seemed destined to turn a railroad crossing into a major world metropolis. Yet nothing much seemed to happen to the self-styled "Pittsburgh of the South." The city struggled along on predominantly local capital despite an industrial enterprise that required large-scale investments. Northern investors shunned this promising city. Perhaps one reason can be found in Andrew Carnegie's statement after touring Birmingham in the late 1880s that "the South is Pennsylvania's most formidable enemy." From then on, Carnegie and his U.S. Steel Corporation began securing control of the city's steel production, not for generating investment profits but rather, as historian Jonathan Wiener asserted, for "controlling Birmingham's competition with Pittsburgh." Carnegie's plot was successful, since the South's proportion of steel production declined from 22 percent in 1893 to 11 percent in 1913. Birmingham's competitive position deteriorated before that date when Carnegie's U.S. Steel Corporation purchased the city's largest producer of steel, the Tennessee Coal and Iron Company, in 1907.

The infamous "Pittsburgh Plus" system imposed by U.S. Steel on Birmingham products severely restricted production and growth. Under the system, the price of steel products was determined by the mill cost at Pittsburgh plus freight charges from Pittsburgh to the consumption point. This pricing mechanism had two major effects. First, it encouraged steel consumers to locate their facilities in proximity to Pittsburgh in order to reduce freight charges. Second, it drastically reduced the effective market area for Birmingham's products. If a New Orleans wholesaler wished to purchase baling wire, he would most likely send an order to Pittsburgh rather than to Birmingham. In fact, Louisiana consumers purchased only 4 percent of their wire from Birmingham; in Texas, Birmingham wire was nowhere to be seen. Had the "Pittsburgh of the South" been allowed to supply southern customers, steel production in that city would have increased by two and one-half times.

Birmingham threatened to upset the colonial pattern of the South's role in the national economy. Heretofore, southern cities were generally only able to perform rudimentary processing of the South's (primarily agricultural) raw materials, and the finished or semifinished products were usually marketed and finished elsewhere. Through local enterprise, particularly that of Henry De Bardeleben, son-in-law of Old South industrialist Daniel Pratt, Birmingham was able to process and market its limited production without relying on northern connections. Northern steel interests, which had previously ignored the Birmingham effort, now became alarmed at the city's potential threat to their monopoly and systematically bought out and restricted this competition. The region was thus deprived of a significant capital-generating enterprise and of the numerous other industrial and commercial activities that would have inevitably sprouted around this new industrial center.

Northern capitalists were initially reluctant to invest in textile milling, and indigenous capital typically financed cotton mill operations in the South prior to 1900. The "Cotton Mill Campaign" of the 1880s approached the status of a religious crusade, especially in the Carolina Piedmont towns along the northern-owned Southern Railway: Charlotte, Greenville, and Spartanburg, among the more prominent participants in the "Campaign."

"Next to God, what this town needs is a cotton mill," bellowed one Piedmont preacher, and a Salisbury, North Carolina, evangelist informed his listeners that "the establishment of a cotton mill would be the most Christian act" they could perform. Southerners evidently took heed: by 1900, one-half of the South's looms were within a one-hundred-mile radius of Charlotte, and the total number of looms in the South grew from 11,900 to 110,000 between 1880 and 1900.

By that latter date, northern capital began to filter into the South's new plants and away from decrepit New England facilities. In Memphis, the leading cotton processor in the Mid-South, northern capital controlled two-thirds of the city's mills in 1905. By 1930, the South's share of active spindles had increased to 58 percent from only 5 percent in 1880. During that same period, New England's share declined from 80 to 35 percent.

These impressive statistics scarcely hid the fact that southern industrialization, accomplished in close partnership between northern and southern entrepreneurs, merely reinforced and exploited regional problems. Southern industry—iron, textiles, furniture, and tobacco—involved the basic processing of raw materials; finishing, distribution, and the greater share of profits occurred elsewhere. In 1900, the South produced proportionately fewer manufactured goods than in 1860, when the region generated less than 10 percent of the national output. These industries did not build cities, as figures cited earlier for North Carolina—an industrial hotbed—indicated. Most important, they restricted the development of human capital by limiting wages and educational opportunities and by maintaining work and living conditions scarcely better than the rural environments from which the labor force came.

Urban boosters were proud of their cheap white labor force and touted it to potential northern investors. A Memphis editor boasted in 1904 that "Memphis can save the northern manufacturer . . . who employs 400 hands, $50,000 a year on his labor bill." Moreover, regional values and conditions ensured a docile work force as well. Commuting to and from their rural homes, mill workers did not look upon themselves as a permanent industrial labor force. In addition, the mill was frequently the only alternative for whites unable to sustain themselves through agriculture. The vast majority of mill workers in the early twentieth century were agricultural dropouts. Finally, they had lived their lives in an unquestioning, hierarchical society—their religion, their tradition, and their experience taught them that this was the way it was supposed to be. Southern boosters assured northern industrialists that union activity or labor unrest was as unlikely as high wages. Such advertising caused southern writer Broadus Mitchell to remark in the 1920s that "the workers are being offered on the auction block pretty much as their black predecessors were."

Textile mill communities offered a prototype for regional labor exploitation. These communities were less new urban forms than versions of an old southern institution, the plantation, and mill owners emulated the combination of paternalism and coercion practiced by William S. Gregg in antebellum Graniteville. Whether as autonomous company towns or as appendages to existing cities, mills and their employees contributed sparingly to urban life. The links between farm and mill were greater than those between mill and city. In some mill towns there was only a small resident population, because workers commuted from nearby farms where labor interchange was common. This pattern existed even in the larger Piedmont cities where entrepreneurs intentionally located the mills on the periphery to provide workers with easier access and fewer urban distractions. Just as planters ruthlessly burdened the soil with exclusive cultivation of staple crops, mill owners fought incursions by other industries that might have led to some industrial diversity and urban growth. Finally, the mills that cluttered the rural countryside and urban periphery damaged the environment and the health of the workers. William Faulkner left us this portrait of a defiled Frenchman's Bend in *The Hamlet*:

> the dry, dust-laden air vibrated steadily to the rapid beat of the engine, though so close were the steam and the air in temperature that no exhaust was visible but merely a thin feverish shimmer of mirage. The very hot, vivid air, which seemed to be filled with the slow laborious plaint of wagons, smelled of lint; wisps of it clung among the soot-stiffened roadside weeds and small bits of cotton lay imprinted by hoof and wheel marks into the trodden dust.

By the early decades of the twentieth century, the cotton textile industry of the nation resided in southern towns and cities. The profits went North, and the human and environmental refuse stayed behind. You could almost hear Grady's rhetorical lament that "the South did not furnish a thing . . . but the corpse and the hole in the ground." The Frenchman's Bends proliferated. The disregard for human capital evident in the provision of urban services and in the maintenance of a biracial society was equally apparent in the quest for industrial growth. The ghosts of Grady and Albert Pike would have been surprised to discover that even in 1920 their respective funeral orations had a timeless quality for the South. So little had changed, yet so much had deteriorated. "We have built as did the builders of the Tower of Babel," an Atlantan observed in 1908. "We have lifted brick and mortar and steel and money into the air that all might see the glory of our city; but what have we done to soften the temper of our people? What have we done toward giving a chance to the lungs of the little children of the poor? . . . We have filled our air with smoke and soot and have provided scantily for the maintenance of the warehouses of pure air."

The industrial dreams spun by New South philosophers had become nightmarish for the region and for its urban civilization. The tentacles of the national economy sunk deep into the southern soul and drained it as deeply. "The soul has fled," a southern philosopher declared glumly. Where it had gone, he did not speculate; but it was not only industrial profits that were flowing northward.

The national economy not only defined and delimited the role of southern industry but of southern commerce as well. The bravado of New South publicists that southern commercial development and consequent urban growth would make "Ninevah, Babylon, Rome—sink into insignificance" remained bluster rather than reality. The colonial status of the urban South and of the southern region that emerged in the antebellum era became institutionalized after the Civil War, and the war itself was a triumph of the national economy headquartered in New York and supported by Washington. The patterns of trade toward the northeast solidified, and southern urban ports suffered correspondingly. During a five-year period between 1856 and 1860, when New Orleans was already beginning its long decline, the city handled 28.4 percent of the country's exports compared with 31.0 percent for New York. During another five-year period, 1894 to 1898, the Crescent City's share had declined drastically to 8.4 percent, while New York's had increased to 43.6 percent. Even though New Orleans succeeded in obtaining railroad connections during the 1880s, it was too late to counter the marketing and credit advantages of the northeast; besides, the same railroads that connected New Orleans to southern towns also connected those towns to the North.

The value of imports, an indicator of colonial status, reflected New Orleans' decline in the national economy. In 1848, the city handled only 7 percent of the nation's value in imports; by 1888, that figure was a miniscule

1.6 percent. No other southern port approached even 1 percent by that latter date. Most shocking was the declining presence of cotton as a commercial commodity. Although staple-crop agriculture was not a catalyst for large-scale urban development, at least it provided southern seaports with a commercial base during the antebellum period. Postwar changes in marketing and processing and the preeminence of northern railroads in the region accounted for the erosion of cotton commerce. In 1858 New Orleans controlled 50 percent of the nation's cotton crop, in 1870, slightly more than 36 percent, and in 1896, only 8 percent. The extensive northern investments in southern railroads is more understandable. The railroad conquered more than any Union army.

Antebellum southerners had called it the Iron Messiah, but New South prophets soon looked upon the railroad as a southern Judas. Its city-building and capital-generating powers had not been overestimated, but the directional flow of these benefits had. By the 1890s, northern capitalists like J. P. Morgan controlled virtually the entire southern railroad network. Urban southerners learned the bitter lessons of their inflated faith in railroads. Northern railroad owners cared little about their southern urban depots beyond freight statistics. Discriminatory rates for some cities in favor of others and the expense of short-haul freight favored the large northeastern terminal points that had numerous competing lines and that depended most on long-distance traffic. Farmers producing strictly for a specific southern market town rarely used the railroad; wagon and river traffic sustained cities like Nashville and Danville despite the good long-distance rail connections enjoyed by both cities. Long distance and high volume were the railroads' specialties, and except for Atlanta and, to a lesser extent, Memphis, southern cities continued to be the "mere way stations" they had been since the antebellum era.

Railroad companies not only abused southern urban economies but urban space as well. The enthusiasm of southern entrepreneurs for the railroad blinded them to the physical blight they created; as with southern industry, urban boosters bartered away the environment for the elusive promise of growth and prosperity. In Nashville, an area appropriately known as "Railroad Gulch" dominated the center of the city. When the Louisville and Nashville Railroad sought to erect a terminal on the site, the city approved and allowed the company to demolish over two hundred buildings and alter the downtown street pattern. As late as the 1950s, Atlanta was simply a jumble of railroad tracks that polluted the central business district. The tracks and the trains thereon were hazardous to pedestrians and to other vehicles, and scarcely a year passed that a child was not killed at one of the many grade crossings. The railroad crossings that determined street patterns, interfered with traffic, and caused injury and death to urban residents were the physical reminders of the triumph of the New South philosophy over common sense.

If urban boosters could not point to industry, commerce, or railroad crossings with much pride, or at least with candor, the national economy allowed them sufficient prosperity to sustain at least a hope for the future. The objective of the northern-dominated national economy was not, of course, to ruin the urban South but to drain it of its resources while maintaining its vital signs. And if southern cities showed little growth, they did demonstrate some economic vitality. Much of this vitality resulted from the aggressive, if misguided, activities of southern entrepreneurs. Atlanta merchants, because of the city's remarkable rebuilding efforts and the publicity generated by Henry W. Grady, achieved a reputation as the most hard-working in the South. As one visitor from a rival city observed: "d--n Atlanta, turn a dollar loose on Whitehall Street and every man is after it." The energy of Atlanta entrepreneurs contributed to the city's rebirth and its subsequent rise in the southern urban system. Atlantans pointed to former urban pacesetters such as New Orleans and Charleston and contrasted their own vigor with the limpid languor of entrepreneurs in those declining ports. A Charleston merchant admitted that his colleagues "have made good husbands," but "the commercial blood of Charleston has not circulated."

Perhaps Charleston's merchants were the wiser, since staple agriculture, the biracial society, and the national economy circumscribed urban development in any case. But Atlanta grew and Charleston languished. Just as urban blacks created their own communities and institutions within the restrictive framework of biracialism, so southern cities generated their own prosperity within an equally confining environment. Since individual black leaders could and did make a difference in strengthening black communities, it is reasonable to assume that energetic entrepreneurs did the same for their cities.

There were several indications that this in fact was the case—local boosters could, through sheer energy, squeeze growth out of a reluctant urban economy. The retail sector was especially sensitive to entrepreneurial innovations. New Orleans and Atlanta pioneered southern cotton and industrial expositions; one such fair in Atlanta in 1909 led to the city's selection as the major automobile marketing center for the South. The successful experiments in quality fashion merchandising by Messrs. Neiman and Marcus in Dallas in 1907 helped to make that city one of the region's major fashion emporia. The erection of business "blocks" and the differentiation of commercial activities reflected the emergence of downtown retail sectors in southern cities by 1900. The establishment of department stores with local capital, such as Rich's in Atlanta, was one of the few urban economic activities that did not redound directly to the benefit of northern capitalists. Atlanta streetcar companies, recognizing the importance of Rich's to their own and to the city's financial success, converged no less than five routes in front of the department store.

Expanded downtown sections accommodated new service and financial functions generated with primarily local capital. By 1910, Peachtree Street was emerging as Atlanta's focus for commercial and financial activity. Thirteen banks were located within a three-block area of a convergence known as Five Points. Atlanta entrepreneur Joel Hurt was the financial angel and energy behind many of these developments. He constructed the South's first skyscraper, the Equitable Building; he owned the city's electric trolley system, and his other interests included banking and steel production. Hurt's projects and the similar efforts of other Atlanta entrepreneurs were part of the reason that city quadrupled its population between 1870 and 1900—a growth rate higher than any other city in the region.

In Memphis at the turn of the century, downtown consisted "mostly of four-story brick buildings, old, unpainted, unattractive, while the sidewalks bent up and down, having been built, apparently, without thought for grading." The rustic appearance of the business district gave way by World War I to several skyscrapers and a new city hall, all built with local capital generated from the cotton trade. One merchant was so excited by the new skyline that he suggested renaming Main Street to "something less provincial."

The statistical indicators of urban progress revealed some favorable trends for southern cities. Manufacturing employment increased to at least one-quarter of the work force in the five largest southern cities by 1920, reflecting a more diverse and balanced economic base. Some southern cities, aided by annexation, registered impressive population gains in the first decades of the twentieth century. Between 1900 and 1920, Atlanta increased its inhabitants by 123 percent; Birmingham, by 365 percent; Knoxville, by 138 percent; Memphis, by 58 percent; and even struggling New Orleans, by 34 percent. Some of these cities also registered extensive geographic expansions. Atlanta increased its territory by 138.2 percent between 1900 and 1920; Birmingham, by 694.8 percent; Knoxville, by 554.9 percent; and Nashville, by 90.5 percent.

The American entrance into the world war in 1917 generated an urban boomlet in the South and indicated the economic potential of the region and its cities, given some federal redistribution of the national wealth. Seaports in particular revived with the granting of naval construction contracts. Norfolk, no longer asleep, was a town, according to Thomas Wolfe, seething with "the toughs, the crooks, the vagabonds of a nation—Chicago gunmen, bad niggers from Texas, Bowery bums, pale Jews with soft palms from the shops of the city, Swedes from the Middle-West, Irish from New England, mountaineers from Tennessee and North Carolina, whores, in shoals and droves, from everywhere." Textile towns took on a temporary brightness as government orders shot up wages and created labor shortages. Some mill families earned $100 a week or more, and mill owners, encouraged by new tax laws, constructed new homes, schools, and YMCAs for their operatives.

It appeared that, by 1920, the old shibboleth "Westward the star of empire holds its sway" now required amending, as Henry W. Grady had suggested in 1886. But the structures of expanding downtowns, the statistics spewing from census reports, and the artificial surge of people and prosperity induced by war—all of which pointed to an unprecedented era of urban growth—actually blurred the context of that growth. The skyscrapers that capped downtown prosperity were symbols more of local pride than of urbanization. Cities like Charlotte, Greensboro, or Columbia "had little more use for them," W. J. Cash noted, "than a hog has for a morning coat—where there was no immediate prospect of their being filled, unless by tenants willing to forgo a meal now and then in order to participate in such grandeur." Their construction was another attempt to "out-Yankee the Yankee." As Sherwood Anderson muttered, "Hating and imitating. Muddled for sure."

The southern city and region actually moved backward in the half century following the Civil War. Whereas statistics indicated progress, there was no real advancement relative to the rest of the nation. By 1920, the South was relatively less urban and less prosperous in comparison with other regions than it had been in 1860. Edmonds stated the reasons for this situation succinctly if unknowingly in 1903: "The South of today . . . is not a new South, but a revival of the old South."

Although some details may have changed, urbanization in the New South followed along antebellum lines, and for the same reasons. Staple agriculture still directed and restricted the type of urban settlement; cotton and tobacco still reigned as agrarian monarchs, and the small southern city remained their most faithful subject. Moreover, the economic mechanisms that superimposed themselves on staple production after the war only increased the grip of staple production on the southern economy. The agrarian influence on accelerating postwar urbanization resulted in more small cities and towns, a hastened decline in the larger antebellum ports, and the continued inability of urban settlements to rise above the functional level of market town.

Crops were not the only agrarian resources guiding urbanization; rural migrants, black and white, provided cities with an agrarian population. Again, this pattern was not different from antebellum migration trends, except that postwar cityward movements were heavier and there were fewer immigrants to break the overwhelming homogeneity of the rural urban population. Agrarian values and crop cycles continued to determine the urban life-style and landscape. The rural condition, whatever it was—poverty, filth, disease, individualism, fatalism—became the urban condition. There were few if any checks on the mercantile orientation of urban governments or on the selective policies they pursued.

The urban biracial society fit neatly into the agrarian city. Although the master-slave relationship no longer obtained, new arrangements ensured the continued separation and subjugation of the Negro race, and the contribution of blacks to urban society could therefore be only limited. The waste of human capital, and so much of it, restricted urban growth and limited the potential of a portion of the white population as well. Du Bois' assertion that blacks had a better "chance" in the city than in the countryside reflected the hopeless condition of black rural life more than the potential of black urban life. The positive aspects and energies of black urban communities lent some respect and dignity to blacks in the city. Unfortunately for the city, the biracial society dictated that those accomplishments would remain confined to the black urban world.

Southern cities spent the last years of the antebellum era attempting to separate themselves from the mechanisms of the national economy. They were, however, ground up by the machinery and spent the better part of the next century as tools of the national economy. The New South boosters rarely spoke of dismantling the machinery but hoped to play the role of vital cogs in the national economic machine. The South and the southern city as providers of raw materials and consumers of finished products played their colonial roles well, but colonialism reinforced staple agriculture and biracialism, and all three reduced the potential for urban growth and regional prosperity. The South's complicity in its own economic subjugation was probably not as overt as the subjugation of its labor force—black and white. Southern cities were relatively more poor, more unhealthy, and more unsightly because the role that boosters carved out for the cities and for the region promoted cheap, coercive labor as the section's best resource next to cotton and tobacco—even better because the labor required considerably less attention.

Despite the rhetoric of success, the New South failed. Staple agriculture, the biracial society, and the national economy remained constrictive forces on southern urbanization and on the region itself. If the boosters wished to blind themselves to the human and economic tragedies of the region, a new formula for urban and regional deliverance would have to be concocted from new sources. The emergence of these new sources and their challenge to the chains encumbering southern urban life is a story that is still in process.

Promenade by the sea: The Battery, Charleston, South Carolina.
Photo by David R. Goldfield

Plantation grace in the city: Stanton Hall, Natchez, Mississippi, erected 1836.
Photo by David R. Goldfield

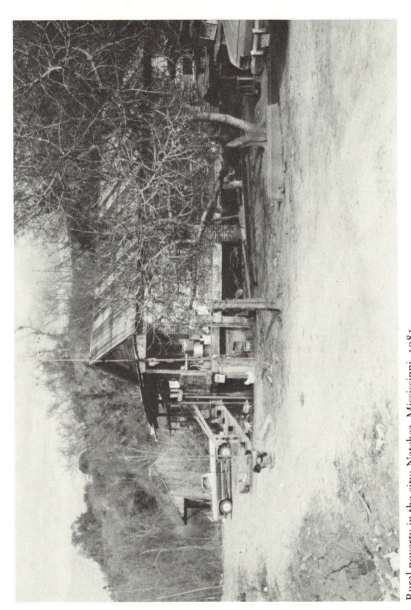

Rural poverty in the city: Natchez, Mississippi, 1981.

Photo by David R. Goldfield

The "Moon Walk": Returning the Mississippi to citizens of and visitors to New Orleans, 1981. *Photo by David R. Goldfield*

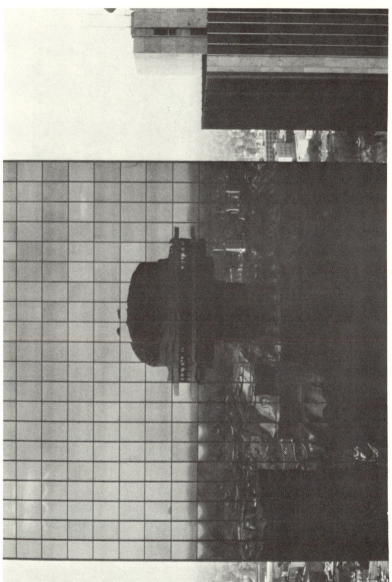

Reflections of Progress: Hyatt-Regency Hotel, Atlanta, 1973.
Photo by David R. Goldfield

Black housing one block from Stanton Hall, Natchez, Mississippi, 1981.

Photo by David R. Goldfield

IV ❧ A Kind of Sunlight

1920–1980

Jeb Stuart's Cavalrymen

The changes that would occur in the South and in southern urbanization over the next several decades hardly seemed evident during the 1920s. Those years were, if anything, a caricature of the previous century. Staple agriculture strangled the region and its cities; racism received renewed vigor as the Ku Klux Klan marched down the main street of every southern city; and the barons of Wall Street and Pennsylvania Avenue were more intent than ever on maintaining their colonial possessions below the Potomac. But cotton, the Klan, and colonialism barely survived the decade. Changes were indeed occurring behind the seemingly glacial facade of southern urban civilization. Historian George B. Tindall called the 1920s "a historical watershed" for the South; the region "stood between two worlds, one dying and the other struggling to be born."

Dorinda Oakley was struggling to survive. In her, wrote Ellen Glasgow, "the spirit of fortitude has triumphed over the sense of futility." Dorinda's fortitude lay in converting the barren ground of her Virginia farm, exhausted by generations of staple exploitation, to a profitable dairy. By disowning staple production and the agricultural practices of her ancestors, Dorinda triumphed. The message came through clearly that staple agriculture was ruinous both to the soil and to human lives, and that diversified, scientific farming would regenerate both.

When staple prices dropped in world markets during the 1920s, it appeared that staple agriculture was undergoing another of its periodic downturns. Glasgow's literary attack was another in a long line of regional criticisms leveled at southern farming methods. The 1920s were different, however. Soil exhaustion was eroding the rich black belt lands of the Lower South, and what exhaustion did not accomplish the boll weevil did. When the depression struck the nation in 1930, southern agriculture already had a head start of several years. The South, already weak from its bout with plummeting staple prices, collapsed and became the nation's basket case during the 1930s.

Still, change was not inevitable. Cotton planters evinced little willingness to abandon the staple, and the complex labor and economic mechanisms that had sustained staple agriculture since the Civil War remained. Through the Agricultural Adjustment Act of 1933, the federal government became the major force for regional agricultural change. Under the act's provisions, not planting became more profitable and more secure than staple cultivation had ever been. By 1938, the AAA had taken more than one-half of the South's cotton acreage out of production. In addition, the proliferation of agricultural extension agents and the devastation of the boll weevil encouraged the now-secure planters to seek other less exhausting crops. Soybeans and peanuts proved to be successful cash crops, and corn hybrids and improved grasses stimulated livestock raising. By the early 1940s, diversified agriculture was at last making some inroads into the South.

The greatest revolution was yet to come—mechanization. As long as planters maintained their coercive labor systems, there was obviously little need for labor-saving technology. In addition, labor was relatively cheap, so there was no economic incentive to introduce machinery, and with farms divided into small parcels for sharecroppers and tenants—and by 1930 more than one-half of all farmers in the South were tenants—mechanization would have been ineffective and expensive. Federal policy again produced a change in southern agricultural methods, because the AAA stipulated that the sharecropper had to share the federal subsidies with the owner. Consequently, planters did not renew sharecropping contracts in 1934 and instead hired the erstwhile croppers as wage laborers, since farm workers on wages were not entitled to any share of subsidy payments.

The decline in sharecropping implied the removal of strictures associated with the system—debt peonage among them. It was as if the federal government had issued a second emancipation edict. Thousands of croppers streamed from southern farms during the late thirties and early forties, and

Leading Southern Cities, 1970

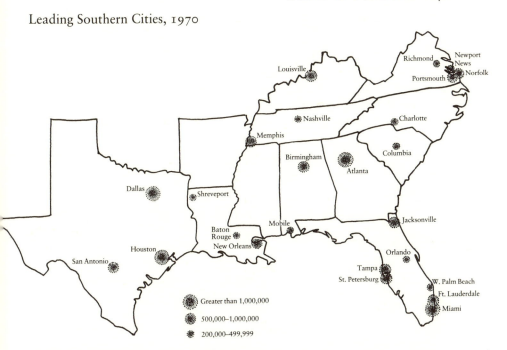

Greater than 1,000,000

500,000–1,000,000

200,000–499,999

suddenly southern agriculture faced a labor shortage. The massive labor requirements for World War II compounded the situation. By 1942, International Harvester was marketing a mechanical cotton picker and the agricultural technology revolution was underway. At the end of the decade, the
exhausted fields presented a new and brighter aspect. As Lillian Smith reported, "tractors and bulldozers, cover crops, and contour plowing have
filled deep gullies and made green pastures of worn-out land." It was barren
ground no more.

Since life in southern cities was inextricably connected with the southern
farm, the developments in southern agriculture—from the depression of the
1920s to the mechanization of the 1940s—were bound to have a significant
impact on the urban South. In Lillian Smith's discussion of the changed aspect of southern farms, she noted matter-of-factly that "people have moved
to town." The migration began during the 1920s. This was nothing new
since fluctuations in the staple market usually produced fluctuations in migration trends as well. But now southerners had better access to a much
wider world, and that world was enjoying relative prosperity during the dec-

ade, offering employment opportunities and improved living conditions to rural southerners who usually lacked both. As a result, despite coercive labor systems, southerners left the farm in record numbers in the 1920s.

The southern city was the beneficiary of some of this mobility as the urban South experienced its greatest growth since the Civil War. The regional population living in cities increased by 6.7 percent over the previous decade, which as a result of a wartime boom helped southern cities register a gain of 5.3 percent. The gains were distributed relatively evenly over the South, indicating a regional rather than a subregional population trend. But it was clear that southern cities were not the choices of most rural migrants: the net migration *from* the region increased to nearly two million during the 1920s, more than 50 percent over the previous decade. The industrial prosperity in northeastern and midwestern cities clearly offered greater attractions than the market towns that dominated the South.

Migration from the region declined during the years of the Great Depression as mobility slowed nationally. Even so, the net migration from the South exceeded 650,000, most after 1934 and the initial impact of the AAA. If these years were "rock bottom" for southern agriculture, they were equally hard for southern cities. The market towns had little to market and few who could afford to buy, and even the larger commercial centers "took on the air of those old dead towns of Belgium and the Hanseatic League." Although there were few opportunities anywhere in the rest of the country, the urban South held the fewest. Urbanization declined to near the level of the dark 1890s.

As southern agriculture was transformed and as employment opportunities opened due to the war effort of the 1940s, the regional exodus quickened. Over two million southerners left the region, usually for cities in the Northeast and Midwest. The changing agricultural base and, more important, the economic revival generated by World War II enabled southern cities to participate in the national trend of increased urbanization. Whereas the region's farm population declined by 20 percent between 1940 and 1945, southern cities gained nearly 30 percent, exceeding the rate of urbanization in other regions. The acceleration of southern urban growth and the diversification of agriculture continued into the next decade. In 1950, South Carolina still grew over 700,000 bales of cotton; by 1960, cotton cultivation had virtually disappeared as the white fields receded before the green wave of pasture, soybeans, and corn. The croppers and tenants who had worked those cotton fields were mostly gone now—over 150,000 of them—to cities like Columbia, Spartanburg, and Greenville. Never before or since the 1950s had the rate of increase in South Carolina's urban population been so great.

What happened in South Carolina occurred in other southern states as well. By 1960, the South was an urban region: more than one-half of the region's population lived in towns or cities. Much of this growth had occurred since 1930, when only three out of every ten southerners lived in cities. Over the next three decades, the region's urban population increased by 156 percent, compared with a national rate of 82 percent. After languishing in the backwaters of American civilization for over a century, the southern city stepped forward into the regional and, soon, the national limelight. People talked and wrote about the Sun Belt and the fantastic growth of its cities as they once did about its poverty and disease.

The southern urban system, which had deteriorated into a string of staple market centers with an occasional overgrown market city here and there, also began to demonstrate a new maturity as the grip of staple agriculture receded. In the 1930s, Alfred Kazin captured these vignettes of the joyless South: "the cars on the unending white ribbon of road; the workers in the mills; the faces of farmers' wives and their children in the roadside camp, a thousand miles from nowhere; the tenant farmer's wife with her child sitting on the steps of the old plantation mansion . . . the Baptist service in the old Negro church." At the same time Kazin drew this rural portrait of the South, sociologist Walter J. Matherly wrote about the development of metropolitan communities in the South and the "health and recreation" attractions of the region that would draw both capital and people from other sections. Matherly concluded by heralding the birth of "an era of metropolitan regionalism" in the South.

If, as George B. Tindall asserted, the South "stood between two worlds," it must have been a very wide straddle. Although there was some accuracy in both the Kazin caricature and Matherly's premature announcement of the Sun Belt's arrival, the truer picture of southern urbanization in the twenties and thirties lay somewhere in the broad middle. Small cities and towns continued to dominate the region's urban system during this period. The influence of staple agriculture lingered, of course, but technology also reinforced the traditional southern urban pattern. The movement to the cities, which resumed in the 1920s after a half century of relative stagnation, occurred simultaneously with the widespread regional use of the auto and of electricity, both of which reduced the necessities for urban concentration and thus complemented prevailing urban patterns. Cities of less than 10,000 still characterized the region's urban growth. In 1940, one-third of the nation's population lived in cities of over 100,000 inhabitants; only one of out eight southerners did so.

During the 1940s, small-city urbanization—the volume of which had made southern urbanization distinctive for over a century—began to decline in importance. That this occurred simultaneously with the transformation of southern agriculture indicated that staple marketing no longer sustained urban development. Industry and service activities would be greater determinants of southern urbanization in the future. For the first time in the South's history, the growth of cities of more than 10,000 people exceeded the rate for cities and towns of less than 10,000 inhabitants. Two genuine metropolises now anchored the southern urban system—Atlanta in the east and Dallas in the west. Both cities owed their early prosperity to cotton, but finance, diversified commerce, and industry built them into regional pacesetters. Finally, the most rapid urban growth in the region was occurring in Florida, where agriculture had only an indirect impact on urbanization. Miami and Tampa-St. Petersburg counted almost a million people between them in 1950, fulfilling Matherly's depression prediction of the region's irresistible health and recreation attractions.

In between Florida and Texas, however, the small city remained the characteristic urban settlement, but these traditional cities were also undergoing changes in their configurations. Low in density, these communities grew horizontally in the 1950s, occasionally spawning satellite towns. Historian C. Vann Woodward termed this semi-urban sprawl "rurbanization"—a phrase that captured well the hybrid form of southern urban settlement. Although urban population increased during the post–World War II era, density did not. This spatial pattern, coupled with vigorous annexation policies, made some southern cities the largest (by area) in the country. Suffolk, a sprawling town in Tidewater Virginia, claimed to be the biggest city in the nation in 1970, and Houston seemed to stretch into the Texas prairie forever. A shocked architecture critic, Ada Louise Huxtable, called the Texas vastness "a nowhere city . . . a spin-the-wheel happening that hops, skips, and jumps outward."

It was not surprising that numbers of the smaller southern cities, in their outward growth, began to grow together. Their identities and functions blended into each other and formed an urban region. Regional airports were the most obvious manifestation of the melding process: Greenville and Spartanburg in South Carolina; Raleigh-Durham (serving Chapel Hill as well); and Tri-Cities Airport serving Kingsport, Johnson City, and Bristol, Tennessee. These urban regions soon grew into other regions, and the chain of small cities became what geographers call a *conurbation*, which really means a formless, horizontal urbanlike settlement sprawling across the southern landscape. By 1960, no less than five conurbations existed in the South, with the largest one (in both area and population) stretching along the Gulf Coast from Pensacola, Florida, to Houston.

The vast Gulf Coast conurbation contained only 3,400,000 people, indicating not only low density but the predominance of small urban centers along the route. While each conurbation possessed one or two major cities that acted as regional focal points—Charlotte in the Carolinas conurbation and Atlanta in the Eastern Inner Core conurbation, for examples—the other urban members rarely included populations over 100,000. The southern conurbations could not compare with the northeastern megalopolis or with the industrial crescent in the Midwest that included Chicago, Cleveland, Detroit, Milwaukee, and Gary, among others. In 1960, when the southern urban population inched above 50 percent of the region's population, it did so primarily because, in both Florida and Texas, three out of every four residents lived in cities. In four states—North and South Carolina, Mississippi, and Arkansas—barely 40 percent of the residents lived in cities. Those conurbations not only contained some very spaced-out cities but a great deal of open space as well.

The southern urban system of the 1970s, then, consisted of several sprawling subregions constantly growing out from one or two subregional centers, with the entire system framed by Atlanta and Dallas (and Houston to a lesser extent). Although cotton, like many southerners, moved to California, the countryside continued to influence urbanization, since low-density development represented a compromise rather than an eradication of the rural landscape. The cities themselves continued to evince rural characteristics because, until the past two decades, population increase has resulted overwhelmingly from black and white rural migrants. In the 1920s and 1930s, writers within and outside the region took the rural character of southern cities for granted. They acknowledged urban growth, of course, but they understood that historically in the region urbanization and agrarianism were complementary rather than contradictory.

William Jennings Bryan's dictum still rang true in the urban South of the twenties and thirties. In Atlanta, where newspaper editors referred to the city as "the New York of the South," they also admitted that "without a strong, thriving rural population to sustain it and back it up, a great city might as well be a city of card-houses. . . . Farms are city-builders." New York—its economy, its population, and its life-style—was so far removed mentally, if not physically, from the countryside that it would be difficult to imagine a similar editorial in the New York *Times*. Southern cities were indeed closer to nature. Novelist Sherwood Anderson, absorbing the somewhat exotic culture of New Orleans during the 1920s, was most impressed, not by the city's urbanity, but by its close relationship to nature. In a letter to his publisher concerning the impending appearance of *Dark Laughter*, a novel he wrote in New Orleans, Anderson wrote that "the Negro, the earth, and the river—that suggests the title." In the book itself, the metaphors on the earthy quality of the city's blacks, the tropical climate, and always the river were the most vivid and expressive. As the narrator stated in Anderson's "A Meeting South," "all good New Orleanians go to look at the Mississippi, at least once a day." This almost mystical urban communion with nature, which struck Anderson as so unusual, had been the southern urban condition for two centuries. Edd W. Parks stated it in a more prosaic but equally emphatic manner when he wrote in 1934 that the urban South was "governed and given character by the country immediately surrounding it."

Nature was never far away, as the floods, the heat, the insects, and their own backgrounds reminded urban southerners. Nor did the decline of staple agriculture after the 1930s appreciably weaken the rural connection for most southern cities. Natchez, with its shining white-pillared homes and generous landscaping, is as lovely now as it was in the 1830s; Savannah is as James Oglethorpe dreamed in 1733. A visitor from the North in 1977 enthused about the city's "air of gracious living" and its "green squares with their moss-draped live oaks and other trees and shrubbery." Perhaps this is to be expected in cities where growth rarely interfered with tradition. But even in Atlanta, the region's urban leader since the Civil War, the cloak of the countryside fits comfortably over residential areas within a ten-minute drive from downtown, where it is still possible "of a late spring evening . . . to breathe the air of a small-town America (not suburbia) of the American past, suffused with the coolness and blossom fragrance of trees and bushes, roses, honeysuckle, and the wet smell of grass and weeds." This is small-town Atlanta and the small-town South. After nearly a half century of rapid urbanization, "the South," wrote Atlanta resident and journalist Pat Watters, "still had no real cities."

Staple agriculture may have gone with the wind, but the rural fragrance lingered on in the presence of millions of rural migrants. The South "had no real cities" because rural values still pervaded the cities, even if cotton did not. Evangelical Protestantism continued to promise Armageddon and heaven to faithful urban parishioners. The Fundamentalist upsurge in the 1920s indicated how far southerners had drifted from the national religious mainstream. The cities' unprecedented growth during that decade spawned evils that required immediate eradication. Evangelists like Billy Sunday and Cyclone Mack became media personalities as they preached damnation and salvation from fashionable urban pulpits—a far cry from the tent-and-dirt-floor days. Their greatest crusade, perhaps, was against the teaching of evolutionary doctrines in the schools. In 1926, the Southern Baptist Convention resolved: "This convention . . . rejects every theory, evolutionary or other, which teaches that man originated or came by way of lower animal ancestry." Thomas Wolfe wrote ironically of a teacher in Altamont (Asheville) who was forced to resign his position as a deacon in the Methodist church when he urged consideration of Darwin's theory: "He was, thus, an example of that sad liberalism of the village—an advanced thinker among the Methodists, a bearer of the torch at noon, an apologist for the toleration of ideas that have been established for fifty years." The evangelical sects ensured that the "savage ideal" would remain in force in southern cities.

Curiously, while evangelical piety rejected biological Darwinism, it embraced social Darwinism, or at least the southern urban boosters' version of that doctrine. As historian Robert M. Miller observed, the southern urban church had "a tremendous stake in the prevailing economic order," and clergymen generally maintained an "uncritical attitude . . . toward the business community." The southern city of the 1920s was hardly the "theocracy" that H. L. Mencken described, but both church and civic leadership supported the individualistic strain of urban society and the weak community welfare activities of government. Even so-called "liberal" churchmen "condemned forces which they felt encouraged religious and social diversity within the city," historian Wayne Flynt asserted.

The connection between religion and commerce was not surprising. Religion provided the ideological base from which the South's rural-transplanted urban residents drew support for their other agrarian values. This was especially so in the smaller communities, which were both philosophically and physically close to the countryside. "Church was our town," recalled Lillian Smith about her own small-town upbringing. In those towns, rural Protestantism survived virtually intact. "Our first lesson about God made the deepest impression on us," Smith continued. "We were told that He loved us, and then we were told that He would burn us in everlasting flames of hell if we displeased Him." Naturally, every child hoped to avoid that fate. "The best way," Smith concluded, "was never to question anything but always accept what you were told."

In the 1920s, a revived Ku Klux Klan became the most vigorous enforcer of these religious values in the urban South. It sought to ensure that unquestioning acceptance and conformity to southern traditions remained at the center of urban society, and it promoted its creed with evangelical zeal. "Fear of change, not vindictiveness or cruelty, was the basic motivation of the urban Klansman," historian Kenneth T. Jackson noted. In this context, the Klan stood alongside the cleric and the booster as urban defenders of southern tradition. The Klan's national headquarters was located in Atlanta, and local boosters there tolerated the Klan because it was a profit-generating enterprise.

The typical Klansman had resided in the city for a relatively lengthy period, so the changes that began in the 1920s were especially difficult to accept compared with the quietude of earlier decades. The Klan was strongest in those cities experiencing the greatest growth and therefore offering the greatest threat to tradition. Like the urban clergy, the Klan directed most of its efforts at enforcing "moral standards" and reducing the impact of diverse groups within urban society. Its influence in the political life of cities like Birmingham and Atlanta did not represent an attack on the traditional ruling elite, who, at the least, accepted the Klan as a political partner and typically sought its endorsements.

The Klan waned because, in the process of upholding agrarian values, it destroyed some others, and its mission became clouded and compromised. This did not happen to the evangelical sects. Their influence, if anything, increased, and they waxed wealthy during the depression years and after, consorting with civic leaders and adopting sophisticated marketing techniques themselves. Although Atlanta novelist Ward Greene despaired of "howling god-hoppers running the town for purity and pep" during the 1930s, revivals were one of the few exciting and lucrative activities in the depression-ridden South. Recalling Lubbock, Texas, of the 1930s, Merton L. Dillon remarked that "they [the ranchers and merchants] and the preachers joined in the enterprise of creating an orderly community safe for churches and secure for business enterprises."

The churches utilized these connections in the decades after World War II to grow prosperous and numerous. The evangelical sects were now prominent urban institutions—gone uptown, so to speak—and aware, as the *Georgia Christian Index* pointed out in 1942, that "many tricks of the advertising trade can be adapted to the promotion of the church and its program." Theologist Langdon Gilkey complained in 1962 that, for Southern Baptists, "being a Christian . . . becomes merely the operation of expanding itself." The success of the evangelical sects in the 1950s and sixties made them a force in the urban economy in their own right, and businessmen looked to the urban churches as a precious market. A young Atlanta account executive confided to Erskine Caldwell in the mid-1960s: "Pick out any of these churches in this part of town and it'll be the best place of all to get acquainted with rich stockholders. . . . When I was selling Bibles and second-hand cars and canned beans, I never thought I'd ever have more of anything than I could use. But that was before I found out what going to church in a churchy town like Atlanta could do for you."

The shared precepts of church and business were evident in the performance of local government, whose main objective was also growth. This philosophy was not different from previous eras, but the extent of rural migration to the cities after 1920 was. The rural migrants were, for the most part, poor and unskilled, and southern cities were not prepared to service their needs. Birmingham leaders, for example, seemingly initiated a perverse inverse correlation between rural migration and public services in the 1920s. The city actually abolished its welfare department, and per capita expenditures for social services declined during the decade. Per capita expenditures for all public services in Birmingham were one-third those of New York City. Other cities, such as Nashville and Macon, had charter prohibitions against allocating more than a certain sum—only $10,000 annually in the case of Nashville—for poor relief. Legislatures had set these limits many years earlier when the press of rural migration was not very great.

The depression overburdened municipal relief efforts throughout the country, but southern cities were the first to succumb under the pressures of poverty during the early 1930s. The problem was not only financial but institutional as well. Southern cities had no bureaucracy and few public facilities equipped to service indigents. In 1930, Atlanta's expenditures for poor relief went directly to private organizations, since the city had no facilities to care for the expanded relief rolls and officials did not attempt to enlarge the few institutions that already existed.

The neglect of poverty in southern cities continued through the post–World War II era. The contrasts between the gleaming skyscrapers erected by oil companies in downtown Houston and the wooden tinderbox shacks literally in their shadow or between the glass monuments of pleasure in central Atlanta that reflected the poverty of the nearby black community may have jolted outsiders, but it barely moved local leaders. In San Antonio in 1970, nearly one out of every three families earned less than $3,000 a year (below the poverty level), and over 6 percent had incomes less than $1,000 a year—a figure that writer Robert Coles termed "almost incredible for an urban center." Only one-fifth of the people eligible for welfare received public assistance because of prescribed limits on city spending for poor relief. No southern city matched or exceeded the national average per capita urban expenditure for public welfare ($11.98), but San Antonio was exceptionally low at 45 cents per capita expenditure. In the Mexican-American ghetto on the city's West Side, living conditions approached those of rural poverty. Coles's tour of the area revealed "unpaved, undrained streets; homes without water; homes with outdoor privies; homes that are nothing but rural shacks." The results of such environmental depravity were predictable: the highest illiteracy, infant mortality, and disease ratios in the city.

The housing in the poor neighborhoods of the urban South has been deficient both in quality and in quantity. Southern cities failed to accommodate the increased rural migration during the 1920s, resulting in severe overcrowding. The migrants took over old town houses in the city, with sometimes as many as eight families living in one house and five persons per room because of the high rents, or they squeezed into flimsy wooden shells called "apartment houses" that were really filthy tinderboxes. In Savannah, migrants crammed into once-fashionable wooden single-family homes, which quickly fell to disrepair. The housing situation worsened during the depression and World War II, and peace did not alleviate the chronic shortages because southern cities abused federal housing programs by building only one new unit for every four destroyed through urban renewal. New slums and more serious overcrowding, particularly within the black community, existed alongside the Sun Belt towers that captivated the media. A New York *Times* reporter in 1978 wandered five minutes from "the citadels of Exxon and Shell" in Houston to discover "one-story shacks with rusting tin roofs, peeling paint, and rickety porches on concrete blocks." Savannah has had a reputation for beauty and grace—"America's most livable city," effused a Washington *Post* reporter in 1977—yet the decrepit conditions of the 1920s have scarcely been remedied, and until recently a vigorous historic preservation movement in the city threatened to decrease even further housing options for the poor.

Southern urban leaders have seemed oblivious to Oliver Goldsmith's dictum that "Ill fares the land to hastening ills a prey / Where wealth accumulate, and men decay." This should not imply, though, that local officials sealed the city treasuries and left citizens to fend for themselves. Southern cities provided services, but they were selective in both type and application. Local officials were indeed cognizant of the expansion their cities were undergoing beginning in the 1920s; their concerns, however, focused on the physical and economic effects of this growth rather than on the social impact. Professional city planning, a national trend in the 1920s, emerged from the City Beautiful and housing reform movements of the early years of this century. Southern cities were interested in the beautification programs but offered little support for more comprehensive treatments of the urban environment. Professional planners, by fostering close ties with business and government leaders (usually the same people in southern cities) demonstrated how their profession could further the city's economic interests—a primary concern of the civic elite. Zoning and transportation schemes became the planners' main contributions to their governments: zoning to preserve the color line and enhance existing property values, and transportation plans to improve downtown circulation and to provide for less chaotic expansion. When several southern cities, including Memphis, New Orleans, and Knoxville, hired Harland Bartholomew to prepare comprehensive plans for their cities, there was a clear understanding between client and planner that "housing and other 'social' concerns" were to be eliminated from the final recommendations.

The plan for New Orleans was typical of the period. The zoning component merely "divided the city into zones with as little change as possible," according to one report; street improvements and open spaces were virtually absent from black neighborhoods, and the plan ignored the quality and extent of other city services such as water supply and education. Planning was a conservative tool designed to order the city, not to change it. There was sincerity in official Atlanta's justification for adopting a zoning plan that rigidly segregated the races: "the protection of property values not the denial of freedom, was the basic intent of the plan."

Transit plans and subdivision regulations sped the decentralization of the already low-density southern city. Richmond, for example, encouraged peripheral growth by extending road systems, sewer lines, and other services into the suburbs, because planners believed that a decentralized metropolis would enhance the central business district by removing competing residential uses and by improving access to the center. By the mid-1940s, Richmond leaders discovered the obvious—that roads went in two directions and that the downtown was becoming deserted—and the city quickly hired Bartholomew in a futile attempt to recapture population and business. Zoning plans and subdivision regulations also stimulated land speculation and rapid geographic growth. Growth, of course, was the main objective of local leaders with regard to the planning function of local government and still is. Open land that might have remained so for years was developed. For many southerners today, childhood memories of a favorite crabbing or swimming hole, meanderings through sun-speckled woods, or the fresh fragrance of an early spring morning are just that—memories. But, as Robert Penn Warren noted in *Flood*, "the trouble was not so much what was not there. It was what was there"—the cheap motels, service stations, fast food emporia, shopping centers, and the highways that made it all possible. This reflected an American, not merely a southern, pattern, but the coincidence of rapid growth during the automobile age and the prevailing planning philosophy exaggerated these trends in southern cities.

The urban South has for the most part escaped the immediate economic consequences of decentralization policies by accelerating its annexation procedures. Richmond's problem, in this view, was not in its erroneous perception of the mechanisms of downtown vitality but in its inefficiency in capturing the peripheral growth for itself. Between 1920 and 1950, Houston tripled in area—in 1978, the city possessed 50 percent more territory than it did in 1963; Charlotte extended its geographic boundaries by over 300 percent between 1940 and 1977; as a result of annexation, Memphis has increased its area tenfold between 1900 and 1970; and between 1950 and 1970, San Antonio added 110 square miles as a result of annexation. By contrast, Boston expanded by only three square miles between 1870 and 1970, and San Francisco increased its territory only nine square miles between 1890 and 1970. Liberal annexation laws in southern states and the abundance of unincorporated communities (an incorporated suburb cannot be annexed) on the periphery have enabled southern cities to escape the fate of northern municipalities ringed by hostile and wealthy suburbs. Annexation accounted for nearly all of the southern urban population increase after 1950. The suburban or semirural quality in southern cities after the decline of staple agriculture resulted primarily from this planned sprawl occasioned by annexation.

Rapid territorial growth generated problems in an urban society accustomed to low service levels and taxes. Wealthy suburban residents were concerned that higher taxes would result from annexation. Residents of recently annexed Clear Lake City outside of Houston complained in 1978 that Houston "will not be able to take proper care of Clear Lake City and provide it with services as those Clear Lake could provide for itself." Clear Lake residents attempted to reverse their annexation and challenged Houston mayor James J. McConn's "growth ethic." Opponents of the growth ethic surfaced within the city of Houston as well. Minorities charged that civic leaders were attempting to dilute their political strength and that already-thin services would virtually disappear in the older areas of the city as the budget was stretched to accommodate new territory. Given the service history of Houston and other southern city governments, the concern over service levels was understandable. When San Antonio annexed forty square miles of territory in 1952, it increased the city's assessed valuation by 27.4 percent; then, rather than expand services, the city reduced the property tax rate by 12 percent and funded its debt. It is not evident, however, that a decline in the growth ethic would result in a corresponding increase in service, especially social service expenditures in southern cities. As sociologist David Harvey warned, "controlling physical growth without controlling anything else merely exacerbates scarcity."

In fact, there was an adjustment to the growth ethic during the 1970s, when, rather than looking for new territories to conquer, civic leaders turned their attention inward toward the city center. The simple cost-benefit formula remains, however. Local officials have discovered that there are profits in decaying downtowns and deteriorated neighborhoods—ironically, the leaders' own planning and service policies initiated this decline beginning in the 1920s.

Novelist Ellen Glasgow was a lonely stoic figure on West Main Street in Richmond. The quiet residential charm of the Victorian era had passed from Richmond and her neighborhood by the 1920s, and she found herself "increasingly adrift in a sea of rooming houses and filling stations"; she noted sadly that "everywhere people were pushing one another into the slums or the country." What residences remained in the city center were decaying; people who could afford to do so began leaving for the suburbs. The residential component of downtown, which had lingered on in a shabby elegance longer in southern cities than elsewhere, was disappearing. One of the most famous central city neighborhoods in the region, Peachtree Street in Atlanta, gave way to the advance of commerce. The Atlanta *Constitution* wrote the following epitaph:

> for many years Peachtree almost up to the center of the city was known as the principal residence street of Atlanta. On it were located many handsome houses, but time and commerce have changed this street perhaps more than any other thoroughfare in the city. Steadily encroaching upon residences, business houses . . . have forced the residences outward until at the present time all but a few of the handsome homes . . . have been dismantled and removed.

"Time and commerce" apparently waited for no city, as even the retail functions of the central business district, caught in the centrifugal whirl of expansion, moved away to the country (suburbs), too. The plans that opened the circulation of the downtown ultimately drained it of its vitality. As early as the mid-1920s, traffic jams and disappearing parking places characterized the central retail area. A Nashville businessman in 1926 complained that "lack of parking space causes purchasers to patronize suburban rather than downtown stores." In Atlanta that same year, Thomas H. Pitts closed his "drugs and sundries store" for good at Five Points in the heart of downtown and explained that "traffic got so congested that the only hope was to keep going. Hundreds used to stop; now thousands pass. Five Points has become a thoroughfare, instead of a center." Some businessmen weathered the rapid geographic expansion by opening branches in peripheral or suburban areas. A Memphis merchant placed the following revealing advertisement in a local newspaper in 1929: "To relieve its customers of the inconvenience of parking in the Downtown congested area, the House-Bond

Hardware Co. is opening neighborhood stores throughout the city. The locations . . . are selected with the plan of offering the present day shopper a convenient spot to park her car without violating traffic regulations." By the time Nieman-Marcus opened a store in a Dallas suburb in 1951, retail decentralization was a common fact of southern urban economic life.

Other businesses began to occupy parts of downtown: seedy bars and strip joints; rooming houses; low-capital, low-quality retail clothing and shoe stores. The low density of the southern city became both an advantage and a disadvantage: the sprawl encouraged retail nodes in the suburbs, but, on the other hand, there was less deterioration in the center simply because there were few large and heavy concentrations of buildings. Where concentrations existed, such as at Five Points in Atlanta, they usually involved financial and administrative activities that did not typically depend on large daily flows of clientele. Moreover, redevelopment was easier because, if clearance was required, there was less to demolish.

Civic leaders had been concerned with the image of their downtowns since the antebellum era. Pursuing the growth ethic, however, their concerns and what limited services government provided were turned outward. When such policies began to confront financial and political resistance, the elite's focus turned inward. Most important, they discovered that downtown redevelopment was a profitable activity. Some southern cities decided to recreate the past, since they were adept at tradition anyway. Besides, tourists, conventiongoers, and residents enjoyed stepping back into the previous century, though the restored areas barely resembled the muddy, cluttered downtowns of yesteryear. By the late 1960s, for example, Richmond's Shockoe Slip, once the center of nineteenth-century Richmond, was in its doddering old age, lined with empty warehouses and closed factories. The area still retained some unique architectural charm, however, beneath the cobwebs and broken glass, and today several blocks of Shockoe Slip have been renewed and house boutiques, restaurants, and studios.

Joe Smitherman, mayor of Selma, Alabama, and once known as "Fightin' Joe" for his combative support for white supremacy, is now fighting for another cause. He is talking about making old hardware stores look like old hardware stores, and he sees "the attraction of visitors to a restored town as the major growth potential for the future." "Preservation for profit" has now moved alongside the "growth ethic" as a major civic elite cliché.

Some cities, evidently less content with refurbishing old hardware stores, have looked deeper in their past to emerge with a profitable restoration theme. While San Antonio neglected its Mexican-American poor, the city redeveloped a mile-and-one-half-long strip along the San Antonio River, known as the Paseo del Rio, along which luxury hotels and Mexican restaurants vie for tourist dollars. Close by, a fiesta fairgrounds, La Villita, provides an excellent setting for convention parties and attractions, and a row of renovated shops known collectively as the Mercado allegedly recreates a nineteenth-century Mexican market.

The most ambitious scheme of downtown redevelopment-restoration belongs appropriately to Atlanta. In the 1960s, the city took several blocks in the original downtown area, then inhabited by railroad tracks, warehouses, and winos, and transformed them into a late nineteenth-century playpen known as Underground Atlanta (much of modern Atlanta is actually built on top of the old downtown area). It opened with fanfare and offered restaurants, ice cream parlors, and shops dressed in Victorian decor. Former governor Lester Maddox even sold autographed ax handles there for awhile. Unfortunately, the only thing the city and its private entrepreneurial partners proved was that, with enough capital, they could transform an old deteriorating area into a new deteriorating area. The poorly policed location eventually became a security problem in the evening, and the quality of shops and clientele declined.

While Underground Atlanta was in the process of creation, the city and private developers—a time-honored partnership in southern cities—decided to create a new downtown. The result was a multimillion-dollar extravaganza known as Peachtree Center, highlighted by the dazzling twenty-one-story Hyatt-Regency Hotel. The hotel, designed by architect-showman John Portman, featured spaceship elevators, a lobby as high as the hotel, and a revolving dome from which tourists and conventiongoers could sip their peach daiquiris and look out over what Henry W. Grady's heirs had wrought. Peachtree Center acted as a catalyst for a development explosion in the area. Beginning in the late 1960s, first-class hotelroom space doubled in eighteen months and downtown office footage increased 30 percent in one year. The city's new skyline included a seventy-story glass silo—the Peachtree Plaza Hotel—which is not only the world's tallest hotel (equipped with a revolving rooftop bar, of course) but includes a one-half-acre lagoon in its lobby.

The curtain began to ring down on the downtown show in 1976. Atlanta had overbuilt. In that year, a massive commercial-residential complex known as Colony Square North, several blocks beyond the new downtown area, went bankrupt. Two years later, the glittering Omni, a complex of expensive boutiques, offices, restaurants, a hotel, and an ice-skating rink on the downtown fringe, went into receivership when the owners could not repay a $90 million debt. Finally, two of the major financiers of downtown redevelopment, Richard Kattel's Citizens and Southern National Bank and Bert Lance's National Bank of Georgia, came under federal investigation after the financial condition of both banks was reported to be insecure. However, Atlanta's irrepressible boosters believe these reversals are temporary, and they are already concocting new schemes for the 1980s.

From a distance, New Orleans' cemeteries look like miniature cities replete with towers, square lots, and dense development. Mark Twain once wrote, in fact, that the city's best architectural achievements were its cemeteries. But today in New Orleans, there is another city of the dead with architectural pretensions. The city leaders, with the exaggerated boosterism characteristic of the urban South, demolished a wide swath of the downtown area to erect the Superdome (we are told proudly that three Houston Astrodomes could fit in New Orleans' domed arena) and a high-rise Hyatt-Regency Hotel mass-produced from the John Portman hotel factory, topped off, naturally, with a revolving dome where you can still sip a peach daiquiri or a more appropriate sazarac. The concrete sea created by these anonymous structures resulted in a huge dead area in the center of the city, frequented by transients, good and bad alike. The complex represented the increasing proclivity of southern cities, pioneered by Atlanta, to turn over their cities to outsiders to be utilized and discarded, rather than transforming decayed areas into citizen-oriented spaces as Boston, San Francisco, and Portland, Oregon, have done.

The leaders' renewed interest in the center of their cities extended to nearby residential areas. Their concern was less for the primarily poor people who had inhabited these neighborhoods for decades than for the potential of these areas as historic tourist attractions and future residences for middle-income taxpayers. Southern urban interest in historic neighborhood preservation dated at least from the 1930s, when the city of Charleston decided to transform the decaying antebellum mansions along the once-fashionable Battery into a model for historic preservation. With the assistance of private groups, the city accomplished this purpose, and the former slum is now a series of wealthy residences and living museums. New Orleans, also in the 1930s, salvaged the Vieux Carré. The most ambitious program evolved in Savannah during the late 1940s and early 1950s, when a group of women demonstrated to the city's business community that preservation could be profitable. The women's organization, the Historic Savannah Foundation, worked within a two-and-one-half square-mile area in central Savannah restoring nineteenth-century homes and stimulating residential investment in the neighborhood. After nearly two decades of work, Historic Savannah claimed a major role in boosting the city's tourist trade from $1 million to $45 million by the mid-1960s.

The financial successes in Charleston, New Orleans, and especially in Savannah stimulated similar joint public-private preservation ventures in other southern cities. In Richmond, for example, the city council declared a deteriorating central city neighborhood, Church Hill, a historic zone in 1957. Historic associations and affluent individuals, protected by the historic district designation, began to purchase homes in the area. By the early 1970s, the neighborhood had become a fashionable residential area. In the meantime, on the west side of downtown Richmond, a primarily private redevelopment effort in a neighborhood known as the Fan District created another residential enclave for professionals.

In the Richmond neighborhoods and in residential areas in the other cities as well, demographic changes accompanied the physical transformations. Generally, affluent white households replaced poor black ones. The inner-city poor, clinging to their central city communities, were neglected for generations, then, when the city discovered them, the preservation movement forced them out of their neighborhoods. As federal funds replace or augment city and private preservation financing, such displacement may diminish, though the extent of federal funding will probably be limited for the foreseeable future. In Richmond, predominantly poor and black Jackson Ward in the center of the city has become a preservation site and, with federal funding, the neighborhood's residents will remain. Similar federal support has occurred in central Savannah's Victorian District.

Downtown and neighborhood preservation were, of course, national urban trends during the 1970s, but southern cities were both pioneers in historic district zoning and in the negative social effects of the preservation movement. Given the southern cities' historic neglect of the poor, the housing alternatives confronting displaced low-income residents were likely to be inadequate. Although cities like Savannah assisted private groups with beneficial zoning and property tax regulations, they did little to aid residents displaced by the process. Were it not for the private efforts of the Savannah Landmark Rehabilitation Project, which, on a limited budget, sought to improve dwellings in the Victorian District and retain the original residents at the same time, it is doubtful whether any portion of the historic district would have ultimately contained blocks of poor residents. The Savannah project succeeded in publicizing its efforts so that federal funding could supplement its own funds.

The persistence of selective implementation and application of public services and policies reflected in part the persistence of southern urban leadership. Until the 1970s, a group of leaders whom historian Blaine A. Brownell called the "commercial-civic elite" continued to dominate local government policies, even if they no longer occupied political offices themselves. The absence of large identifiable ethnic groups, the prevalence of rural values, the weakness of organized labor, and the tradition of white solidarity enabled the commercial-civic elite to maintain control in urban government long after the influence of their northern colleagues had waned. Although the connections between business and government were most obvious in the smaller urban places, similar patterns prevailed in even the most sophisticated southern cities. Atlanta's William B. Hartsfield, the city's booster-mayor for twenty-three years beginning in 1937, admitted to Pat Watters that "in his every act, his every decision as mayor, he always kept in mind that Atlanta was headquarters of the Coca Cola Company." Floyd Hunter's study of the city's power structure during the early 1950s indicated that the relationship implied by Hartsfield's statement was a dominant force in Atlanta politics and hence in public policy. Hunter's "policy-making influentials" were typically the leaders of the city's mercantile and financial community. Although most of Hunter's elite did not hold elective office, the city's mayors from the 1920s to the early 1970s were usually eminent businessmen such as Ivan Allen, Jr., in the fifties and sixties and his successor, insurance executive Sam Massell.

The pattern that Hunter described was not unique to Atlanta. The Citizens' Charter Association, a group of leading Dallas businessmen, has controlled decision-making in that city since the 1930s. The Good Government League of San Antonio, an organization of the city's Anglo businessmen, has nominated and elected 94 percent of the city councilmen since 1955. Into the 1970s, southern urban governments remained "adjuncts to the business and economic community." The South, according to political sci-

entist Peter A. Lupsha and planner William J. Siembieda, "has never been
. . . a region where interclass coalitional politics and union influence . . .
turn the political tide."

This exclusive commercial-civic elite has been adept at proclaiming the
ecumenicism of its policies while accomplishing little (especially in the
realm of public services) to prove it. The booster, a rhetorical proponent of
change, is actually afraid of and opposed to change; *progress* has been a
euphemism for *tradition*. Urban leaders converted new methodologies like
planning, for example, to conservative objectives designed to preserve the
existing social and political structure. They also dissembled to avoid pursuing policies that could threaten their hegemony. When the Memphis Chamber of Commerce boasted in early 1941 that "there is no housing shortage
in Memphis. . . . Memphis is well-housed," the city had one of the worst
housing shortages in the nation and nearly four out of every five blacks and
one out of three whites were living in substandard housing. The deceit on
disease and the falsehoods about race were other conscious deceptions to
ensure the status quo and to present an attractive image to potential investors. Above all, the boosters claimed to be the keepers of the community's
welfare. Although boosterism was a phenomenon of main-street America,
as Sinclair Lewis demonstrated, huckstering southern-style was a distinctive
variation. In a region that specialized in inflated political oratory inflicted on
largely unsophisticated rural audiences, boosterism created a political dem-
agoguery of its own based on an identity between community welfare and
the leaders' policies. In this manner, as historian Richard Sennett has noted,
"the image of community is purified of all that might convey a feeling of
difference, let alone conflict, in who 'we' are. . . . The myth of community
solidarity is a purification ritual." Boosterism, like its partner evangelical
Protestantism, thus "purified" the southern city of its class and racial di-
visiveness, uniting all under the banner of the growth ethic. Occasionally a
fellow southerner would see through the boasts and lay bare the poverty of
thought and action they represented. Thomas Wolfe, writing to his mother
in 1923, made the following comments on booster rhetoric in his home
town of Asheville:

> I will not hesitate to say what I think of those people who shout "Progress, Prog-
> ress, Progress"—when what they mean is more Ford automobiles, more Rotary
> Clubs, more Baptist Ladies Social unions. I will say that "Greater Asheville"
> does not necessarily mean "100,000 by 1930," that we are not necessarily four
> times as civilized as our grandfathers because we go four times as fast in auto-

mobiles, because our buildings are four times as tall. What I shall try to get into their dusty little pint-measure minds is that a full belly, a good automobile, paved streets, and so on, do not make them one whit better or finer,—that there is beauty in this world,—beauty even in this wilderness of ugliness and provincialism that is at present our country, beauty and spirit which will make us men instead of cheap Board of Trade Boosters, and blatant pamphleteers.

The "cheap Board of Trade Boosters" won the argument from Wolfe, of course, and the better men whom Wolfe hoped for would need to wait another generation. In the meantime, the veneer of rhetoric and the glitter of new buildings and population statistics dominated the southern urban stage. It was a romantic drama, as the purple booster rhetorical flights implied, embellishing the irrelevancies with homages to the past:

Before the Dawn of Christianity
The Boast of Man was
          "I am A Roman"
Today
The Same Man Would
Have Said
          "I am A Memphian!"

W. J. Cash heard in this rhetoric of growth "the gallop of Jeb Stuart's cavalrymen," deriving from "the native genius of an incurably romantic people enamored before all else of the magnificent and spectacular."

Romanticism, the hostility toward new ideas, the parsimonious social conscience, and the shadow of rhetoric without the substance of accomplishment—these were characteristics of the antebellum South, characteristics of an agrarian society. There was never any New South; "let's never call it that," a Birmingham booster wrote in the 1920s. Indeed, agrarian values, like the rural migrants, still undergirded southern urban society. Southern cities still bore the physical reminders of their rural roots into the 1970s; they carried their rural ideological baggage as well. There were churchmen and businessmen, of course, who chafed under and struggled against the prevailing conservatism of their respective institutions. The black churches were in the forefront of southern regional and urban change during the 1950s and sixties, and there were white churchmen who joined them. There were civic leaders, especially journalists, who departed from the party line frequently at personal or professional peril. I have, however, attempted to describe a trend, the dominant philosophical and economic forces operating in southern cities during the half century beginning in 1920. And these forces, generally, stood as bulwarks against diversity, dissent, and a better way of life for a significant proportion of the urban population.

The South was changing in the 1920s: the decline of staple agriculture, accelerated migrations into the cities, the widespread use of electricity and the automobile, and the growing urban skyline. For the erstwhile agrarian residents, these changes, though barely discernible, must have seemed almost revolutionary after decades of placidity and stagnation. The fright extended up to the elite as well, and their calls for community solidarity became more fervent during the decade. The southern people in the 1920s, Thomas Wolfe wrote, had emerged "into a kind of sunlight of another century. . . . They heard wheels coming and the world was in, yet they were not yet wholly of that world."

And there was resistance against moving into "that world" of the twentieth century, especially in the cities, because they seemed poised on the brink, as Tindall observed, ready to step into the sunlight and leave the shadows behind. The Fundamentalist crusade and the recrudescence of the Ku Klux Klan were in part reactions to these changes. But there were also more thoughtful responses from those for whom the alternatives for southern city and region were more complex and less definable in terms of "good" and "evil." The Southern literary renaissance—the works of Wolfe, Faulkner, and Glasgow, in particular—indicated a fear of the new world as well as an impatience with the traditions of the old. Flem Snopes may have been "the soulless incarnation of a commercial civilization," yet Faulkner was clearly uncomfortable with the old regime of waste, racism, and narrowmindedness. Thomas Wolfe, in *You Can't Go Home Again*, exposed the folly of boosterism in his native Asheville, where "a spirit of drunken waste and wild destructiveness was everywhere apparent. The fairest places in the town were being mutilated at untold cost." But as Wolfe railed against the new, he felt betrayed by the old—the stifling religiosity of his community, the web of family status, and the mindless cruelty and despair of Niggertown.

In the 1930s, the group of Vanderbilt University intellectuals known collectively as the Nashville Agrarians similarly attempted to balance the new world with regional traditions. They believed that those traditions, metaphorically at least, resided in the Old South, and they laid out the benefits of a simpler agrarian civilization. At their best, the Agrarians urged southerners to challenge booster hyperbole, to think, and "to look very critically at the advantages of becoming a 'new South' which will be only an undistinguished replica of the usual industrial community." John Crowe Ransom was among the earliest humanists to decry the region's "boundless destruction of nature," epitomized by urban sprawl, depleted natural resources, and industrial pollution. Stark Young, perhaps the most equanimous of the Agrarians, wrote in their famous manifesto *I'll Take My Stand*: "We can accept the machine, but create our own attitude toward it."

Alas, the Agrarians provided no specific program to accomplish this unique balance of modernism and southernism. Another group of southern intellectuals, primarily social scientists at the University of North Carolina in Chapel Hill, sought to utilize the coming age of urbanization and industrialization to improve the quality of the South's population through education, health facilities, and more diverse employment opportunities. The Regionalists, as this group was called, were the first southerners systematically to study the region, expose its problems, and suggest remedies. If Howard W. Odum and his colleagues erred, it was in placing too much faith in the benefits of modern technology and urbanization for regional deliverance. As Louis D. Rubin, Jr., assessed them: "They were activist prophets, and they led the way out of the swamp—with, however, little concern for whether the swamp might have any attractions of its own."

The most heartening aspect to this flowering of respondents to the question of "whither the South?" was that it marked the first significant challenge to the civic-religious leadership since Progress became enthroned as a regional objective after the Civil War. Unfortunately, southern writers were perhaps better understood and appreciated outside the region, and both the Agrarians and Regionalists wrote and spoke to a limited regional audience. After World War II, white southerners seemed less likely to take up the cudgels against the prophets of Progress. The civil rights drama monopolized regional attention, and in the 1970s many appeared mesmerized by the Sun Belt publicity, convinced perhaps that the southern millenium had arrived.

The subsidence of literary and academic criticism after World War II was ultimately not surprising, given the artificial nature of the debate to begin with. The participants of the thirties were not only questioning, but confused and angered as well. What they did not see, or perceived only dimly, was that Progress and Tradition were not opposites to be reconciled within the southern milieu. Rather, Progress and Tradition, city and countryside, were complementary and self-reinforcing mechanisms in the South. The discussants were for the most part carrying on a one-sided debate. W. J. Cash understood this when he recounted in *The Mind of the South* how southern leaders after the Civil War utilized the rhetoric and policies of Progress to uphold and transmit Old South traditions. The civic-religious elite sought and encouraged some changes—in census figures, economic growth, and geographic expansion—because these changes reinforced their position and the rural values of urban society. These changes, in fact, changed very little of southern urban society. In the 1950s, for example, Richmond officials graciously accepted federal funds for the construction of an expressway that dislocated 10 percent of the city's black population. Almost simultaneously, they rejected a federal grant that would have improved the housing conditions of some poor Richmonders. Though planners favored the project, one editor warned citizens of the "Shadow of Marx" that hung over this proposal. The Richmond decisions, which local leaders probably did not view as contradictory, underscored the observation of a civil rights worker who wrote in 1962 about the alleged changes that were occurring in southern society: "The new does not supplant the old. The new merely is superimposed on the old."

Changing southern cities were still southern cities and inextricably part of their region. This was so because, as W. J. Cash noted perceptively in the 1940s, the farmer and his values were still "at the center" of southern civilization. Cash's catalog of the shortcomings of the rural personality described the values prevalent in urban society as well: "violence, intolerance, aversion and suspicion toward new ideas . . . an exaggerated individualism and a too narrow concept of social responsibility, attachment to fictions and false values, above all too great attachment to racial values and a tendency to justify cruelty and injustice in the name of these values."

Above all, as Cash noted, the values of the biracial society reigned over the region. They were the most vigorous vestiges of a waning staple agricultural society. The attachment of white urban southerners to biracial values was a foundation for their "murderous entrenchment against all new life." In the confrontation between biracialism and the sunlight of the twentieth century, however, the darkness pervading the hearts and minds of urban southerners would slowly and tentatively be lifted.

Stirring the Antbed

The situation of blacks in southern cities by the 1920s had changed little since the dark years of the 1890s. The proportion of urban blacks remained stable and even declined in some southern cities. The industrial boom of

World War I created new employment opportunities in northern cities, and a steady stream of blacks from the farms and the cities of the South filled out work-force requirements in the North. Southern urban newspapers that had urged the blacks to remain in the countryside now decried their disappearance from the southern urban labor force. The removal of labor mobility restrictions in the rural South during the 1930s led to the exodus of nearly half a million blacks to northern cities, even though employment was almost as scarce in those cities as in the South—the black migrants were evidently content enough with escape from the biracial society. Renewed employment opportunities resulting from World War II labor requirements generated a new wave of black migration to northern cities. Blacks of the depression generation were obviously modifying Du Bois' dictum about the advantages of southern urban life over southern rural life: their migration patterns declared that blacks preferred the advantages of northern urban life over the alleged benefits provided by *any* southern environment. In fact, until the 1960s the region continued to lose black population, and its cities experienced little increase in the proportion of their black populations, though annexation, more than outmigration, accounted for the stability of the black urban population.

The migration trends of blacks reflected the burdens of biracialism in the South. The overwhelming concentration of blacks in the lowest urban occupational categories, for example, remained unchanged from the 1920s to the 1970s. While blacks made significant incursions in the 1960s into previously all-white industries such as textile milling, their entrance into these industries was at the lowest rung of the job ladder. In some areas of the southern economy, black occupational participation has not yet attained pre-World War I levels. The erosion of "nigger work" during the 1920s was especially severe in the unskilled building construction trades. A banner at a Klan parade in Atlanta in 1930 delivered the message: "Niggers, back to the cotton fields—city Jobs are for White Folks."

The black economic situation worsened in the depression, when whites received preference both for employment and for relief. In Houston, local officials refused to accept welfare applications from blacks or Mexicans; in Richmond, blacks were asked, in effect, to bear the burden of the depression. While white employment rose slightly during the 1930s, black employment declined by 6 percent. Nor did federal relief efforts provide blacks with an equitable apportionment of welfare funds. In Jacksonville, Florida, black families outnumbered white families on relief by a ratio of three to one, yet the black households received only 45 percent of the welfare funds. Relief allotments for blacks in the urban South were invariably less than for whites: in Atlanta, blacks received $19.29 per month compared with $32.66 for whites, and in Houston the respective payments were $12.67 and $16.86. The depression confirmed that the biracial society was indeed separate and unequal.

The economic inequities of the biracial society persisted long after the depression ended. Blacks continued both to earn considerably less than whites and to be confined to a narrow range of unskilled occupations. In Atlanta, a city that Mayor Hartsfield characterized as "too busy to hate," black college graduates as late as the 1960s were unable to secure employment outside of teaching, the post office, or in black businesses. In 1960, the median income of black Atlanta families was half that of white families, despite the fact that the city possessed one of the wealthiest black communities in the urban South.

Economic statistics from other southern cities revealed similar disparities. In Memphis, where blacks comprised 38 percent of the population, they represented 58 percent of all families with annual incomes less than $1,000 in 1949, 70 percent of such families in 1959, and 71 percent of those families in 1969. In 1959, 69 percent of the city's blacks were below the poverty level as defined by the United States Census Bureau, compared with 14 percent of the white population. Ten years later, the comparative poverty-level figures were 44 percent and 8 percent respectively. By 1970, the black family median income was only 56 percent of the white family income. While Memphis whites participated in the prosperity of the 1960s, a good portion of the black community remained outside the city's economy.

The best indicator of the blacks' inferior status in the southern urban biracial society remained the black neighborhood. There it was possible to see not only the impact of economic inequality but of social and political discrimination as well. Residential clusters rather than the emergence of a single black ghetto continued to characterize black residential patterns in the urban South. The residential pattern was typically one large cluster, usually in the most decrepit area near the center, surrounded by smaller clusters moving outward toward the periphery. In some of the older cities like Savannah and Charleston, reminders of the antebellum past persisted into the 1920s and 1930s where long fingers of black residences intruded into white neighborhoods on the narrow lanes behind the major residential thoroughfares. These vestiges disappeared as whites began to abandon the centers and patterns emerged similar to those in newer southern cities. Birmingham, for example, had a primary black neighborhood adjacent to the downtown area, and several smaller clusters scattered throughout the city wherever poor land existed. Black neighborhoods in Nashville and Atlanta evinced similar patterns.

Residential patterns, like the blacks' low economic status, persisted in subsequent decades with only slight modifications. If anything, the isolation from the white residential areas increased, although racial residential segregation was decreasing in northern cities. By 1960, only 5.5 percent of the southern urban population resided in integrated neighborhoods, compared with 31.8 percent for the Northeast. Between 1964 and 1967, the percentage of southern urban blacks residing in tracts that were more than 75 percent black increased from 65 percent to 78 percent in Memphis, 57 percent to 67 percent in Louisville, 79 percent to 90 percent in Shreveport, and 86 percent to 88 percent in Nashville. Although black neighborhoods in the South are more dispersed than those in northern cities, they are usually more segregated. In addition, southern urban blacks are more likely to be peripheral or suburban residents than their northern counterparts. This is not an index of increased affluence or residential permissiveness, however; the relatively dispersed cluster pattern is one explanation, and another is that, as southern metropolitan areas have expanded, they have incorporated poor rural blacks barely eking out a living on small garden plots. In 1970, 14 percent of the South's metropolitan black population resided on the metropolitan periphery, compared with only 3 percent in the Northeast.

The complicity of southern urban governments in institutionalizing racial residential segregation accounted in great part for the persistence and increase in these patterns. The civic elite's early embrace of urban planning, for example, originated partly out of planning's utility for preserving a biracial urban society. Zoning was one of the most frequently employed tools of local leaders to order the urban environment and, not incidentally, racial residential patterns as well. Although the United States Supreme Court had declared racial residential zoning codes unconstitutional in 1917, southern cities discovered that a thin veil was sufficient to ensure codification of residential segregation. Some local leaders openly admitted that zoning laws were framed partly "to keep the negroes to certain districts." The absence of zoning in Houston, though, did not prevent a pattern of racial residential segregation; there, private deed restrictions were employed as an effective substitute for zoning.

Transportation policy, the other major planning emphasis of local governments besides zoning, also indicated the racial motivations behind city-planning actions. As blacks began to move into the previously white sections of Atlanta in the late 1930s, city planners devised a transportation scheme to halt the black residential advance. The plan called for the construction of a landscaped parkway 190 feet wide. Clearly marked by symbols "*w*" and "*c*" on the planners' maps, the areas to the west and east of the parkway would be white and black residential areas respectively. In order to reinforce the intent of this scheme, the city planning commission proposed the erection of a cyclone fence on both sides of the parkway.

The residential confinement and concentration of the southern urban black population received new impetus during the 1950s and 1960s under federal housing policies. Urban renewal legislation authorized federal grants to city governments, which would then decide on the location and extent of both slum clearance and public housing. In the hands of southern civic leaders and their planner-associates, these grants became effective mechanisms for eliminating, regrouping, and concentrating black residential neighborhoods. The typical sequence involved the destruction of a black slum and a subsequent failure to erect replacement housing, a policy that forced blacks to crowd into adjacent areas, thereby creating worse conditions and concentrations than before. In Atlanta between 1957 and 1967, the city demolished 21,000 housing units, most occupied by blacks, and constructed only 5,000 new units during that same period. In Charlotte, the city tore down an average of 1,100 black-occupied housing units per year from 1965 to 1968 but erected only 425 new units during that time. When southern cities actually built public housing, it was invariably located on the worst sites and consequently in already-existing black neighborhoods.

Local officials, in fact, viewed the federal program as another scheme to enhance the growth ethic and maintain the inequities of the biracial society. New downtowns, not new public housing, characterized the leaders' implementation of federal urban renewal. The simultaneous emergence of the civic elite's renewed interest in downtown and the application of federal funds for slum clearance was more than coincidence. During the 1960s, an Atlanta booster declaimed proudly about the exorcism performed on a black neighborhood in that city: "Old slums have been transformed into handsome, productive property . . . [and] the blight of the old Buttermilk Bottoms [*sic*] has become an impressive array of motels, office buildings and high rise apartments." The editor of a black Atlanta newspaper viewed the renewal project from a different perspective, complaining that blacks had "lived for years in 'Buttermilk Bottom' . . . until the powers saw a great real estate value and then most of us were shifted to areas just as bad, if not worse."

It is possible to imagine the living conditions that prevailed in the remaining black enclaves after such major reductions in low-income housing stock. This was another version of the official neglect that had plagued black residential areas for generations. Relaxed or nonexistent building codes in southern cities had permitted the proliferation of the "shotgun shacks" and shanties that had characterized black residential "architecture" since the nineteenth century. These dwellings were "prime investments in southern towns," as George B. Tindall noted; "they required small outlays and bore low assessments but brought handsome returns from areas where neglect of sanitary provisions was 'as proverbial as . . . exorbitant rents.'"

The southern city scarcely provided more suitable accommodations than private developers did. Savannah erected a black development in 1948 that provided six hundred identical two-bedroom, unheated cinderblock homes on fifty-by-one-hundred foot lots. They sold for $4,200. In the meantime, accommodating zoning laws enabled developers to convert a portion of a black neighborhood in central Savannah into commercial property, a decision that forced displaced blacks into adjacent areas, creating serious overcrowding and consequent deterioration of the housing stock. Not yet neglected in peace, blacks were forced to move again when Historic Savannah, supported by favorable urban legislation, purchased, renovated, and sold some of these dwellings. Little wonder that black neighborhoods in southern cities continued to demonstrate other indices of official neglect such as illiteracy, premature death, and criminal behavior. The spare statistics delivered without comment by the Richmond Council of Social Agencies in 1929 spoke volumes about life in the black community:

Death Rate	Average Age at Death
Black 20.43 per 1,000	Black 37.2 years
White 11.54 per 1,000	White 52.1 years

Black-White Illiteracy	14 : 1
Black-White Arrests	3 : 1

Mary Mebane described southern black urban life in the 1930s, a description that probably obtained for another generation: "Life became a cycle, a ritual—birth, existence, death. One worked for subsistence wages, or below, partied on Saturday night to relieve the harshness and monotony of daily existence, and on Sunday prepared his soul to die."

Such were the costs of the biracial society to southern urban blacks. Yet, despite the terrible monotony of their low existence, blacks, as they had in the past, took as much initiative in their neighborhood lives as possible. While the white community sought to destroy and confine, the black community strove to build and expand. The control that black residents exercised over their neighborhood businesses and institutions remained the major, perhaps the only, advantage of residential living in a biracial society. Since the 1920s, the black community of Atlanta has demonstrated how far self-help can transport a black neighborhood that is isolated and confined from white society. By the 1920s, three black clusters had evolved in Atlanta, east, west, and south of the downtown area. The west side black neighborhood soon became the city's, if not the region's, most prominent example of self-help. Black businessman Heman E. Perry and his Standard Life Insurance Company purchased three hundred acres of land in the area for the purpose of building a predominantly middle-class black neighborhood. Since white lending institutions refused to sell mortgages to blacks, Perry provided the necessary financing for home purchases. By 1930, 37 percent of the city's black population lived on the west side and 55 percent of the area's residents were homeowners, compared with a 15 percent home-ownership rate for the total black Atlanta population. Almost one-half of the west side population consisted of homeowning professionals and skilled workers.

The neighborhood evolved into the institutional center for black urban life. Three black colleges and six churches located there as early as the 1920s. In the following decade, the vast Atlanta University Center—a conglomerate of six black colleges and universities—was formed. The university, in addition to its educational functions, provided land for residential development and for the construction of primary schools. Unlike most black neighborhoods in the nation, the west side community was constructed by blacks for blacks. By the 1960s, according to *Fortune* magazine, the west side had helped to make Atlanta "the largest single depository of Negro capital in the U.S."

The development of black businesses and institutions in Atlanta and in other southern cities helped to perpetuate the isolation and separation of the black community. It was part of the perversity of the biracial society that black enterprises, especially real estate, insurance, and banking firms, developed significant stakes in maintaining residential segregation. Credit and insurance practices of black businesses occasionally took advantage of the poor and largely unsophisticated black population.

The west side of Atlanta, though certainly a unique southern black community, demonstrated that there were possibilities and initiatives within the black neighborhood. But for blacks to expend their energies and talents within the confines of a biracial society was to advance only a little; the strictures of confinement and the darkness of discrimination had to be removed before significant racial progress could occur. Blacks had challenged the biracial system before without much success, and they knew that they could not depend on the assistance of the white southern urban community, where the substance of action frequently disproved the shadow of rhetoric. With more tactical leaders and with strategic allies from outside the South, some of the ancient structures of the biracial society would finally crumble.

The prevalent belief, especially in southern cities, is that the white civic elite played a major role in facilitating the changes that occurred in the biracial society during the 1960s and 1970s. Again, shadow is confused with substance. The rhetoric of the white business community was moderate, even liberal, on race relations, but the white elite covertly worked to enforce the status quo in this area as in most other aspects of urban life. It is true that during the early 1920s white initiatives resulted in an important break in the structure of southern urban racism. In the midst of racial violence throughout the nation in 1919, troubled whites in Atlanta organized the Commission on Interracial Cooperation, which was designed to begin a dialogue with black community leaders. Whites and blacks in other cities followed the Atlanta example, and some of the accomplishments of those commissions were impressive, if short-lived. Occasionally, segregated streetcars became integrated, black welfare agencies received appropriations from the Community Chest, commissions provided basic legal services, and some of the poor public services in black neighborhoods were even upgraded. But major distractions such as the depression and World War II halted these efforts. In the late 1940s, what Lillian Smith called "the twisting turning dance of segregation" still held forth, and the white leadership called the tune.

Indeed, it seemed to southern urban blacks in the late forties and fifties that they were captives in what sociologist Leonard Reissman called "the fortress of tradition that was meant to protect the biracial society." Segregation and the accompanying racism were givens in southern cities. As an Atlanta *Constitution* editorial stated in 1948: "Only a fool would say the Southern pattern of separation of the races can, or should be overthrown."

There were apparently enough "fools" in black communities throughout the urban South—and in Washington, D.C.—who thought otherwise. The 1954 Supreme Court decision in *Brown* v. *Board of Education of Topeka, Kansas*, had an enormous psychological impact on the urban South, even if concrete results were at least a decade or two away. For one thing, it galvanized the white power structure into a strong, if sometimes covert, defense of the biracial society. Journalist Hodding Carter, a racial moderate, warned in Atlanta that "it will be tragic for the South, the Negro, and the nation itself if the government should enact and attempt to enforce any laws or Supreme Court decisions that would open the South's public schools and public gathering places to the Negro." Henry Edmonds, one of the urban South's most liberal white theologians, complained in Birmingham that the *Brown* decision "ended the era of good feeling in the South between the races and halted the progress that was being made . . . under the earlier formula of equal but separate facilities." In the South's characteristic small urban places, resistance took more vigorous form as civic leaders organized White Citizens' Councils to enforce the biracial society as it was. Pat Watters recalled how "frightening" it was "to go into a small city and to realize that not merely the semiliterate poor white gas station attendant, but also the bankers, the mayor, the editor, even some of the preachers, all those who are personages in such a place supported it [the Citizens' Council] fervently."

But the black community was equally determined to capitalize on federal support for their efforts to challenge the biracial society. The movement began when Rosa Parks refused to obey a white Montgomery bus driver's order to move to the back of a city bus. The ensuing Montgomery bus boycott catapulted the Reverend Martin Luther King, Jr., into national prominence and prompted federal judge Frank M. Johnson, Jr., to issue comprehensive desegregation orders that ultimately transformed Montgomery into one of the most integrated cities of its size in the country. It was an alliance—blacks and the federal government—that would win numerous battles in the civil rights civil war over the next two decades.

Perhaps the greatest struggles occurred over school desegregation. The schools were a bulwark of biracialism, since illiteracy and the separate and unequal educational systems in southern cities were important in maintaining the subservient position of the black community. Moreover, racial mixing in the schools conjured up latent southern fears and sexual bugaboos. One of the earliest confrontations occurred in Atlanta in 1961. Black and white religious leaders organized OASIS (Organizations Assisting Schools in September) to counteract MASE (Metropolitan Association for Segregated Education) and Lester Maddox's GUTS (Georgians Unwilling to Surrender). The tactics of OASIS, assisted by white editor Ralph McGill, were clever in that they appealed to the city's growth ethic and booster tradition rather than to concepts of racial justice. OASIS placed advertisements warning that disorder would damage the city's reputation, and McGill lectured that Atlanta "has always tried to look forward and not backward." The peaceful desegregation of Atlanta's schools occurred on August 30, 1961, seven years after the *Brown* decision. It was at this time that Mayor Hartsfield coined the phrase that Atlanta was "a city too busy to hate." Peaceful integration became another item in the booster catalog of Atlanta progress.

The victory in Atlanta over segregation and the biracial society was not clear-cut, however. When Martin Luther King, Jr., won the Nobel Peace Prize in 1965, Atlanta's civic leaders threatened to boycott the dinner in his honor until an interracial committee convinced them that, by honoring King, they were also honoring the city. More revealing, by 1970 Atlanta's schools were no more desegregated than schools in the rest of Georgia. A survey in 1966 indicated that segregation in the city's schools was more widespread than at the time of the *Brown* decision in 1954.

The so-called white "moderates" were ultimately most dangerous to black aspirations for an equitable role in southern urban society; they framed their rhetoric and proposals with liberal homilies, but their actions came from the biracial tradition. The desegregation of public schools in Greensboro, North Carolina, indicated not only the effectiveness of white moderate subterfuge, but of black determination as well. Greensboro's black community had an activist tradition dating back to the 1920s, and white community leaders were considered moderates by southern urban standards. It was not surprising, therefore, when the school board issued a compliance resolution almost immediately after the *Brown* decision. But resolution did not signify implementation. The attitudes of the white moderate school board members gave some hint of this when they expressed concern that desegregation would be "traumatic for the average white southerner" and that "the average Negro did not want desegregation" anyway. In the meantime, white religious and business leaders remained silent. The black community was not silent, however, and by 1957 the school board had devised a desegregation plan.

The plan required black applicants for transfer to white schools to complete a series of complicated forms, all notarized, and for white parents to secure automatic transfers from desegregated schools if they wished to continue their children's education in a segregated environment. Under this formula, a total of six black children enrolled in previously all-white schools. Greensboro's moderate white leadership boasted that their city was the first in the South to desegregate its public schools. The city's blacks were obviously not satisfied with the plan, however, and filed suit against the school board in 1959. In a successful attempt to avoid litigation and an almost certain adverse decision, the school board merged an all-black school with an all-white school to which blacks had applied. Several months later, the school board transferred all of the white students out of the latter school and redrew district lines so that it now became an all-black school with an all-black faculty. Since the blacks were now enrolled in the school to which they had applied, the legal question no longer existed, though segregation did.

Historian William Chafe followed the Greensboro desegregation saga as it unfolded and concluded that "the one priority that dominated all others in white Greensboro was the desire to 'keep the lid on'—to preserve the city's reputation for progressiveness and moderation without having to engage in substantive change." It was the familiar southern urban story of shadow, not substance, of the "hostile . . . entrenchment against all new life." Not until 1969, after desegregation had occurred in allegedly much less moderate communities in the South, did significant integration occur in Greensboro's schools. As Chafe noted, it was the "good" South that delayed integration the longest, whereas schools in places like Mississippi had been integrated since the middle of the decade.

The white economic and political leaders whom Chafe identified as the major culprits in the Greensboro episode could not continue their holding action for long. Pat Watters characterized the South in the 1960s as "an antbed which has been most thoroughly stirred by a stick"—and blacks were stirring the most. In Greensboro itself, while the white-dominated school board was carrying out its desegregation charade, black university students were directing a frontal attack against the "twisting turning dance of segregation." Early in 1960, four black students sat down at a Woolworth's lunch counter in downtown Greensboro, and within days the "sit-in" movement spread to fifty-four southern cities. A concerted half decade of protest against the biracial society had begun, only this time the stage was not the school board meeting room or the lunch counter. An entire nation watched the final violent gyrations of the segregation dance.

When Martin Luther King, Jr., and his black and white followers marched across Pettus Bridge into Selma and into the troops and dogs of Police Chief Jim Clarke, an era was drawing to a close. The march to Selma resulted in the Voting Rights Act of 1965, as the federal government belatedly caught up with their black partners and blacks received a voice in a biracial society where only the hollow rhetoric of white leaders had echoed before. Although subsequent federal civil rights legislation would ensure blacks' equal participation in housing and employment, the Selma drama was the last collective action of the southern black community played to a national audience. The laws were or soon would be passed; the time had come to consolidate the gains and utilize the laws as battering rams to assault the remaining bastions of white supremacy. Though some walls of separation stubbornly withstood the attack, blacks and the federal government had succeeded in throwing the biracial society into disarray. The South and southern cities would never be the same again because, as Pat Watters asserted, "the civilization of the South was no longer undergirded by law that, in its deepest meaning—dehumanization of Negroes—was based on murder, based on the antithesis of the meaning of law and civilization. That was crucial. Southerners were free at last."

Make no mistake—the blacks and those omnipresent "outside agitators" were the liberators. As one southerner admitted in 1973, "it was not our good will and robust, warm, nature, but agitation, pressure, and federal power that brought this about. These are not accomplishments, they are compliances." Because southern whites seemed reluctant to acquiesce in their own freedom from biracialism, the urban black communities had to apply constant pressure to avoid being locked behind the walls of a separate and unequal biracial society again. The urban political system, not the streets, became the mechanism for black pressure during the late 1960s and 1970s.

Supported by federal law and by their own numbers, blacks have become the major political force in several southern cities and in many smaller communities in the agricultural black belt. The black mayors of Richmond, Atlanta, Birmingham, and New Orleans are the most visible evidence of black political power, and black city councilmen are no longer oddities in many southern towns or cities. As with most other assaults on the biracial society, blacks have secured only a minimum of support from the local white community. In 1979, when Birmingham elected its first black mayor, Richard Arrington, only 10 percent of the white voters supported him. In Atlanta, where blacks have voted through the twentieth century, the political alliance between wealthy whites and the black community dissolved in 1969 when blacks, led by attorney Maynard Jackson, sought greater representation in the city's higher elective offices. Four years later, with 10 percent of the white vote, Jackson won the mayoral race.

Southern urban whites acknowledge but clearly are wary of black political power. Nevertheless, white candidates now make pilgrimages to black churches and other community institutions to secure black support. The scenes emerging from some of these campaigns are surreal: Birmingham's Bull Connor, whose dogs and fire hoses were a few years earlier directed at those same people with whom he now held hands and sang "We Shall Overcome"; and George Wallace, in the very church where Martin Luther King, Jr., preached in Montgomery, just a block or so away from where Wallace rang out with "segregation forever," now being serenaded by a black congregation singing "The Battle Hymn of the Republic."

What, if anything, do these vignettes of southern urban political life signify for the conditions of blacks in the region's cities? They ensure, for one thing, that a regression to the policies that prevailed prior to the 1970s is unlikely. The conscious public effort to destroy, contain, isolate, and dominate the black community will probably not recur. But they also signify that black political strength and security depend on sheer numbers, not necessarily upon the changing attitudes of the white community. Several southern cities have already attempted to push through reapportionment, at-large elections, annexation, and consolidation schemes under the guise of political reform, when actually these policies are aimed at diluting black political strength. Increasing black political power has tended to conservatize the southern urban whites.

The stakes of urban political power, however, are becoming smaller and smaller. When blacks finally ascend to the highest offices in urban politics, they soon discover that, as political historian James C. Cobb noted, they have inherited "more of a problem than a prize." As the pace of annexation slows and as white residential and commercial removal from the southern city continues, economic problems mount. Despite the hoopla about the Sun Belt, southern cities remain the most impoverished of the nation's urban centers, and service levels, never especially great, are not likely to increase with blacks in high office because of growing financial difficulties. Although the presence of black political leadership will result in a more equitable distribution of federal grants, even here black city government officials are constrained by the types of projects they can fund and by the political importance of demonstrating that black political power does not necessarily signify white exclusion, as white political power invariably implied black exclusion.

In the still-numerous cities where whites control the political apparatus, the federal government's emphasis on local initiative and discretion in the allocation of funds under the Community Development Act of 1974 places little burden on white political leaders to improve services, housing, and employment opportunities in the black community. Despite language in the preamble of federal legislation emphasizing benefits to the poor and minorities, in practice city governments have discretion as to the neighborhoods that will receive federal funds.

Most important, black political power is circumscribed by the absence of black economic power. Since the antebellum era, urban economic and political elites have usually been identical, and the biracial society was an important pillar in support of this power structure. The weakening of biracialism has loosened this alliance, though in some of the newer cities in Florida and Texas it persists. It is not yet clear how economic leaders will respond to their black political leaders, but if they withdraw from participation, and perhaps from the city as well, as has happened in the North, economic exigencies will further reduce black political options.

Some southern cities, of course, continue to experience economic growth, but black political power divorced from economic power may not be able to accomplish much for the chronically poor, low-paid black. Increases in the prices of real estate and of consumer goods that have accompanied growth have tended to concentrate wealth in the economic elite, with the poor (primarily black) suffering most from inflation—and usually from accompanying pollution and higher taxes as well. In industrial Durham, for example, blue-collar wages and employment have lagged behind white-collar employment and wages. One consequence is that factory workers (a majority of whom are black) can no longer compete for housing. Economists have suggested that residential segregation may actually increase even if black economic status is rising because, in growth economies, white economic status has traditionally increased faster. So, quite apart from political power, the mechanisms of the Sun Belt economy may severely limit black economic advance.

Urban race relations have traditionally taken their character from the countryside. Indeed, the differentials in black advances in various cities throughout the region, analysts believe, are due in great part to the racial conditions of the adjacent countryside. Urban sociologists term this phenomenon "bilateral cultural movement," but regardless of the phrase, it represents a traditional rural influence on urban development. Whereas the decline of staple agriculture released thousands of blacks from a dim rural future, it may actually have heightened racial tensions in the towns and small cities that received a portion of this migration. These urban places would be the slowest to change in any case, and if the small city is still the characteristic southern city, then it is premature to write an epitaph for the biracial society.

The black is still part of the rural-urban culture as well. His religion, kinship patterns, language, name, and even deprivations are part of his rural traditions. He is black, but he is also a southerner. This is one reason why maintenance of the biracial society was and is so tragic. By rejecting the black man, the white southerner was rejecting a part of himself as well. White and black are two separate worlds, yet they are one. As historian Joel Williamson described it, it is a "duality that is also, paradoxically, a unity." When Pat Watters declared in the wake of black civil rights victories in the mid-1960s that "Southerners were free at last," he meant *all* southerners. Robert Coles experienced this duality when he talked with a black child who braved angry white mobs to attend a New Orleans public school. The rural southern values floated from this urban child like the scent of honeysuckle: "I hope I never leave Louisiana, because we have the best flowers here, and my grandmother grows them better each year, she says. We have sun and rain, enough of both; and every time I get discouraged I do what my grandmother says, I go look at the azaleas and I sit in her chair under our little palm tree and catch the sun and then move to the shade. My daddy says that we haven't got much, but we have a good backyard, with soil that will grow anything and with weather to match."

If southern cities were poised between two civilizations at the beginning of the 1920s, then southern urban blacks are astride two eras in their long history in the region at the beginning of the 1980s. In New Orleans again, Robert Coles provided this vignette from the biracial society: "Late November in New Orleans the rain comes down hard. With it a chill can challenge the city's sense of itself as deeply southern. . . . For the poor those damp, cold days are particularly difficult; so children go to school shivering or even wet, because they haven't good sweaters, and often enough lack a raincoat; and families hover around old and dangerous gas burners, the only source of heat for many who live in the port city's black slums." A friend of mine who had a lonely, sometimes frightening time as a white fighting the biracial society in Alabama during the 1960s related another scene, this one from Montgomery at a Christmas night parade in 1973. The parade snaked its way down from the Capitol to Martin Luther King, Jr.'s church and up Montgomery Street past the Elite Café, marching through several jumbled eons of southern history. There was nothing unusual about the parade—it contained the usual assortment of baton twirlers, school bands, student honor guards, and local dignitaries. Lanier High School—the old white-establishment high school in Montgomery—was represented by its band, now about one-third black, their blue and white flags snapping in the crisp, though not cold, December evening breeze, performing a little dance step popularized by southern black university bands. Nothing unusual.

The rich black resources are there for the future of the urban South. The blacks challenging an entrenched system and society have achieved remarkable victories. Much, of course, remains to be done, but, as the black New Orleans youth said, "We've been here for a long, long time, you know." It is likely he would have added, "and we'll stay here." And that is the hope for the future of the South, and of the southern city.

Fast Trains to Texas

As the years after World War II have brought freedom to urban blacks and whites enmeshed in the web of a biracial society, they have also meant a partial liberation for southern cities bound in a national network of economic subserviency. The southern city had long played the role of the black in the national economy: confined to "nigger work" and allowed to contribute only so far as such contributions would help others. The decline of staple agriculture, the increasing economic role of the federal government, and the discovery of black human capital have breached the hierarchical structure of the national economy.

First came the collapse. In 1929, Richard H. Edmonds, who had been generating New South propaganda for nearly half a century, declared that "the South was writing an Epic of Progress and Prosperity in Letters of Gold." One year later, the epic came to an abrupt conclusion as the region plummeted into economic disaster. If wishes were fast trains to Texas, how the boosters would ride—but the boxcars were filled with homeless southern refugees heading nowhere, like the region. Staple agriculture and a colonial economy were weak supports to help the South and its cities weather the economic storm. The Roosevelt administration called Birmingham the "worst hit" city in the country. Men who could find work in the U.S. Steel colony received ten to fifteen cents per hour, and loan sharks hovered about those who could not. Workers in the steel mills received script for salary, redeemable only at the company store. The murder rate soared, and in 1931 Birmingham led the nation in murders. The city established other dubious records during the decade. Local government, virtually broke, had the lowest per capita public expenditure for cities of similar size in the nation, and in 1933 civic leaders attempted to sell the city parks to raise money. What one editor described as "that great absentee landlord, the U.S. Steel Corporation," did little to clear away the city's economic wreckage.

But other southern cities vied with Birmingham as urban welfare cases. Half of the businesses on Atlanta's famed Peachtree Street lay vacant; the situation was so desperate during the early years of the depression that some local leaders concocted a "back-to-the-farm" movement, as if a retreat to the city's agrarian origins would alleviate the burdens of a national economic breakdown in the twentieth century. Actually, the movement was going the other way. Hundreds of cotton farmers from rural Georgia roamed the city streets looking for employment because they could not sell their crops. This merely added to the human misery already prevalent in the city. At the other end of the state, in Savannah, the mayor was buying wood to sell to indigents and appealing to fishermen to donate fish to the poor.

Some southern cities managed to limp through the depression years with relatively little economic misery. Louisville and Richmond, on the strength of their cigarette industries, maintained the lowest unemployment rates in the region—cigarette production reached an all-time high in 1937. Cities in Florida coasted through the depression despite the collapse of the real estate boom in the late 1920s, and in the mid-thirties, a revolution in Cuba and a succession of especially severe winters in the North revived the economy of Miami and neighboring Miami Beach. The latter city experienced a building construction explosion in 1936 with forty-seven new hotels, seventy-four apartment buildings, and 252 homes; the city matched these figures during the following year as well. These were unusual cases, to be sure. Most southern cities, like cities elsewhere, floundered in penury and confusion. The national economy had broken down. It soon became clear that the economic salvation for urban America, especially for the devastated urban South, lay not in waiting for New York to revive, as had been the Republican hope in the early 1930s. The solution lay in Washington. The active participation of the federal government altered both the national economy and that economy's impact on the urban South.

Between 1933 and 1939, three New Deal agencies—the Federal Emergency Relief Administration (FERA), the Public Works Administration (PWA), and the Works Progress Administration (WPA)—sent nearly $2 billion to the South, most of it to the region's cities. In the process, the federal grants alleviated unemployment and poverty to some extent and altered the urban skyline and the physical city. Sewers, parks, new or renovated government office buildings, hospitals, bridges, and playgrounds—the types of services that southern cities would not have provided even in good times—appeared on the urban landscape through federal benevolence.

Washington pumped $361 million into a prostrate Birmingham over a four-year period beginning in 1933; the WPA initiated the city's first general street-improvement program, erected buildings, and gave work to the city's unemployed. Tampa, not as seriously affected by the depression as Birmingham, nevertheless benefited from federal largesse: in 1935, the WPA constructed a municipal airport, improved Bayshore Boulevard—a major thoroughfare—and even repaired some of the city's hotels. In Richmond, the PWA erected a bridge over the James River and helped to construct the Virginia State Library, a high school, and a hospital. In short, the federal government paid for the capital facilities in southern cities that northern cities had paid for themselves in earlier decades and on which they were still pay-ing off the debt. The almost-free modernization received by southern cities would prove to be an important economic advantage in subsequent decades.

The massive federal relief effort in southern cities was, of course, meant to be temporary, but there were few signals emanating from the urban South by the end of the 1930s indicating that southern cities were on the verge of economic self-sufficiency. Meanwhile, Congress was becoming more wary of massive government expenditures, staple agriculture was in shambles, and such commercial inequities as Pittsburgh Plus, differential freight rates, and unfavorable credit practices remained in place. Colonial patterns persisted. As Texan Maury Maverick observed in 1937: "The South actually works for the North; mortgage, insurance, industrial, and finance corporations pump the money northward like African ivory out of the Congo." With the beginning of World War II, however, all thought of a federal retreat from the national economy faded, and southern cities became strategic centers for the war effort.

The federal government had discovered southern cities and their environs as likely sites for shipyards and military bases during World War I. Newport News Shipbuilding and Dry Dock Company on the Virginia coast became a major supplier to the navy during and after World War I. Fort Sam Houston, adjacent to San Antonio, became the nation's largest army base during the twenties and helped the city's stricken economy during the thirties. By the early 1940s, the federal government had numerous and positive experiences with military operations in and near southern cities. In addition, both President Roosevelt and his National Resources Planning Board favored southern sites because of the area's chronic economic problems. Wartime industries that required "large numbers of workers . . . available for unskilled work or for training" matched the southern urban labor profile. What local private enterprise and southern urban governments could not or would not do, the federal government did by raising wage scales and helping to diversify the urban economy, moving it further away from its dependence on agriculture.

Accordingly, Charleston and Houston shipyards received major naval contracts. The aircraft industry became an almost-exclusively southern activity, with B-24s manufactured in Dallas, B-29s in Marietta, Georgia, and assorted assembly plants in Nashville, Birmingham, and Miami. Ellington Air Force Base in Houston eventually became NASA's Johnson Space Flight Center. The federal government spent over $1.5 billion in Florida from 1941 to 1945—the largest sum appropriated to any state in the nation; almost one-half of this expenditure went to shipbuilding operations at Jacksonville, Miami, Tampa, and Panama City. The total federal outlay for southern military facilities amounted to $4 billion, or more than one-third of the national facilities budget, and assistance to war-related industries in the South accounted for another $4.5 billion in federal funds.

There was no Pittsburgh Plus for government war contracts in Birmingham. The U.S. Steel plant in suburban Fairfield produced five million artillery shells, and city steel mills in general accounted for over three-quarters of all war materials manufactured in the South. The southern steel industry was an obvious beneficiary of wartime production requirements, but newer industries located near the newly opened oil fields of Texas also grew, and with them cities as well. During the 1920s and 1930s, natural gas was treated as a dangerous waste product that was disposed of through burning flares. Refineries had to contend with other noxious waste gases and chemicals as well. Advancing technology and World War II stimulated the expanded production of chemicals. Houston, with superior transportation links to nearby abundant raw materials, was in an ideal position to become not only a center of chemical production but of petro-chemicals as well. Soon Houston added steel-making to its industrial arsenal and by the 1960s was challenging Birmingham for the region's steel production lead.

Southern cities strained under the sudden impact of war and prosperity. As in the First World War, seaports experienced the greatest dislocations: between 1940 and 1943, Charleston's population increased by more than one-third, Norfolk's by nearly two-thirds. The growth ethic reached its illogical conclusion as primitive services and increased population generated chaos in some communities. Hattiesburg, Mississippi, doubled its population in six months from 20,000 to 40,000 people with the opening of Camp Shelby in 1940. Annual rents increased thirteenfold by 1944; bank deposits increased by five times; and bank clearings tripled. But public institutions collapsed; private charities, individual households, religious institutions, and the federal government actually ran Hattiesburg during the war years.

This was nothing, however, compared to the chaos in Mobile. The increased personnel requirements for wartime industries and shipyards nearly doubled the city's population to 201,369 by 1944. John Dos Passos, elbowing his way through the city in 1943, reported that Mobile appeared "trampled and battered like a city that's been taken by storm. Sidewalks are crowded. Gutters are stacked with litter. . . . Garbage cans are overflowing. Frame houses on treeshaded streets bulge with men in shirtsleeves. . . . Cues wait outside of movies and lunchrooms." The city stopped functioning, its traditionally meager public services overwhelmed at the first crush of migrants. Water came out of taps by single drops, and crime and vice flourished as the nineteen-member police force was overwhelmed by the demands placed upon it. The federal government rescued the city in 1944 by providing housing and services for its beleaguered citizens.

Washington was in the process of redistributing the national wealth, thereby placing the different regions of the country on a more equitable footing in the national economy. The military bases were, in reality, the least of the stimuli that federal expenditures afforded to the southern urban economy. Personnel levels at such installations fluctuated. Moreover, the government closed a number of the southern urban bases in the 1950s and again in the 1970s. Hunter Army Airfield in Savannah, for example, opened in 1940, closed in 1946, reopened in 1950, closed in 1966, reopened in 1967, and closed in 1974. Since the military was the largest single employer in the city by 1969, the deactivation of Hunter Field hurt Savannah's economy.

It was the federal assistance to southern urban industry that achieved a pump-priming effect on the urban economy. The federal government helped to stimulate new industries, as in Houston, and released old ones from colonial restrictions, as in Birmingham. Military spending in southern cities encouraged the development of electronics research and manufacturing firms, scientific equipment companies, and aeronautics machinery plants. The growth of high-technology industry has had a positive impact on a region traditionally burdened with low-technology, low-wage rural industries. By 1960, low-wage industries accounted for only two out of every five manufacturing jobs in the region. Between 1940 and 1960, the high-wage industrial sector increased by 180 percent in the South, compared with a national rate of 92 percent. During this time, the industrial labor force grew by 1,520,000 in the region, and almost 90 percent of these jobs were in the high-wage group of industries.

However, the multiplier effect of federal economic policy did not ensure complete regional deliverance from the inequities and unbalanced development of the old industrial regime. Just as vestiges of the biracial society cling like Spanish moss to the urban South, traditional industrial patterns based on a rural, colonial economy linger on.

The textile industry has woven its spell across the southern landscape in dozens of hard, grim towns and in the larger cities as well. It is a microcosm of the cruelties of biracialism, the strictures of staple agriculture, and the limitations of a colonial economy. Following the nineteenth-century pattern, as the staple regime tottered in the 1920s, the textile industry experienced its greatest period of expansion. This time, it was not only a question of investment money funneled into textiles during a slack agricultural period. The demands of World War I generated huge profits for the southern textile industry; when world demand for textiles remained high during the 1920s, entrepreneurs sank these profits back into their mills in the form of physical and mechanical expansion. In addition, the federal government, that growing benevolent presence in the southern midst, allowed special tax breaks for new housing and improvements in the textile mill villages, so textile-mill fever struck small southern towns in epidemic proportions. Boosters in Gaston County, North Carolina, urged themselves to "organize a mill a week." By 1929, they had transformed the county into the leading textile area in the South. The growth did not result primarily from the relocation of aging New England textile mills, but rather from the expansion of indigenous mills and the creation of new mills. And southern capital helped contribute to this expansion.

This encouraging indication of self-help within the national economy was not accompanied, however, by an alteration in the nature of the southern textile industry—that is, milling remained a predominantly rural activity. Community cow stalls and pigpens were typical sights in the company towns, and in other areas, the pattern of rural commuting prevailed. Cheap, coercive labor still characterized the mill village work force: like coal, oil, iron ore, and topsoil, mill labor was considered a regional resource for exploitation. Macon, Georgia, boosters touted their labor force as "thrifty, industrious, and 100% American"; in Spartanburg, labor was "of purest Anglo-Saxon stock, strikes unknown"; and in Kingsport, Tennessee, there were no "inter-racial and international difficulties to complicate the social and political scheme of the community." Boosters assured entrepreneurs that their work force would be trouble-free.

Trouble-free, and cheap besides—this was an irresistible combination for growth in an industry characterized by vigorous competition and over-production. In 1922, mill workers in Massachusetts earned an average of 40.9 cents per hour, compared with 21 cents per hour for workers in Alabama mills. Cost-of-living differentials accounted for some of the disparity, but not for all. In Charlotte, at the hub of the Piedmont textile belt, the minimum standard of living for a family with three children in 1920 was $1,438; in 1921, North Carolina's textile workers earned an average of $624 per year. With no work on depressed farms, mill owners had a captive labor market. Long hours accompanied low wages: eleven-hour days and six-day work weeks were common in the southern textile mill industry during the 1920s. Efficiency experts—the overseers of the industrial plantation—patrolled factory aisles, assuring that production quotas and schedules were kept. If fatigue did not warp the body, cotton lint and dust did. The deafening din of machinery and the constant 80- to 100-degree temperatures inside the mill further assaulted the already-weak physical constitutions of the workers.

Life away from the mill—what life there could be, given these working conditions—offered little sustenance to the laborer, especially in the mill villages. Sinclair Lewis described a "packing box on stilts," with no indoor plumbing and newsprint for wallpaper in Marion, North Carolina. Workers subsisted on a debilitating diet of cornbread, fatback, and pinto beans. Psychological deprivations added to physical problems. The company towns were isolated communities, and their workers were ostracized as "cotton mill trash," intellectually, physically, and socially inferior. Moreover, they labored in an industry where woman and child labor had higher value than adult male labor—a pattern that cut deeply into southern family traditions in the mill towns.

Nor was there much likelihood of escape from this rural-urban half-light. Mill owners included some paternalistic masters: they ensured jobs for families so that generations could work at the mill, sold coal to heat the workers' houses, extended credit to workers for worthy causes, and deducted charitable contributions, debts at the company store, and utility bills from the workers' weekly salaries. Although some mill owners, like the Calvinist God, would punish sin (such as a child born out of wedlock) harshly by evicting the offending family from the company house (and therefore from employment as well), they would also show a more benevolent side by erecting a church for workers at company expense. One worker in a North Carolina company town expressed his "appreciation" for his employer's sense of religious duty this way: "At the Baptist Church, the superintendent of the Mill was the superintendent of the Sunday School; the foremen were the teachers; . . . deacons were foremen. One thing I didn't like about it. . . .

It was run like a mill." Like the slaves on the antebellum plantation, the mill workers imbibed a distinctive Christianity whose prayer began, "Lord, we do not ask you to remove our difficulties and sorrows; we just pray you will give us grace to bear them in a manner that will honor you."

Mill workers evidently bore their burdens well, since company towns were models of medieval hierarchy into the 1960s. During that decade, one North Carolina company town resident summarized what the mill meant for him: "The Mills have give a lot of people a place to work, and well, it raised me, [but] they like to let us starve to death. . . . The people . . . kept us going." The South lost at least two generations of rural whites to the mill villages. At least blacks were able to build the semblance of communities; mill workers—also isolated and prohibited from contributing in a meaningful way to southern urban life—had the communities built for them.

Breaking these constraints would have meant breaking agrarian traditions, and mill workers were well-schooled in those peculiarly southern precepts. Such education went beyond memorizing prayers. Rural society was a hierarchical society, and religious life and daily experience reinforced deferential attitudes. Southern rural society was frequently a milieu of scarcity, which was also a dominant force in the mill villages. Scarcity meant dependence if you were poor. Depressions and seasonal slumps resulted in part-time operations and occasional closures; temporary layoffs were common, whether to enable other sections of the factory to "catch up" in the production process or for violation of company rules, which ranged from women wearing shorts in public to fighting; and wages depended on company store prices and the quality and quantity of work for a particular week. Unemployment meant no place to go, since most mill operatives had already fled from agricultural ruin. Under these conditions, union activity or collective protest action was unlikely. The highly individualistic, fearful, and deeply religious rural white southerner was easily manipulated by mill owners and their booster comrades. A Tupelo, Mississippi, editor warned mill workers in 1937 that "if you join the CIO, you will be endorsing the closing of a factory." Or, as a Greenville, South Carolina, minister informed worshipers in that mill town, "CIO means Christ is Out." The same hostility to change that motivated boosters also infected the rural white labor force of the mill towns.

That union activity flared occasionally in these isolated communities testified to the desperation of the workers' situation. After a series of wage cuts, production increases, and firings of "trouble-makers," workers walked out of mills in Gastonia, North Carolina, in April, 1929. They were assisted in the strike action by the Communist-led National Textile Workers Union. The apparatus defending agrarian tradition swung into immediate and violent action. Civic leaders posted advertisements in the local press asserting that the NTWU instigated the strike "simply for the purpose of overthrowing this government and to kill, kill, kill." Although the adverse publicity broke the strike, union activity continued with local leadership, such as mill worker Ella May Wiggin, a twenty-nine-year-old mother of five. The union died in a cotton patch outside Gastonia on a September evening in 1929, when Ella May and a group of fellow workers were gunned down. It would be a long time before workers stood together again in Gastonia.

Just as there were those urban southerners in the 1920s who felt that relieving some of the inequities of the biracial society would not cause southern civilization to crumble, some entrepreneurs believed that dignity and healthful surroundings for mill workers would not necessarily trim profits and production. Planning, which had already proven its usefulness to civic leaders, emerged as a tool to alleviate some of the hardships of mill existence. While planners in the North built garden suburbs, those in the South erected company towns. Charlotte planner Earle S. Draper devised some of the most progressive mill town plans during the 1920s. Such requisites to civilized life as electricity, sewers, and decent housing were characteristic of Draper's towns. Chicopee, Georgia, a subsidiary of a Massachusetts textile firm, was Draper's most notable creation. Curvilinear, tree-lined streets, paved pedestrian walks, brick single-family homes, and a greenbelt buffer around the community were some of the planning amenities that Draper installed when the town opened in 1927. Few southern-based textile firms, however, possessed the capital or the inclination to create at least a comfortable physical environment for their work force.

The textile culture survived depression, war, and labor defections. The industry greeted New Deal wage-and-hour legislation by firing workers, increasing the tasks of those remaining (called a "stretch-out"), installing new machinery, or ignoring the regulations entirely. Eventually, labor shortages and wartime profits eliminated the worst abuses of the textile regime. The industry emerged from World War II dominant in the South and typifying the region's emphasis on low-wage, low-skilled labor, despite the advances in high-technology production achieved under federal direction during the war. Regionalist Rupert B. Vance wrote in 1946 that "only 0.5 percent of the workers in the South's cotton textile industry can be regarded as technically skilled personnel."

Between 1947 and 1958, employment in the South increased most in the lowest-wage category of labor. Only in 1977 did the region's employment in high-wage sectors exceed the low-wage sectors—38.6 percent compared with 35.8 percent. But low-wage employment still characterizes more than one-half of all manufacturing employment in North and South Carolina, and nearly that much in Mississippi, Arkansas, and Georgia. The impact ramifies considerably beyond the employees, as a North Carolina economist pointed out in 1972: "This [low-wage labor] helps to explain the below-average levels of income and retail sales, the more limited tax base, and the more modest expenditures for public instruction. Lower educational levels in turn make it more difficult for the state to attract high-wage firms which require more highly skilled personnel."

The prevalence of low-wage industry was attractive to northern and foreign investors faced with huge labor bills in a labor-intensive industry in their own locales during the 1960s and seventies. Northern, German, and French investors became a major presence in the textile heartland of the Carolina Piedmont. The expansion of textile giant J. P. Stevens and Company during the early 1970s required capitalization from Wall Street—the South continuing its poor record of capital accumulation—and today only one southerner sits on the Stevens board of directors.

Urban boosters seemed chronically unwilling or unable to distinguish between those industrial investments that would contribute positively to community growth and those that would follow the exploitative path blazed by the textile industry. The profits of textile milling in the 1920s blinded civic leaders to the negative effects not only of textile manufacturing, but of similar types of processing industries as well. Southern cities entered into vigorous competition to attract industry through tax exemptions, free sites, and outright bonuses, despite the fact that as early as the 1930s Regionalist research indicated only marginal benefits accruing from these inducements. Savannah booster Robert M. Hitch wrote in 1929 that "industrial enterprises are among the greatest builders of cities," and accordingly Savannah "has assiduously fostered the prosperity and expansion of the industries she has, and is pursuing an undeviating policy of encouraging the coming of others." Savannah's "undeviating policy" included a five-year tax exemption, free water, and cheap labor.

During the 1930s, Savannah boosters succeeded in attracting such industries as Dixie Asphalt Products and American Cyanimid. These and similar enterprises polluted the Savannah River, which soon became one of the foulest water courses in the nation. Further, their location on the urban periphery accelerated the deterioration of the downtown area as workers and businesses deserted the center. Finally, these industries followed the textile culture by exploiting both labor and natural resources. Staple agriculture had scorched the southern earth; now basic industry was doing the same thing not only to the earth but to the water and the sky as well.

After World War II, groups of southern counties gathered together to form regional planning boards whose major function was, Pat Watters noted, "as an industry-luring vehicle"—as organizations that served as data-collecting agencies for prospective industrialists rather than as genuine planning institutions. Individual communities continued to offer incentives, and local leaders worked closely with manufacturers to develop the most attractive package of inducements. As had happened so frequently in the southern urban past, local government and private enterprise entered into close and cooperative partnership, and boosters espoused the growth ethic with little cognizance of the ultimate costs and benefits of industrial growth to the city.

The Hammermill Company, for example, located a paper mill in Selma, Alabama, in 1965 after working on plans for the factory with city officials. Selma offered the company a permanent 50-percent deduction on property taxes. A revenue bond issue financed the construction of the plant. Selma, in other words, built the mill, then leased it to Hammermill, which, through favorable state legislation, secured tax benefits as if it owned the structure. When Hammermill and similar companies required skilled labor, they imported it, leaving the local work force in a low-skill, low-wage status, adversely affected by the inevitable inflation that accompanied such industries. Public services were unlikely to improve, since cities had donated away most of whatever tax advantages they might have accrued through industrialization.

Has the growth ethic as espoused by civic leaders suckered and victimized the South again? Has the desire to outdo the growth of other cities and sections merely reinforced the shortcomings of a colonial economy? Is it, as Pat Watters believes, a "misguided effort of the South to catch up to something that was essentially sorry and shabby in the rest of America"? Perhaps South Carolina holds the answer. West German flags fly in Spartanburg, Kuwaiti money flows on Kiawah, and boosters prattle innocently, yet revealingly: "what we've done here ought to be done in the underdeveloped countries. We established a good political atmosphere and showed we had a real commitment to economic growth." And indeed, the industrialization that came in a wave during the 1960s and 1970s has transformed South Carolina from a poor agricultural state to a poor industrial state. The state presently ranks forty-sixth in per-capita income, and the average mill worker earns 20 percent less per hour than the national average. South Carolina continues to lead the nation in illiteracy and infant mortality. Manufacturing remains primarily a nonmetropolitan, *i.e.*, small-town activity. The new has merely been superimposed on the old.

Contemporary urban labor patterns reveal further the persistence of exploitative activities in the southern economy. In 1978, sociologists David C. Perry and Alfred J. Watkins wrote in the New York *Times* that jobs were the major source of urban poverty in the South, an indication of the predominance of cheap labor. Residents of southern urban slums are poorer, based on per-capita income, than slum dwellers in northeastern cities, yet almost one-half of the northeastern poor are unemployed, compared with only one-quarter jobless in poor southern urban neighborhoods. There is thus little economic incentive in southern cities today to establish comprehensive social service programs, because the poor, rather than being an economic burden, are a resource in the form of cheap labor.

Subemployment rates—figures for those working below a government-defined living wage—were significantly higher in southern inner cities than in the North. In Memphis in 1970, for example, 21.5 percent of the inner-city work force earned less than two dollars an hour, compared with 8.6 percent for workers in Newark, one of the most economically crippled cities in the nation. In fact, no southern inner-city subemployment rate was lower than any northern city's rate. The persistence of low-wage industries and the relative absence of labor unions—both regional traditions—account in great part for this situation.

Some analysts contend that the recent growth of high-wage, high-technology enterprises and the gradual shift to service industries such as health, education, and government will weaken the persisting colonial patterns in labor and traditional industry. While recent urban industrial trends may mitigate some of the exploitative aspects of the region's urban economy, it is not clear that other features of colonial dependence will be affected as well. Local industrial enterprise, for example, has been limited. Besides Coca-Cola and the tobacco industry, few large corporations have their origins or headquarters in the South. Pittsburgh, Philadelphia, and New York financiers dominated the Texas oil boom of the 1930s, as Carnegie had controlled Birmingham steel a generation earlier. In 1946, one journalist referred to Texas as "New York's most valuable foreign possession." While the growth of air and truck transport after World War II reduced the railroads' dominance over southern cities, other aspects of the national economy have a distinctly northerly flow. The region's cities continue to depend upon northern banks to finance large-scale operations—most of Houston's corporations list a New York bank as their principal bank—and any firm in the urban South dealing with international business connections invariably goes through New York banks. Corporations in southern cities patronize New York and Washington law offices; they also use New York accounting firms. All of this means that northern interests still control large-scale investment in southern cities.

This, in turn, indicates that the inability to accumulate significant capital resources continues to afflict the region and its cities. Economist Charles F. Haywood asserted in 1978 that "the South has long been a region of capital shortage. It remains so today and will be so for some years to come." Haywood suggested that the connection of the major southern urban corporations with the national banking network would not necessarily impede their growth. However, those activities "that are heavily dependent on local sources of funds—housing, local businesses, and . . . local government," may experience some difficulty. This prediction reinforces the South's traditional pattern of low services, small investments in human capital, and limited urban growth.

Sun Belt sophistry has replaced the New South Creed as the prevailing rhetorical ruse in the region and, like its philosophical predecessor, has obscured the region's economic and social problems. It has also masked the extent and quality of urbanization. Southern cities continue to be economic second fiddles in the national economic symphony directed from the Northeast. It is true that functional diversity has boosted southern urban growth to unprecedented levels, as cities in Florida and Texas attest. However, numerous southern cities are merely spectators and only very occasional participants in the Sun Belt prosperity, as the statistics on poverty and subemployment imply.

Since the 1950s, it has been more appropriate to speak of metropolitan rather than of urban growth in the South. Metropolitan areas in the South are growing, but not the cities within those areas. This, of course, is a national trend, but it is usually associated with economically declining areas in the North. Between 1970 and 1975, Atlanta, for decades the southern urban bellwether, declined in population at a faster rate than both Newark and Detroit. New Orleans and Norfolk lost population faster than New York during the same period. Savannah suffered an absolute decline of over 20 percent between 1960 and 1970, while its metropolitan area grew by nearly 5 percent. During the 1960s, Atlanta's population increased by 1.9 percent, while its metropolitan area was growing at a rate of 36.7 percent.

The region's economic growth has diverted to the suburbs. The petrochemical industry, for example, has located north of New Orleans along the Mississippi River, too far away to help the city's workers. Southern cities can no longer capture these economic activities through easy annexation. The white-collar migrants who are moving south with the economy are familiar and comfortable with the suburban life-style. Some of them are escaping the social problems of northern cities and have few incentives for relocating in a southern city where such problems exist as well. The irony is that southern urbanization was for generations circumscribed by the region's role in the national economy, among other factors. Now that the South's role has become more important, the region's cities are barely sharing in the prosperity. Its workers are still relatively low-paid; its economic base, although more diverse, still maintains dependence on the North for important functions; and the traditional absence of decent and sufficient public services is reducing the quality of life and inducing further economic and demographic decline.

This was not how it was supposed to be. Since the nineteenth century, southerners have looked upon urbanization as a guarantee of regional social and economic progress. Especially since the 1920s, when general urban growth became evident after a long dormant period, southerners—and not only boosters—viewed urbanization as the great change-agent for the region's relative backwardness. The city was supposed to cure everything from pellagra to poverty. During the 1930s, the Regionalists argued that southern culture was "immature." Since that culture, its values, and its organization followed from the region's agrarian way of life, urbanization would result in cultural maturation and hence would alter the values of the region. The Regionalists predicated their conclusions on the assumption that the urban environment represented a milieu distinct from the rural environment, therefore the different cultural results.

This assumption marked future assessments of the impact of urbanization on the southern region. In the 1950s, urban analyst Robert Earl Garren predicted that urbanism as a "new way of life for the South" would solve "difficulties now present in human relationships" (*i.e.*, race relations). This would be so because, according to Garren, money was an essential lubricant to urban social relations, which therefore tend to be more impersonal, objective, and less emotional. Deep-seated racial prejudices have little role in such interpersonal contacts. Skills and abilities have the highest priority in "an efficient money . . . economy," not race, religion, or ethnicity. Garren continued that such impersonalism, characteristic of the city, would have a beneficial impact on labor relations because it would end the stifling paternalism of rural labor relations. He concluded that urban development would help to make the South "a first-rate region within the nation."

During the 1960s and 1970s, when urbanization was perhaps more noticed, scholars grew enthusiastic over the region's prospects as a result of urban growth. In the mid-1960s, sociologist Edgar Thompson averred that "the city everywhere is the natural habitat of the liberal mind, and the southern liberal is increasing in number and making himself heard." Liberalism, he predicted, would bring racial peace and political harmony to the region. Another sociologist, Leonard Reissman, declared at the same time that urbanization was destroying the social homogeneity of the South. The solid South was not so any longer. A decade later, sociologists Thomas H. Naylor and James Clotfelter made the same point that urban growth was "undermining the unity of the region." Political scientists echoed V. O. Key's assertion that "urbanization contained the seeds of political revolution in the South." Now, cities were in a position to provide regional political leadership, which meant an end to the "tradition-bound" politics of the agrarian past. Almost all of these scholars predicted an epitaph for Dixie.

After a half century of urban growth, however, most of these predictions remain at best only partially fulfilled. The prophecies have foundered because, in their unwitting environmental determinism, the experts assumed that southern cities were distinct from their region. They were and are not. Since the colonial era, southern cities were inextricably tied to and in some aspects indistinguishable from the southern countryside. What southern cities did not do for the region in the twentieth century and, more specifically, since World War II is a measure of the continued strength of this connection. In a region covered with tradition, the agrarian character of urbanization is probably one of the oldest.

Cities shared the values of the countryside. Rural values dominated southern cities because rural people inhabited southern cities. To expect, therefore, a revolution in regional culture because of urbanization is to expect a sudden and unlikely transformation of a rural society's cultural baggage. Urban society had not produced any significant alterations in the biracial patterns of the region for over a century, for example. In fact, cities adopted biracialism wholeheartedly. Were it not for the persistence of the primary victims of the biracial society—the blacks—and the timely if somewhat halting assistance of the federal government, urban society *per se* would not have removed many of the obstacles that biracialism signified for blacks. Resistance to integration was perhaps more sophisticated in southern cities, as the Greensboro case indicated, but it was nevertheless as effective, if not more so, than in the countryside.

Labor relations have improved only as federal and state legislation have decreed them to improve. The textile culture—low wages, poor benefits, and hostility to unionism—still characterizes an important segment of the southern urban economic base. Above all, the exploitative mentality, signified by the boosters' growth ethic, persists. Environment, labor, and service equity are subservient to the current definitions of economic progress. The march of staple agriculture robbed the soil and created a vast labor dependency. The urban environment changed some of the parts of that saga, but the results were the same.

In terms of politics, black faces on the city council and in mayors' offices represent a significant change from just a decade ago, but it is not clear whether such changes in personnel have resulted in a more liberal political region or whether these black urban leaders have any political power outside their own towns and cities. Two-party politics in southern cities and in the region has not resulted in liberalization—perhaps the opposite. It was possible to have a southern president, but Jimmy Carter hardly represented the ascendancy of the urban South. Blacks voted for Carter primarily because of his racial policies, whereas the majority of southern whites voted for Gerald Ford in 1976 and Ronald Reagan in 1980. In southern cities themselves, whites tend to vote overwhelmingly for white candidates, rarely for black politicians. The biracial society is obviously much less of an obstacle to black political aspirations, but the blacks' visibility in southern cities is due more to black and federal efforts and to white flight than to the mechanisms of urban society.

Finally, there were hopes that southern cities would lead the region to that elusive economic equality sought after for over a century. The pursuit, however, has been, as Pat Watters suggested, "misbegotten and misguided." The growth ethic has perhaps resulted in regional parity statistically, but for cities and many of their residents, the changes are hardly noticeable. The cities, in fact, rather than being regional leaders, are lagging behind regional growth. In addition, the southern city still performs a secondary role in the national economy, especially in the area of capital investment and financial services. So it was not possible for the southern city to push the region to equality because the mechanisms of the national economy still controlled both southern city and region.

Consider the image of an urban southerner rocking on his porch, surrounded by the sweet smells of the rural, small-town South while the skyscrapers of Atlanta loom in the near distance. It is possible, even in the inhospitable red clay of northwest Georgia, that cotton once grew where the steel and glass towers now stand, but the skyscrapers are more a change of scenery from the cotton field than a change in culture. Of course, our friend on the porch is well aware of the changes in his city and his region over the past two decades. There is a black mayor at city hall; a subway has opened up (what better indication of urban civilization could there be?); there is a new, sprawling international airport—you can actually get to Europe from Atlanta now; and the Atlanta Braves, Falcons, and Hawks make this a major-league city by any standard, even if their respective records make the major-league status of the teams a matter open to question.

It probably does not occur to the porch-sitter that the same values that floated over the cotton fields still hover about the skyscrapers; that Atlanta might have flights to Europe but purchases its loans from New York banks; that the sophisticated new subway system is more a commuter railroad serving suburban residents who flee the city after work than an urban transportation system; and that the new stadium and sports arena were constructed at public expense while the city's abundant poor required special appeals to secure what was left over. It is early April now, and the magnolias never smelled as sweet; the iced tea tastes good in the late afternoon glow that hints of summer evenings to come; and the smells from the kitchen, oh my, take him back to his childhood on his grandparents' farm. There is nothing quite like the smell of homemade biscuits just coming out of the oven. . . .

Bibliographical Essay

The urban South is an outpost of southern historiography. Whether it will remain an outlier or transform into an exciting new frontier of study remains to be seen. I have attempted to place southern cities in the mainstream of southern history as the best approach for examining and understanding those cities. Accordingly, the bibliographic support for the book transcends the urban South and encompasses the region, and even beyond. The essay that follows, however, will not be a comprehensive bibliography of works on the southern region, but rather a compilation of those sources that I found useful to the writing of southern urban history.

General Works

The history of southern urbanization as advanced in this book supports the view of the continuity of southern history. This, of course, is not a unique interpretation. I have been most influenced by the following works that expound this theme. W. J. Cash, *The Mind of the South* (New York: Alfred Knopf, 1941), is a masterpiece of literary grace and historical insight. It is an agonizing portrait of a region loved and lamented, with the flaws of an author too close to his subject, yet correct concerning the persistence of southern culture and the identity between Progress and Tradition. Though Carl Degler, *Place Over Time: The Continuity of Southern Distinctiveness* (Baton Rouge: Louisiana State University Press, 1977), hedges the continuity theme and overemphasizes racism, the book is a useful comprehensive analysis on that theme. Louis D. Rubin, Jr., ed., *The American South: Portrait of a Culture* (Baton Rouge: Louisiana State University Press, 1980), provides a narrower focus for the continuity thesis, though its essays on southern literature are a valuable introduction for the historian. Rubin's own introduction, "The American South: The Continuity of Self-Definition," and conclusion, "The Boll Weevil, the Iron Horse, and the End of the Line: Thoughts on the South," are the strongest essays in the volume. On another aspect of regional culture, Samuel S. Hill, Jr., ed., *Religion and the Solid South* (Nashville: Abingdon, 1972), provides excellent treatment on the persistence of religious values, especially as revealed by the evangelical sects. Hill's introduction to the volume and his two essays, "The South's Two Cultures" and "Toward a Charter for a Southern Theology," were the most helpful for me. Hill's most recent contribution to understanding the connection between southern religion and society is *The South and the North in American Religion* (Athens: University of Georgia Press, 1981), which emphasizes southern theology's general abdication of social responsibility in favor of an "ethos without ethic." The divergence between southern and northern religion became most marked after the Civil War. The book presents a strong argument for southern distinctiveness in religious thought and practice. On the origins and persistence of regional violence, another cultural characteristic, see Sheldon Hackney, "Southern Violence," *American Historical Review*, LXXIV (February, 1969), 906–25. All of these works imply or state explicitly the distinctiveness of the southern people. The best brief statement of that is George B. Tindall's "Beyond the Mainstream: The Ethnic Southerners," *Journal of Southern History*, XL (February, 1974), 3–18.

The only general work on southern cities covering the entire period of southern history is a volume edited by Blaine A. Brownell and myself, *The City in Southern History: The Growth of Urban Civilization in the South* (Port Washington, N.Y.: Kennikat Press, 1977), consisting of five original essays. The essays, particularly mine and Blaine's, tend to overemphasize the similarity of southern cities with those elsewhere in the United States. Our major objective was to indicate the possibilities of southern urban historiography and to call attention to the fact that there were indeed cities amidst the crepe myrtles and crinolines. A more recent edition of my views on southern urbanization, emphasizing the attributes of a regional perspective, is "The Urban South: A Regional Framework," *American Historical Review*, LXXXVI (December, 1981), 1009–34. Don H. Doyle, "The Urbanization of Dixie," *Journal of Urban History*, VII (November, 1980), 83–91, offers a fine review of recent literature on the subject. Gerald M. Capers, "The Rural Lag on Southern Cities," *Mississippi Quarterly*, XXVI (Spring, 1973), 253–61, represents an early attempt at explaining the rural influence on southern cities. Other articles that are strongly suggestive of the close relationship between city and country and the latter's influence on the former are: Yi-Fu Tuan, "The City: Its Distance from Nature," *Geographical Review*, LXVIII (January, 1978), 1–12; Robert Redfield and Milton B. Singer, "The Cultural Role of Cities," *Economic Development and Cultural Change*, III (October, 1954), 53–73; and Richard Dewey, "The Rural-Urban Continuum: Real but Relatively Unimportant," *American Journal of Sociology*, LXVI (July, 1960), 460–66. For a general discussion on the difficulties of distinguishing rural from urban in non-American cultures, see Brian J. L. Berry and John D. Kasarda, *Contemporary Urban Ecology* (New York: Macmillan, 1977). This scholarship demonstrates the limited usefulness of Louis Wirth's "Urbanism as a Way of Life," *American Journal of Sociology*, XLIV (July, 1938), 1–24, which presents the city as a distinctive and separate environment. The newer works also demonstrate the persistence of rural culture in an urban setting. For a clear statement of the cultural retention argument, see Kathleen Neils Conzen, "Immigrants, Immigrant Neighborhoods, and Ethnic Identity: Historical Issues," *Journal of American History*, LXVI (December, 1979), 603–15.

General works on the American city, especially on the evolution of the American urban system, are numerous, but two helpful sources are a book by myself and Blaine A. Brownell, *Urban America: From Downtown to No Town* (Boston: Houghton Mifflin, 1979), and James E. Vance, Jr., "Cities in the Shaping of the American Nation," *Journal of Geography*, LXXV (January, 1976), 41–52.

Colonial Era

The literature on the colonial urban South is relatively sparse. A bookshelf containing works on urban life in colonial America would doubtless lead the uninitiated to assume that everything outside of Massachusetts was wilderness. Carville Earle and Ronald Hoffman have done more and better than perhaps any other scholars to remedy this situation. Their survey of the period is "The Urban South: The First Two Centuries," in Brownell and Goldfield, eds., *The City in Southern History*, 23–51. John C. Rainbolt explores the reasons for the laggard pace of urbanization in one colony in "The Absence of Towns in Seventeenth-Century Virginia," *Journal of Southern History*, XXXV (August, 1969), 343–60. Joseph A. Ernst and H. Roy Merrens, "'Camden's Turrets Pierce the Skies!': The Urban Process in the Southern Colonies During the Eighteenth Century," *William and Mary Quarterly*, 3rd Series, XXX (October, 1973), 549–74, is the best account available of interior urban settlement in the Carolinas. John W. Reps, *Tidewater Towns: City Planning in Colonial Virginia and Maryland* (Charlottesville: University Press of Virginia, 1972), is not only attractive, but its erudite text provides an excellent survey of the physical development of towns in the area.

Carl Bridenbaugh's works, especially *Cities in the Wilderness: The First Century of Urban Life in America, 1625–1742* (New York: Ronald Press, 1938), and *Cities in Revolt: Urban Life in America, 1743–1776* (New York: Capricorn, 1955), contain material on Charleston and Savannah, though his strictly narrative format omits discussion of the process of urbanization and its relationship to larger regional developments. Historians have served the Chesapeake better than other southern colonial areas. One work that deals with tobacco cultivation and marketing, as well as the impact of wheat on trade patterns, is Paul G. E. Clemens, *The Atlantic Economy and Colonial Maryland's Eastern Shore: From Tobacco to Grain* (Ithaca: Cornell University Press, 1980). Gerald W. Mullin, *Flight and Rebellion: Slave Resistance in Eighteenth-Century Virginia* (New York: Oxford University Press, 1972), provides some idea of slavery's evolution in a colonial urban setting, though the best overall survey, which also compares southern colonial slavery to the northern variety, is Ira Berlin, "Time, Space, and the Evolution of Afro-American Society on British Mainland North America," *American Historical Review*, LXXXV (February, 1980), 44–78. Berlin relates cultivation patterns to differences in slave treatment and life, much in the manner that Earle and Hoffman have fixed upon crop types as leading explicators of urbanization.

Antebellum Era

W. J. Cash wrote in his epic that "the South . . . is a tree with many age rings, with its limbs and trunk bent and twisted by all the winds of the years, but with its tap root in the Old South." What happened (and did not happen) in the antebellum era set a precedent for the region and its cities for more than a century. From the region's cities, which began their long relative downward spiral, to the system of biracialism and to the pattern of colonial relations, the roots indeed lay in this period. The general urban survey of the period is my essay "Pursuing the American Dream: Urban Growth in the Old South," in Brownell and Goldfield, eds., *The City in Southern History*, 52–91. Leonard P. Curry, "Urbanization and Urbanism in the Old South: A Comparative View," *Journal of Southern History*, XL (February, 1974), 43–60, is an interpretive view of the urban South up to 1850, arguing that there were strong similarities between northern and southern urbanization with respect to both quality and quantity. Together with my essay, these two pieces represent the strongest statements for that interpretation. Although the question seems both stilted and time-worn, Lyle W. Dorsett and Arthur H. Shaffer, in "Was the Antebellum South Antiurban? A Suggestion," *Journal of Southern History*, XXXVIII (February, 1972), 93–100, were among the earliest historians to provide evidence of both the existence and importance of antebellum southern urbanization.

There are few scholarly studies of single antebellum southern cities apart from the hortatory volumes issued by local civic groups or amateur historians. Two exceptions are D. Clayton James, *Antebellum Natchez* (Baton Rouge: Louisiana State University Press, 1968), which offers a comprehensive view of urban growth and decline with a particularly strong discussion of the city's dependence on the cotton culture, and Kenneth Wheeler, *To Wear a City's Crown: The Beginnings of Urban Growth in Texas, 1836–1865* (Cambridge, Mass.: Harvard University Press, 1968), which analyzes the urban rivalry of four Texas cities and their thirst for growth through internal improvements and the connections that they would afford with the national economy. Richard C. Wade, *The Urban Frontier: Pioneer Life in Early Pittsburgh, Cincinnati, Lexington, Louisville, and St. Louis* (Chicago: University of Chicago Press, 1964), offers helpful material on regional trade patterns, especially the impact of transportation technology and the development of political and social institutions in the early antebellum period.

The central and controlling role of agriculture for urbanization and the southern economy is best explained by Carville Earle and Ronald Hoffman, "The Foundation of the Modern Economy: Agriculture and the Costs of Labor in the U.S. and England, 1800–60," *American Historical Review*, LXXXV (December, 1980), 1055–94, where they argue that a region's agricultural pattern determines the nature and cost of urban labor. Another statement on the influence of agriculture in southern cities is Michael P. Johnson, "Planters and Patriarchy: Charleston, 1800–1860," *Journal of Southern History*, XLVI (February, 1980), 45–72. John Radford's "The Charleston Planters in 1860," *South Carolina Historical Magazine*, LXXVII (October, 1976), 227–35, is a fine essay on how the "plantation ethos" permeated that city. Antebellum travelers invariably noted the pastoral aspects of southern cities, and a useful compilation is Eugene L. Schwaab, ed., *Travels in the Old South: Selected from the Periodicals of the Times* (2 vols.; Lexington, Ky.: University Press of Kentucky, 1974). Articles relating travelers' observations of particular cities too often resemble catalogues of minutiae, though a model of the best of that genre is Ivan D. Steen, "Charleston in the 1850s: As Described by British Travelers," *South Carolina Historical Magazine*, LXXI (January, 1970), 36–45.

The most pervasive rural influence was the rural migrant. Unfortunately, I did not come across any literature relating to cultural transference in the antebellum South, except tangentially. Still, I found two helpful studies from which to extrapolate: Dickson D. Bruce, Jr., *Violence and Culture in the Antebellum South* (Austin: University of Texas Press, 1979), avers that a particular world-view conducive to violence was part of normal child-rearing patterns in the Old South. Bruce also analyzes the works of several southern writers who utilized violence as a major theme. A related work is Michael Stephen Hindus' comparative effort, *Prison and Plantation: Crime, Justice, and Authority in Massachusetts and South Carolina, 1767–1878* (Chapel Hill: University of North Carolina Press, 1980). South Carolina evinced a greater degree of interpersonal violence, legal redress was frequently a private affair, and the plantation was the surrogate for public penal institutions. This situation, which continued after the Civil War, reflected the capricious application of the legal system to blacks and the relatively high incidence of violence throughout the region.

Anne C. Loveland, *Southern Evangelicals and the Social Order, 1800–1860* (Baton Rouge: Louisiana State University Press, 1980), is the best analysis of southern evangelical religion in the Old South. She traces the transformation of the region from the most "unchurched" section to a region overcome with revivalist fervor by the time of the Civil War. Loveland also discusses the advantages of a city location for evangelists. E. Brooks Holifield offers a different view of antebellum religion in *The Gentlemen Theologians: American Theology in Southern Culture, 1795–1860* (Durham: Duke University Press, 1978). Holifield focuses on the "elite Southern town clergy" bent upon promoting a more genteel and urbane image and theology for their flocks. However, this "reasoned faith" was clearly on the wane by the 1850s.

While southern religion was undergoing a change in the late antebellum era, the options for southern thought in general were constricting; dissent and diversity, two common aspects of urban life, were narrowing or disappearing altogether. Two books reveal the reduced range of cultural and literary expression: Drew Gilpin Faust, *A Sacred Circle: The Dilemma of the Intellectual in the Old South, 1840–1860* (Baltimore: Johns Hopkins University Press, 1977), indicates the difficulties that thinking men had in finding acceptance for their ideas in an increasingly hostile environment. While Carl N. Degler, *The Other South: Southern Dissenters in the Nineteenth Century* (New York: Harper & Row, 1974), demonstrated that "the South is not and never has been a monolith" (and few would argue with that statement), the main impression is the scarcity of dissent in the antebellum era.

The narrowed southern mind benefited urban leaders who were able to pursue a ruthless selectivity in the provision of urban services without fear of political repercussions. The equation of economic growth with patriotism ensured implementation of their policies. Public health, perhaps more than any other service, reflected the dominance of economic motives in the form of suppressed information and haphazard enforcement of health regulations. Three articles that deal particularly with this theme are David R. Goldfield, "The Business of Health Planning: Disease Prevention in the Old South," *Journal of Southern History*, XLII (November, 1976), 557–70, which covers several southern cities; and two more specific studies, John Duffy, "Nineteenth Century Public Health in New York and New Orleans: A Comparison,"*Louisiana History*, XV (Fall, 1974), 325–37 (Duffy's book, *Sword of Pestilence: The New Orleans Yellow Fever Epidemic of 1853* [Baton Rouge: Louisiana State University Press, 1966], is an excellent account of the interplay of business and urban services), and M. Foster Farley, "The Mighty Monarch of the South: Yellow Fever in Charleston and Savannah," *Georgia Review*, XXVII (Spring, 1973), 56–70.

Slavery also accounted for both the narrowed mind in the South and the meager public services. Historiographical controversy on urban slavery revolves around the extent to which urban slavery was a "step toward freedom" and whether or not the institution was in decline by 1860. Most recent literature adopts the view that whereas treatment of urban slaves, especially hirelings, might well have been more harsh than the treatment of plantation hands, there were more diverse employment opportunities in the city and at least a chance for the exercise of greater freedom. Also, urban slavery, rather than declining, probably was evolving into a more mature and specialized labor system by the 1850s. This latter viewpoint challenges the pioneer work of Richard C. Wade, *Slavery in the Cities: The South, 1820–1860* (New York: Oxford University Press, 1964). Though methodologically flawed, Claudia D. Goldin, *Urban Slavery in the American South, 1820–1860: A Quantitative History* (Chicago: University of Chicago Press, 1976), is the most direct attack on Wade's thesis, emphasizing the strength of the institution in an urban setting, the dependence of the urban slave labor force on agricultural conditions, and the growing skills of urban slaves. On the "step toward freedom" hypothesis, see Clement Eaton, "Slave-Hiring in the Upper South: A Step Toward Freedom," *Mississippi Valley Historical Review*, XLV (March, 1960), 663–78.

Two works that are helpful in demonstrating the versatility of slave labor in an urban industrial setting are Charles B. Dew, *Ironmaker to the Confederacy: Joseph R. Anderson and the Tredegar Iron Works* (New Haven: Yale University Press, 1966), and a more comprehensive volume dealing with rural and urban industries, Robert S. Starobin, *Industrial Slavery in the Old South* (New York: Oxford University Press, 1969). Starobin's book is an exhaustive study of industrial slave living and working conditions, and though he concludes that slavery was "incompatible in the long run with full industrialization," his evidence points to a successful marriage of slavery and industry during that early stage of southern industrialization. Herbert G. Gutman's "The World Two Cliometricians Made: A Review Essay of F+E=T/C," *Journal of Negro History*, LX (January, 1975), 53–227, also contains some material on urban slavery and on the urban labor force in general.

Slaves were not, of course, the only urban-dwelling blacks. The classic work on free blacks in the Old South is Ira Berlin, *Slaves Without Masters: The Free Negro in the Antebellum South* (New York: Pantheon Books, 1974). Since free blacks were the most highly urbanized segment of the southern black population, I learned a great deal about the role of free blacks in southern cities. Berlin's exposure of their economic and social life comprises the book's strongest sections.

Two historians have discussed more specific aspects of black life in antebellum southern cities. John T. O'Brien, "Factory, Church, and Community: Blacks in Antebellum Richmond," *Journal of Southern History*, XLIV (November, 1978), 509–36, stresses the importance of religious institutions in urban black life—a foundation for postbellum black society. Marianne Buroff Sheldon analyzes an earlier period covering the Gabriel conspiracy and its impact on race relations in "Black-White Relations in Richmond, Virginia, 1782–1820," *Journal of Southern History*, XLV (February, 1979), 27–44. Scholars have paid more attention to biracialism in Richmond than in other southern cities. Richmond's unique economic base, though, especially in the 1850s, makes it difficult to generalize to other cities such as Charleston (where Christopher Silver's fine but as yet unpublished work provides comprehensive coverage) and New Orleans with its free black elite.

Goldin's book touched off speculation and research on the elasticity of demand, *i.e.*, the "substitutability" of slave labor in the city. In other words, how did cities fill their labor requirements when agricultural prosperity recalled some urban slaves? European immigrants, much more a factor in antebellum than in postbellum southern urban populations, were important additions to a work force periodically depleted and replenished by agricultural cycles. For a general discussion of the immigrants' role, see Randall M. Miller, "Immigrants in the Old South," *Immigration History Newsletter*, X (November, 1978), 8–14. Gutman's aforementioned essay contains a cogent discussion of this point. Earl F. Niehaus, *The Irish in New Orleans, 1800–1860* (Baton Rouge: Louisiana State University Press, 1965), is an adequate survey of one immigrant group in a southern city, though uninformed by geographical research methods. For a portrait of an individual immigrant, see Bennett H. Wall, "Leon Godchaux and the Godchaux Business Enterprises," *American Jewish Historical Quarterly*, LXVI (September, 1976), 50–66.

Perhaps the greatest fact of economic life in antebellum America was the formation of a national economy controlled from the Northeast. Among the most useful general works analyzing this development is Allan R. Pred, *Urban Growth and the Circulation of Information: The U.S. System of Cities, 1790–1840* (Cambridge, Mass.: Harvard University Press, 1973), which demonstrates how communication and hence business advantage accrued to New York in almost geometric fashion. Pred's most recent work on this theme, *Urban Growth and City-Systems in the United States, 1840–1860* (Cambridge: Harvard University Press, 1980), also underscores how the evolving urban system, aided by transportation technology and subsequent alterations in patterns of commerce, left the South relatively isolated from western and eastern trade routes, a situation further compounded by the South's immature intraregional urban network. Thomas C. Cochran's "The Business Revolution," *American Historical Review*, LXXIX (December, 1974), 1449–66, is an imaginative piece of scholarship that convincingly demonstrates how New York came to monopolize the way of doing business from factorage to finance, a development as important perhaps as the industrial revolution. Not only information and business procedures concentrated in the Northeast, but canals and railroads converged on the major economic citadels. The result was a portentous drawing-away of trade from the Mississippi River corridor to a more west-to-east direction following the new railroad lines. Louis B. Schmidt, "Internal Commerce and the Development of the National Economy Before 1860," *Journal of Political Economy*, XLVII (December, 1939), 798–822, offers a clear analysis of the shifting pattern of trade.

Scholars have not dealt directly with the southern regional response to this new economic reality, but there are specific studies of states and cities in the region. My own *Urban Growth in the Age of Sectionalism: Virginia, 1847–1861* (Baton Rouge: Louisiana State University Press, 1977), details the various policies devised to secure urban growth and not incidentally to attain equality within the national economy. Merl E. Reed, *New Orleans and the Railroads: The Struggle for Commercial Empire* (Baton Rouge: Louisiana State University Press, 1966), presents the general incompetence, indecision, and division among local and state officials torn between a congenital alliance with the Mississippi River and the purported wave of the future embodied in the railroad. Carter Goodrich, "The Virginia System of Mixed Enterprise: A Study of State Planning of Internal Improvements," *Political Science Quarterly*, LIV (September, 1949), 355–87, demonstrates how public-private funding endeavors enabled cities to benefit from major railroad and canal projects. The article also indicates how a rural-dominated state legislature viewed urban interests as coterminus with its own. That there was more to southern railroad-building than merely enhancing urban treasuries is evident from Jere W. Roberson, "The South and the Pacific Railroad, 1845–1855," *Western Historical Quarterly*, V (April, 1974), 163–86, which reveals the sectional hope of constructing such a railroad and the great fear that the region would be submerged economically if a northern route were favored instead. James P. Baughman, "The Evolution of Rail-Water Systems of Transportation, 1836–1890," *Journal of Southern History*, XXXIV (August, 1968), 357–81, and Earl F. Woodward, "Internal Improvements in Texas in the Early 1850s," *Southwestern Historical Quarterly*, LXXIV (October, 1972), 161–82, discuss the perpetual rivalry between Houston and Galveston and the role of Houston entrepreneurs in enabling that city to forge ahead of its coastal rival. Both articles show that southern economic nationalism had as great obstacles from the region's own fiercely competing cities as from the national economy. For a general overview of the railroad-building era in the Old South and its frequent labor, capital, and management problems, see James A. Ward, "A New Look at Antebellum Southern Railroad Development," *Journal of Southern History*, XXXIX (August, 1973), 409–20.

Internal improvements were but one means of improving the urban South's economic position in the national economy. Urban entrepreneurs and their planter colleagues invested in an array of industrial and commercial enterprises in the two decades before secession. The southern performance in these efforts has yet to be related in book-length form, but there are several articles that touch upon narrower aspects of economic development. John A. Eisterhold, for example, has made a thorough investigation of the South Atlantic and Gulf Coast lumber trade and of the attempts of port cities to search out direct trade routes for their product. His findings appear in "Lumber and Trade in the Lower Mississippi Valley and New Orleans, 1800–1860," *Louisiana History*, XIII (Winter, 1972), 71–92; "Savannah: Lumber Center of the South Atlantic," *Georgia Historical Quarterly*, LVII (Winter, 1973), 526–43; and in "Charleston: Lumber and Trade in a Declining Port," *South Carolina Historical Magazine*, LXXIV (April, 1973), 61–72. Southern industrial efforts are covered in part by Richard W. Griffin in "The Origins of the Industrial Revolution in Georgia: Cotton Textiles, 1810–1865," *Georgia Historical Quarterly*, XLII (December, 1958), 355–75, which indicates the cyclical rural financial support for the mills; and by Thomas S. Berry, "The Rise of Flour Milling in Richmond," *Virginia Magazine of History and Biography*, LXXVIII (October, 1970), 388–408, which traces that city's rise to one of the country's leading mill towns, though Berry inadequately discusses the seasonal problems and capital shortages that plagued even successful enterprises.

The southern economy—urban and rural—was highly productive in the 1850s. Rather than altering the pattern of trade to its own benefit, however, the South became more dependent upon the Northeast and less involved with the West as a trading partner. Schmidt's article and Pred's book, both cited earlier, document the growing economic estrangement between West and South, as does Colleen M. Callahan and William K. Hutchinson, "Antebellum Interregional Trade in Agricultural Goods: Preliminary Results," *Journal of Economic History*, XL (March, 1980), 25–32, which focuses on foodstuffs and contends that southern self-sufficiency, in effect, drove western farmers to eastern markets. Sam Bowers Hilliard reaches a similar conclusion in *Hog Meat and Hoecake: Food Supply in the Old South, 1840–1860* (Carbondale, Ill.: Southern Illinois University Press, 1972). Both of these studies indicate that, besides the growing interregional railroad network, cultivation patterns influenced trade as well. Forrest McDonald and Grady McWhiney, in "The South from Self-Sufficiency to Peonage: An Interpretation," *American Historical Review*, LXXXV (December, 1980), 1095–1118, present additional evidence of self-sufficiency in discussing the role of the "plain folk" in southern agriculture. Ironically for the South, food self-sufficiency removed another economic link with the West. After the Civil War, the lack of this self-sufficiency placed the region in even worse economic condition. It was the type of "no-win" situation that characterized the South in the national economy for more than a century. While the South was losing the West, northern tentacles buried deep into the region's economy. John R. Killick, "The Cotton Operations of Alexander Brown and Sons in the Deep South, 1820–1860," *Journal of Southern History*, XLIII (May, 1977), 169–94, details the business transactions of a northern mercantile firm, primarily in Gulf Coast ports, collecting cotton assignments for shipment to Liverpool. Their business grew steadily despite direct trade campaigns launched by southern economic nationalists.

J. D. B. De Bow was probably the foremost of these nationalists, and Otis C. Skipper, *J. D. B. De Bow: Magazinist of the Old South* (Athens, Ga.: University of Georgia Press, 1958), adequately recounts his life. A fuller appreciation of De Bow and his ideas is available in *De Bow's Review*, especially Volumes III (1847) to

XXVIII (1860). *Hunt's Merchants' Magazine*, a New York-based publication, also includes numerous articles and statistics on southern commerce and industry during the 1840s and 1850s, though obviously less passionate than its New Orleans competitor. The *Southern Planter*, edited by Virginia agricultural reformer Frank G. Ruffin, is interesting for the evidence it presents on the close relationship and cooperation between city and farm. George Fitzhugh's two books, *Cannibals All! or, Slaves without Masters* (Richmond: A. Morris, 1857) and *Sociology for the South; or the Failure of Free Society* (Richmond: A. Morris, 1854), were, besides attacks on northern capitalism and defenses of the "peculiar institution," programs for southern economic advancement through urbanization and industrialization.

The growing economic dominance of the North, despite southern endeavors to the contrary, generated great concern in the South and added to the already-intense and bitter sectional debate. It contributed to the general feeling in many parts of the South that the Republican party represented a genuine threat to southern liberty. Slavery involved only part of the threat, since the Republicans were more anti-southern than antislavery. The Republicans' staunch economic nationalism was part of a broad perceived threat to southern institutions. I have relied on several works covering the political crises of the 1850s to formulate this hypothesis, among them, Robert R. Russel, *Critical Studies in Antebellum Sectionalism: Essays in American Political and Economic History* (Westport, Ct.: Greenwood Press, 1972). The essays in this volume include clear statements of the southerners' fears of Republican economic motives. Richard L. McCormick, "The Party Period and Public Policy: An Exploratory Hypothesis," *Journal of American History*, LXVI (September, 1979), 279–98, presents an excellent analysis of growing federal power, especially in the economic sphere—a power some southerners doubtless believed the Republicans would exercise against their region. Thomas B. Alexander, "The Civil War as Institutional Fulfillment," *Journal of Southern History*, XLVII (February, 1981), 3–32, focuses in part on the growing power of the executive, which reduced southern faith in the national government, despite southern control of Congress.

Two books were particularly helpful to me in presenting the political framework of southern distrust and hostility toward the Republicans: Michael F. Holt, *The Political Crisis of the 1850s* (New York: John Wiley & Sons, 1978), which outlines the southerners' loss of faith in the national political system with the advance of the Republicans; and J. Mills Thornton III, *Politics and Power in a Slave Society: Alabama, 1800–1860* (Baton Rouge: Louisiana State University Press, 1978), which presents detailed and convincing evidence for Alabama to support, essentially, Holt's hypothesis. From the collective evidence revealed by these authors, it would seem that southern fears, far from being paranoid, were justified with respect to what the Republicans stated and, ultimately, to what they did.

The Postbellum Era to 1920

Despite the theme of continuity that runs throughout the book, significant changes occurred in the South as a result of the Civil War. The region's accommodation to these changes invariably modified regional characteristics and, therefore, urbanization. The New South versions of these regional elements, though, indicated more of a change in degree than in kind. King Cotton reigned, more so than ever; slavery was gone, of course, but a biracial society persisted in the framework of new institutions; and the national economy was more than ever a presence within the region.

Two general surveys of the period provide a useful framework in which I pursued my regional themes and their impact on southern urbanization. C. Vann Woodward's *Origins of the New South, 1877–1913* (Baton Rouge: Louisiana State University Press, 1951), remains the classic statement for this period despite numerous challenges to several interpretations advanced in the book. Woodward devotes several sections to urbanization and to economic development that impacted directly upon southern cities, especially chapter 5—"The Industrial Revolution"; parts of chapter 6 on "The Divided Mind of the New South"; parts of chapter 8— "Mudsills and Bottom Rails"; and chapter 11 on "The Colonial Economy." Urbanization and industrialization were, of course, two key tenets of the New South Creed, and Paul M. Gaston's intellectual survey of the period, *The New South Creed: A Study in Southern Mythmaking* (New York: Alfred Knopf, 1970), exposes the New South prophets and profiteers. The last chapter, particularly, "The Emperor's New Clothes," reveals the irony of creed programs that actually led the region to greater economic dependence. The best general urban survey of the period is Howard N. Rabinowitz, "Continuity and Change: Southern Urban Development, 1860–1900," in Brownell and Goldfield, eds., *City in Southern History*, 92–122. The essay provides excellent coverage on blacks and on urban economic development.

The quality of single-city surveys for this period is little better than for the antebellum era. The most comprehensive account is James H. Russell's "Atlanta: Gate City of the New South," a doctoral dissertation from Princeton University, 1972, which unfortunately is unpublished. Russell's best sections deal with the city's economic redevelopment following the Civil War, concentrating on entrepreneurial decision-making. William D. Miller's *Memphis During the Progressive Era, 1900– 1917* (Memphis: Memphis State University Press, 1957), is less an account of Progressive reform in that city than a traditional urban biography with little attempt to place Memphis urbanization within the larger regional context, especially the impact of the heavy white migration from rural Mississippi. Joy L. Jackson, *New Orleans in the Gilded Age: Politics and Urban Progress, 1880–1896* (Baton Rouge: Louisiana State University Press, 1969), is a narrative of the colorful politics, inefficient services, and general corruption that demonstrated, at least for New Orleans, that there was continuity between the Old South and the New. William D. Henderson, *Gilded Age City: Politics, Life and Labor in Petersburg, Virginia, 1874–1889* (Lanham, Md.: University Press of America, 1980) is a portrait of a stagnating, relatively minor city that could offer useful comparisons with studies of Memphis, New Orleans, and Houston, but does not. Marilyn M. Sibley, *The Port of Houston: A History* (Austin: University of Texas Press, 1968), discusses the background to the opening of that city's momentous Ship Channel in 1914 and, in the process, presents an adequate biography of Houston during the previous thirty years. The book chronicles the close interrelationship between public and private sector leadership characteristic of southern cities since the antebellum era. Perhaps the best available single-city survey in print is Michael Chesson's exhaustive *Richmond After the War* (Richmond: Virginia State Library, 1981), which covers every aspect of life in the city and attempts to place Richmond within the postbellum southern urban system and region. The Chesson book and Russell's dissertation provide an interesting comparison of two cities damaged by war, yet experiencing somewhat different fates in peace. One difference was the dynamism and capital investments of local entrepreneurs in Atlanta.

Both Chesson and Russell provide some background discussion of their respective cities during the Civil War, but the most useful survey remains Emory M. Thomas' *The Confederate State of Richmond: A Biography of the Capital* (Austin: University of Texas Press, 1971), which recounts the struggle of municipal government to cope with the exigencies of war and population expansion. Marion Brunson Lucas' *Sherman and the Burning of Columbia* (College Station: Texas A&M University Press, 1976), is a narrower and less successful effort, basically confirming James Ford Rhodes's judgment eighty years ago that incompetent Confederates and not Sherman were responsible for the conflagration. Clifford Dowdy's *Bugles Blow No More* (Dunwoody, Ga.: Norman S. Berg, 1937), is one of numerous fictive accounts of life in besieged southern cities, this one focusing on Richmond and more than others interspersing some interesting descriptions of urban life and living during the four turbulent years of war. Dale A. Somers' unfortunately brief scholarly career was marked by several well-researched interpretive articles concerning various aspects of urban life during the Civil War. His work frequently demonstrates a lighter side to life in the war-riven South than the older generation of scholars were wont to depict. Two useful pieces are his editing of "New Orleans at War: A Merchant's View," *Louisiana History*, XIV (Winter, 1973), 49–68, and his article, "War and Play: The Civil War in New Orleans," *Mississippi Quarterly*, XXVI (Winter, 1972–73), 3–28. Also in marked contrast to the school of historical melodrama is Perry A. Snyder's "Shreveport, Louisiana: 1861–1865, From Secession to Surrender," *Louisiana Studies*, XI (Spring, 1972), 50–70, which depicts a relatively thriving if somewhat nervous river port during the war years. The food and clothing shortages that plagued Richmond were not visited on Shreveport, and even as late as 1864 the social season came off with its usual vigor. Joseph H. Parks also presents a relatively thriving community in "A Confederate Trade Center Under Federal Occupation: Memphis, 1862 to 1865," *Journal of Southern History*, VII (August, 1941), 289–314.

Some cities may have fared better during the war than afterwards. The regional devastation initiated a period of economic reversal halted only in the 1880s. By then, a basic agricultural pattern had been established across the region that represented both an impoverishment and an accommodation to new economic realities. The dominance of cotton monoculture had significant import for southern urbanization. The various agricultural labor and tenure systems that evolved after the Civil War and their regional significance are fast becoming a historical quagmire with differing class and race interpretations. For an excellent overview of the conflicting literature, see Harold D. Woodman, "Sequel to Slavery: The New History Views the Postbellum South," *Journal of Southern History*, XLIII (November, 1977), 523–44. Skirting the mud, I was interested primarily in how labor and tenure affected the southern urban system, investment patterns, and labor mobility. Accordingly, my selection of appropriate works may seem eclectic, if not contradictory, on the larger historiographical issues. Gilbert C. Fite presents an unusually clear survey of tenure patterns and cultivation trends, even delving into rural educational developments, in "Southern Agriculture Since the Civil War: An Overview," *Agricultural History*, LIII (January, 1979), 3–21. This issue contains several useful articles on southern agriculture, with Fite's as the most comprehensive. Jonathan M. Wiener, one of the leading Marxist interpreters of postwar southern agriculture, argues an interesting case for the "labor-repressive character of class relations in the postwar South," particularly the continuity of planter leadership and their "prebourgeois" values. Supporting arguments developed by Barrington Moore, Wiener contends that a chronic labor shortage and a desire to maintain control led planters to evolve labor systems that severely restricted labor mobility, in contrast to the North's decision to resolve the shortage through technology and productivity increases or, as Wiener calls it, the "classical capitalist method." Though actual events took a less calculating turn than Wiener would have it, his interpretation coincides with the anemic pace of urbanization and industrialization, slowed in part because of agricultural labor restrictions as before the Civil War. The clearest rendition of this hypothesis is in his "Class Structures and Economic Development in the American South, 1865–1955," *American Historical Review*, LXXXIV (October, 1979), 970–92. This article is also useful for its discussion of federal agricultural policy and its regional impact in the 1930s—an impact that resulted in a wave of migration off the farms. Wiener's *Social Origins of the New South: Alabama, 1860–1885* (Baton Rouge: Louisiana State University Press, 1978) is a more specific and detailed examination of planter control of labor and of investment patterns. Dwight B. Billings, Jr., *Planters and the Making of a 'New South': Class, Politics, and Development in North Carolina, 1865–1900* (Chapel Hill: University of North Carolina Press, 1979), presents the North Carolina version of Wiener's argument. Billings argues for the continuity of planter leadership and the establishment of textile mills with planter capital to support the planter regime. Roger L. Ransom and Richard Sutch, *One Kind of Freedom: The Economic Consequences of Emancipation* (Cambridge: Cambridge University Press, 1977), on the other hand stress race and the failure of Reconstruction to provide freedmen with land and credit, which resulted in the debilitating labor and cultivation systems. Ransom and Sutch also discuss the country store and its role in reinforcing the agricultural system. "The curse of King Cotton," they conclude "was the lack of prosperity he imposed upon the South."

On specific aspects of the labor and tenure systems, see Pete Daniel, "The Metamorphosis of Slavery, 1865–1900," *Journal of American History*, LXVI (June, 1979), 88–99. He surveys the coercive policies utilized by landlords and merchants on black and white agricultural labor—policies that reduced labor mobility and the quality of human capital, and consequently limited regional economic and urban development. Daniel treats in more detail the system of peonage, the most coercive labor pattern, in *The Shadow of Slavery: Peonage in the South, 1901–1969* (Urbana, Ill.: University of Illinois Press, 1972). Thomas D. Clark's article, "The Post–Civil War Economy in the South," *American Jewish Historical Quarterly*, LV (June, 1966), 424–33, discusses the transactions of the country store. A portion of the article deals with Samuel S. Fels, whose parents operated a country store in Yanceyville, North Carolina, before Fels moved on to Philadelphia and Fels-Naphtha fame.

The combination of the Lost Cause and the economic hardships reflected by the deteriorating labor and capital situations on southern farms provided a conducive climate for evangelical Protestantism. Charles Reagan Wilson, in "The Religion of the Lost Cause: Ritual and Organization of the Southern Civil Religion, 1865–1920," *Journal of Southern History*, XLVI (May, 1980), 219–38, offers valuable insights into the secularization of evangelical Protestantism and its narcotizing effect on the mind of the postbellum South. "The religion of the Lost Cause was a cult of the dead," Wilson writes. It was the pervasiveness of this phenomenon throughout the region that provided one of the major lines of division between North and South. Bishop Warren A. Candler was one of the pillars of Lost Cause religion, and Mark K. Bauman's *Warren Akin Candler: The Conservative as Idealist* (Metuchen, N.J.: Scarecrow, 1981) provides a sometimes frightening look into the reactionary mind of the bishop who battled against everyone from immigrants to Yankees and everything from evolution to federal child-labor legislation. Violence continued to flourish in southern city and region as well, as William D. Miller relates in "Myth and New South City Murder Rates," *Mississippi Quarterly*, XXVI (Spring, 1973), 143–53.

The relative absence of urban services, reinforced by regional values, insufficient capital, and a leadership with priorities elsewhere, characterized New South cities, as in the Old South. The general treatments mentioned earlier, particularly the Jackson book on New Orleans, follow this interpretive line. Additional material may be found in Eugene J. Watts, "The Police in Atlanta, 1890–1905," *Journal of Southern History*, XXXIX (May, 1973), 165–82, which stresses the politicization of that city's police force and consequent low performance. John H. Ellis, "Businessmen and Public Health in the Urban South During the Nineteenth Century: New Orleans, Memphis, and Atlanta," *Bulletin of the History of Medicine*, XLIV (May–June, 1970), 197–212, presents a not-surprising picture of continued municipal negligence in health services leading to at least one major disaster, the Memphis yellow fever epidemic of 1878. Although services improved somewhat during the 1880s, there was little in the next several decades to challenge Ellis' statement "that the lower classes were literally and directly drained upon from above."

The leadership that implemented these policies has received more scholarly attention than their antebellum predecessors. Two major studies of postbellum southern urban leadership are Carl V. Harris, *Political Power in Birmingham, 1871–1921* (Knoxville: University of Tennessee Press, 1977), and Eugene J. Watts, *Social Bases of City Politics: Atlanta, 1865–1903* (Westport, Ct.: Greenwood Press, 1978). Harris challenges Floyd C. Hunter's "power-elite" concept of urban leadership by analyzing policies and the relative influence of three economic interest groups in formulating these policies. Though he uncovers divisions within the leadership structure, his findings do not refute Hunter entirely. The bickering within the elite may have been more characteristic of a city with Birmingham's particular industrial economic base. Harris concludes, unsurprisingly, that "political power was roughly proportional to economic power." Watts's Atlanta may be more typical of southern cities in that a "social filter" kept power in the hands of a relatively select group of economic elite throughout the period of study, in contrast with the changing character of leadership taking place in northern cities. Similar to Watts's interpretation, Samuel M. Kipp III, "Old Notables and Newcomers: The Economic and Political Elite of Greensboro, N.C., 1880–1920," *Journal of Southern History*, XLII (August, 1977), 373–94, discovers a "unified local elite" who, like an interlocking directorate, dominated all aspects of Greensboro life. Kipp suggests that this pattern was typical of other rapidly growing "once-small towns," but, as Watts indicates, it may hold true for larger southern cities as well.

Watts's findings raise the question of the need for progressive reform, when generally the same interests controlled power. The answer may be that progressive political reform served to rationalize administration and reinforce the hegemony of the leadership. This is not to belittle these reforms or the improved service levels (however selective they were) that resulted from greater attention to fiscal and administrative efficiency. A fine example of such results is Harold L. Platt, "The Modernization of an Urban Polity, Houston, 1892–1905," in Michael H. Ebner and Eugene M. Tobin, eds., *The Age of Urban Reform: New Perspectives on the Progressive Era* (Port Washington, N.Y.: Kennikat Press, 1977). The reforms, ironically, led to greater control of the city by northern capitalists.

City planning or, more accurately, "City Beautiful" was a concept that southern urban leaders adopted and adapted from their antebellum predecessors. Few leaders would argue with the philosophy behind the slogan "Beauty is Our Money Crop," coined by a Georgia urban booster in an azalea-festooned story by Flannery O'Connor, "The Partridge Festival," in O'Connor, *The Complete Stories* (New York: Farrar, Straus and Giroux, 1971), 421–44. Atlanta, as a New South leader, vigorously pursued beauty and order, as Elizabeth A. Lyon in "Frederick Law Olmsted and Joel Hurt: Planning for Atlanta," and Rick Beard, "Hurt's Deserted Village: Inman Park, 1885–1911," indicated in Dana F. White and Victor A. Kramer, eds., *Olmsted South: Old South Critic/New South Planner* (Westport, Ct.: Greenwood Press, 1979), 165–93 and 195–221, respectively. These essays demonstrate that Progressivism was not "for whites only," but only for certain whites—an interpretation confirmed quantitatively by J. Morgan Kousser, "Progressivism—for Middle-Class Whites Only: North Carolina Education, 1880–1910," *Journal of Southern History*, XLVI (May, 1980), 169–94. Education was a particular regional and urban failing, and progressive reform accomplished little to alter this fact, as Kousser demonstrates, and as Wayne J. Urban argues for Atlanta in "Progressive Education in the Urban South: The Reform of the Atlanta Schools, 1914–1918," in Ebner and Tobin, eds., *Age of Urban Reform*, 131–41. Urban concludes: "The business-efficiency aspect of progressive education in Atlanta was apparent in several reform policies, each of which indicated the priority of curtailing expenses in the reform agenda." Apparently, little had changed in public service philosophy since the antebellum era. Even New Orleans had its Progressive-type reformers, but there the issue was more of "ins" versus "outs" rather than of administrative efficiency, according to Raymond O. Nussbaum, "'The Ring is Smashed!': The New Orleans Municipal Election of 1896," *Louisiana History*, XVII (Summer, 1976), 283–97.

A much broader view of southern Progressivism is Dewey W. Grantham, "Review Essay: The Contours of Southern Progressivism," *American Historical Review*, LXXXVI (December, 1981), 1035–59. Grantham, however, places virtually every change in southern society from the white primary to social work under the rubric of Progressivism—a definition that reduces the usefulness of the term. Although he perceives an active reform movement in the South, particularly in the cities, the actual achievements of the "reformers" were minimal—and it is arguable whether prohibition, black disfranchisement, and blue laws were "reforms" in the usual sense of the word.

The biracial society was obviously not a target of Progressive reform and, in fact, those reforms—whether in administration, planning, or education—generally reinforced prevailing racial trends. Until recently, most post–Civil War historiography on race has focused, understandably, on the transition from slavery to freedom in a rural setting. The urban environment required certain adjustments to the antebellum biracial system. The definitive work in this area is Howard N. Rabinowitz, *Race Relations in the Urban South, 1865–1890* (New York: Oxford University Press, 1978), which modifies Woodward by demonstrating convincingly an early transition from exclusion to segregation after the Civil War. The book is an exhaustive account of the evolution of race relations in five southern cities, especially the impact of segregation on black urban life. The material on black economic status, service levels, residence, and leadership is the most comprehensive found anywhere. That Rabinowitz does not analyze rural black influences in the city or place his exclusion-to-segregation theme in a regional context of biracialism are relatively minor points in an otherwise-complete study.

Zane L. Miller's "Urban Blacks in the South, 1865–1920: The Richmond, Savannah, New Orleans, Louisville, and Birmingham Experience," in Leo F. Schnore, ed., *The New Urban History: Quantitative Explorations by American Historians* (Princeton: Princeton University Press, 1975), 184–204, is an upbeat survey of the period, utilizing a variety of census figures to demonstrate the emergence of an urban black middle class and a general improvement in opportunity, however marginal, of blacks moving from country to city.

In addition to these general works, there are several valuable accounts of black life in specific southern cities. John W. Blassingame's *Black New Orleans, 1860–1880* (Chicago: University of Chicago Press, 1973), is probably the best of this genre. He presents evidence that blacks fared better in cities than in the countryside and, at least until 1880, were involved in a variety of occupations, though "job bustin'" (segregating blacks into certain menial occupations) became evident at that time. Generally, free blacks, rather than former slaves, tended to occupy leadership positions, though on the whole the status of the free black elite lowered considerably after the Civil War. Dale A. Somers, "Black and White in New Orleans: A Study in Urban Race Relations, 1865–1900," *Journal of Southern History*, XL (February, 1974), 19–42, is actually a sequel to Blassingame, since it details the deterioration of race relations after 1880. Robert E. Perdue, *The Negro in Savannah* (Hicksville, N.Y.: Exposition Press, 1973), is less helpful than Blassingame's study of New Orleans, though it confirms free black leadership and a lively social life in the Crescent City. Unfortunately, none of these surveys approaches the sophistication and insight of such studies of northern black communities as David M. Katzman, *Before the Ghetto: Black Detroit in the Nineteenth Century* (Urbana, Ill.: University of Illinois Press, 1973), or Kenneth L. Kusmer, *A Ghetto Takes Shape: Black Cleveland, 1870–1930* (Urbana, Ill.: University of Illinois Press, 1976), both of which employ comparative analysis, geographic research methods, and an awareness of the interrelationship between urbanism and blacks. The studies of southern urban blacks tend to push the city into the background.

Leadership and segregation have received considerable treatment in the journals. Some of the more helpful articles are: David C. Rankin, "The Origins of Black Leadership in New Orleans During Reconstruction," *Journal of Southern History*, XL (August, 1974), 417–40, which confirms Blassingame's observations about free black dominance, particularly that of light-skinned free blacks, in postbellum black leadership. Raymond Gavins, "Urbanization and Segregation: Black Leadership Patterns in Richmond, Virginia, 1900–1920," *South Atlantic Quarterly*, LXXIX (Summer, 1980), 257–73, analyzes the interplay between growing segregation and racial hostility, and the rise of a new black leadership—the black bourgeoisie—by darker men engaged in professional and business occupations serving blacks. These new leaders merged with rather than replaced the old mulatto elite who relied on white clientele for their financial support.

Segregation, as Rabinowitz forcefully demonstrates, was the great fact of black urban life after the Civil War. Residential segregation was one of the most vicious aspects of the biracial system, and here the southern urban pattern sharply diverged from the large ghetto type that emerged in the northern cities, especially after 1900. John Kellogg, "Negro Urban Clusters in the Postbellum South," *Geographical Review*, LXVII (July, 1977), 310–21, is an excellent treatment of these residential patterns, generally unencumbered by geography jargon. The cluster pattern of settlement—primarily on the least desirable sites—characterized living quarters for the southern urban black. Kellogg also indicates that for many northern black ghettos filtering into formerly white housing stock was a typical neighborhood succession phenomenon, whereas in the southern cities black residential areas were more usually first-occupancy neighborhoods. Roger L. Rice, "Residential Segregation by Law, 1910–1917," *Journal of Southern History*, XXXIV (May, 1968), 179–99, analyzes the legal aspects of residential segregation, with the judicial system providing little support for black housing rights.

Blacks typically reacted to segregation by attacking it and forming their own institutions. The epidemic of streetcar boycotts that visited southern cities between

1900 and 1906 was a plague for the traction companies, but segregation laws escaped relatively unscathed. The best survey of the boycott is August Meier and Elliott Rudwick, "The Boycott Movement Against Jim Crow Streetcars in the South, 1900–1906," *Journal of American History*, LV (March, 1969), 756–75, which outlines the conservative protest that produced some modest temporary gains but ultimately failed to stop the "dance of segregation." The article also demonstrates that the conservative business and professional black leaders were in the front ranks of protest leadership. Howard N. Rabinowitz, "The Conflict Between Blacks and Police in the Urban South, 1865–1900," *Historian*, XXXIX (November, 1976), 62–76, argues that blacks were far from passive victims against a frequently corrupt and abusive white police force. They filed suits alleging police brutality and, in Atlanta at least, physically challenged the police, with the latter eventually refusing to enter a black precinct because of potential personal danger.

Self-help was ultimately the most productive strategy utilized by blacks. One fine example of this is discussed in Edyth L. Ross, "Black Heritage in Social Welfare: A Case Study of Atlanta," *Phylon*, XXXVII (Winter, 1976), 297–307, which relates the rise of the Neighborhood Union, a professional social-work agency organized by and for blacks.

The large and increasing presence of blacks in southern cities had some impact on the dwindling proportion of foreigners. The precise nature of this impact remains to be told. Richard J. Hopkins may have provided some clues in "Occupational and Geographic Mobility in Atlanta, 1870–1896," *Journal of Southern History*, XXXIV (May, 1968), 200–13, when he discovered that occupational mobility among immigrants approached that of native whites, while black mobility was extremely low. The fact that blacks were the most stable portion of Atlanta's population was perhaps the most surprising finding of the Hopkins analysis, a finding that William Harris contradicts in "Work and Family in Black Atlanta," *Journal of Social History*, IX (Spring, 1976), 319–30. Harris, in a fine comparative analysis, also shows that the occupational status of Atlanta's blacks actually was better than that of the Boston Irish and the Detroit blacks, though lower than the status of Atlanta's own immigrant population. The issue of black influence on immigrant mobility is skirted in Stephen Hertzberg, *Strangers Within the Gate City: The Jews of Atlanta, 1845–1915* (Philadelphia: Jewish Publication Society of America, 1978), which recounts the general success and relative absence of anti-Semitism implied in Hopkins' account and an even greater mobility than that of native whites. A process of self-selection probably operated in Atlanta, since few Jews came there directly from Europe. Accordingly, they were already adapted to New World patterns and brought skills and capital with them. At least one effort at direct immigrant importation to the South failed, according to Gary Dean Best, "Jacob H. Schiff's Galveston Movement: An Experiment in Immigrant Deflection, 1907–1914," *American Jewish Archives*, XXX (April, 1978), 43–79. Schiff blames the presence of blacks for Jews' unwillingness to live and compete in the urban South, but, in view of evidence presented by Hopkins and Hertzberg, that very presence should have enhanced Jewish chances. The black presence may have also affected immigrant residential patterns, as Ronald H. Bayor implies in "Ethnic Residential Patterns in Atlanta, 1880–1940," *Georgia Historical Quarterly*, XLIV (Winter, 1979), 435–47. As in the black case, clusters rather than one large ghetto for a particular ethnic group emerged. The large black population and the relatively small immigrant population may have accounted for this residential pattern. Segregation tended to increase among the former and decrease among the latter, similar to northern urban trends.

While the impact of black populations upon urban immigrant life remains unresolved, there is little doubt that the general poverty and low literacy levels of the freedmen contributed little consumer purchasing power or capital accumulation to the region and its cities. This situation enhanced the field for northern capital and control and reinforced the South's colonial economic position. The region's poor record of capital formation was merely one aspect of colonialism, as related by William N. Parker in "The South in the National Economy, 1865–1970," *Southern Economic Journal*, XLVII (April, 1980), 1019–48, which argues that the root of southern economic inferiority lay in the agricultural system fashioned after the Civil War, though, as I have indicated, the region's subsidiary position antedated the war. The best surveys of the southern economy during this period remain the standard accounts by Woodward, Cash, and, to a lesser extent, Gaston.

The historiographical effort lavished on race and agriculture has obscured the importance of providing analysis of the South's role in the national economy, especially with the advance of methodology since Woodward wrote *Origins of the New South*. Wiener provides some evidence of colonialism with the selectivity of northern investments, though it is surprising that Marxist historians have not picked up on this theme to a greater extent. Maury Klein, *The Great Richmond Terminal: A Study in Businessmen and Business Strategy* (Charlottesville: University Press of Virginia, 1970), chronicles the northern capital takeover of one of the South's major railroad empires. Less helpful is his *History of the Louisville and Nashville Railroad* (New York: Macmillan, 1972).

Historians have been more concerned with local issues of economic growth. Some examples include Sarah McCulloh Lemmon, "Raleigh—An Example of the 'New South?'" *North Carolina Historical Review*, XLIII (Summer, 1966), 261–83, which narrates the organization of the chamber of commerce in 1888 and subsequent efforts to make Raleigh "a large and important manufacturing centre." Lemmon does not place Raleigh in the larger context of the region or within the national economy, and she does not consider the limits that economy placed on Raleigh's ambitions. A similar problem affects Durward Long, "The Making of Modern Tampa: A City of the New South, 1885–1911," *Florida Historical Quarterly*, XLIX (April, 1971), 333–45, which discusses the city's industrialization, especially cigar-making. A more realistic view of the New South boosters' complicity in colonialism may be found in Carl Abbott, "Norfolk in the New Century," *Virginia Magazine of History and Biography*, LXXXV (January, 1977), 86–96, which employs the Jamestown Exposition of 1907 as the framework for a discussion of misplaced boosterism. A less interpretive work is Gary Bolding, "Change, Continuity, and Commercial Identity of a Southern City: New Orleans, 1850–1950," *Louisiana Studies*, XIV

(Summer, 1975), 161–78, which narrates the city's decline and resurrection as an industrial center, where the local wisdom announced with pride that in the "once-magnolia-scented land there is a new odor: the pungent smell of grease and factory smoke." Apropos, perhaps the best insight that scholars can obtain into the economic mind of the New South is Richard H. Edmonds' *Manufacturers' Record*, which performed the same service in the New South as *De Bow's Review* (which actually continued until 1867) performed in the Old South, with a bit more chicanery and puffery.

Don H. Doyle, "Urbanization and Southern Culture: Economic Elites in Four New South Cities (Atlanta, Nashville, Charleston, Mobile) 1865–1910," in Vernon Burton and Robert C. McMath, Jr., eds., *Toward a New South? Studies in Post–Civil War Southern Communities* (Westport, Ct.: Greenwood Press, 1982), is a valuable comparative analysis of the philosophical and practical foundations of booster policy in two cities of growth and two of relative decline. Although Doyle perhaps places too much emphasis on the importance of entrepreneurial leadership, he is successful in noting the uneven character of southern urbanization and some of the structural reasons for such development in differing economic environments. His work may represent a transition from the now-overworked booster case studies to a more sophisticated discussion of booster thought and policy and a broader comparative and regional context.

The Modern Era, 1920 to the Present

A voluminous literature from not only history but all of the social sciences confronts the historian working in this period. In fact, historians, by the very nature of their craft, and southern historians, by nature of their preferences, have produced a relatively small proportion of the relevant literature on southern city and region. It is an unfortunate compartmentalization of disciplines because, as Cash noted, the historian can contribute a great deal to understanding the vagaries of a southern life that straddled two vastly different worlds, and even up to the present there is still some question as to where the foot would fall. George B. Tindall provides an excellent framework for much of the period in the volume that follows Woodward's in Louisiana State University Press's History of the South series, *The Emergence of the New South, 1913–1945* (Baton Rouge: Louisiana State University Press, 1967). As big as a telephone book but reading much better, *Emergence* integrates southern urbanization with regional history to an even greater extent than Woodward's book does, probably because of the city's more evident presence in the recent period. Thus most chapters in the book contain material pertinent to southern urbanization: the booster spirit of the 1920s (chapter 3); the improved yet still selective urban services (chapters 7, 8, and 14); the labor strife in the cotton mill towns (chapter 10); the New Deal and southern cities (chapters 11 and 12); urban and regional life within a colonial economy (chapter 13); urban blacks (chapter 16); the response of concerned southerners in the 1930s to boosterism and traditionalism (chapters 17 and 19); and the impact of World War II on cities (chapter 20). Perhaps it is asking too much, considering the quality of the Woodward and Tindall contributions, but a volume similar in format and coverage for the period after 1945 is one of the great historiographical voids in modern southern history. Numerous dissertation topics have been plucked out of the Woodward and Tindall volumes, and challenges to particular interpretations have enlivened and informed historical writing for the past generation. These comprehensive works are not only significant in themselves, but also for the inspiration they provide to other scholars.

The general volumes that cover the post–World War II era are either anthologies or relatively brief overviews and personal memoirs that furnish important material but lack the range or interpretive insight of the comprehensive volumes produced by Woodward and Tindall. John C. McKinney and Edgar T. Thompson, eds., *The South in Continuity and Change* (Durham: Duke University Press, 1965), assemble an impressive cast of scholars, but there is too much "presentism" in the anthology, which tends to evaluate regional indicators as heralding an epitaph for Dixie. This is particularly evident in Leonard Reissman's "Urbanization in the South" (pp. 79–100), and Thompson's "The South in Old and New Contexts" (pp. 451–80). Nevertheless, the volume produces useful information on urbanization and migration trends, especially the geographic expansion of the southern city. A more realistic collection is Ernest M. Lander, Jr., and Richard J. Calhoun, eds., *Two Decades of Change: The South Since the Supreme Court Desegregation Decision* (Columbia: University of South Carolina Press, 1975), in which several essays note the significant though still relatively circumscribed gains by blacks and unions.

In personal reminiscences of the region's recent history, too often the writer intrudes upon his subject. This is not the case with such accounts as Robert Coles, *Farewell to the South* (Boston: Little, Brown, 1972), and Pat Watters, *The South and the Nation* (New York: Pantheon Books, 1969). The biracial society, its partial demise, and its persistence form major themes in both works, since the authors recall their roles and observations during the turbulent 1960s. The urban South occupies an important role in these recollections both as a mirror for regional problems and as a reflection of regional strengths. Watters devotes one-quarter of his book to a discussion of cities and towns, but the remainder of his narrative pertains to urbanization as well—an indication that artificial divisions between city and region are not appropriate devices for understanding either city or region.

The attention that both Coles and Watters devote to urban settings (Watters evinces a greater appreciation for the distinctive process of urbanization in the South) implies more scholarly devotion to southern cities than I have noted for earlier periods. The best concise survey of part of the period is Blaine A. Brownell, "The Urban South Comes of Age, 1900–1940," in Brownell and Goldfield, eds., *The City in Southern History*, 123–58. Brownell places urbanization in a regional context, demonstrating that urban racial and religious trends in particular possessed rural roots. Rupert B. Vance and Nicholas J. Demerath, eds., *The Urban South* (Chapel Hill: University of North Carolina Press, 1954), purports greater coverage both in time and topics than it delivers. The volume generally does not reflect the usually high standard of Regionalist endeavors either in interpretation or statistical projection, and the contributors generally seem content to present their statistical extrapolations without much interpretation. Nevertheless, the volume provides basic information on the metropolitanization of the South, migration patterns, and city-planning trends. The strongest essay is T. Lynn Smith, "The Emergence of Cities" (pp. 24–37), which presents a statistical overview of a century and a half of southern urbanization in concise and readable form.

Perhaps the problem that confronted Vance and Demerath was that southern scholars are not accustomed to dealing with urbanization as a research entity. Two essays that provide less information on urbanization than on the mind-set of the writers and their social-scientist colleagues are Walter J. Matherly, "The Emergence of the Metropolitan Community in the South," *Social Forces*, XIV (March, 1936), 311–25, and Robert Earl Garren, "Urbanism: A New Way of Life for the South," *Mississippi Quarterly*, X (September, 1957), 65–72. Matherly, a frequent contributor to Regionalist research, predicts a metropolitan era—or, as he calls it, "metropolitan regionalism"—for the South, spurred not only by industry but by the region's unique recreational and climatic attributes. Here we have an early vision of the Sun Belt. Garren is even more sanguine about the prospects for southern urbanization, forecasting a social revolution in the region as a result of urban growth.

Much of this optimism emanated from Chapel Hill, where Regionalist publications dominated southern social sciences from the 1930s to the 1950s. The Regionalists, however, were far from being intellectual versions of the urban booster. Two works in particular demonstrate their exhausting, painstaking research and their analytic powers: Howard W. Odum, *Southern Regions of the United States* (Chapel Hill: University of North Carolina Press, 1936), and Rupert B. Vance, *All These People: The Nation's Human Resources in the South* (Chapel Hill: University of North Carolina Press, 1945). Odum's monumental (nearly 700 pages) work represents the first systematic study of the region, and it is a bold, learned statement of what had gone wrong with the New South Creed. Regionalism was a program to bring the South to parity with the rest of the nation through enlightened regional and national policies. The abundant charts, graphs, and tables depict a dreadful condition of poverty, illiteracy, and ill-health—confirming all of the worst stereotypes about southerners. Yet through all the gloom came at least some hope that national leadership would acknowledge and combat southern problems, and that industry and cities would maximize human and natural resources to help right regional wrongs.

The optimism is even stronger, though still guarded, in the Vance book, another social science epic. World War II had altered the dire regional picture to some degree, and Vance makes it clear that what was needed for the future was an end to colonialism and a continuation of the national partnership begun in the New Deal. These works are more primary documents of their time than secondary sources. Although politicians and even colleagues vilified them, the Regionalists plowed forth, armed with their statistics. Yet the Regionalists usually pointed out and rarely demanded, especially in referring to the biracial system. Given the intellectual climate produced by the "savage ideal," perhaps this was understandable.

There are other social scientists today carrying on the spirit of the Regionalist school. The Southern Growth Policies Board, despite its booster-sounding name, has been one rallying point to counteract the latter-day prophets of progress. Their recent report, *The Future of the South* (Research Triangle Park, N.C.: Southern Growth Policies Board, 1981), edited by Pat Watters, urges restraint and "looking inward" for the 1980s in terms of regional economic development, and points to continuing problems in service levels, urban decay, and race relations. The board also functions as a statistical archive.

Historians, with the notable exceptions of Woodward and Tindall (who contributed to the *Future of the South* volume), have generally been absent from this regional reassessment. While southern social science was exposing regional ills, southern historians in the thirties and forties were still licking fictive Reconstruction wounds. Even the Agrarians, however unrealistic, were at least fighting the very real threat of dehumanizing modernism, but the southern historians were still fighting the Yankees and would continue to do so through the 1950s. A new generation of southern historians has appeared, however, and though they are reluctant to venture beyond that historical barrier of World War II, their insights on specific aspects of twentieth-century southern history, particularly on urbanization, are of major import for contemporary southerners.

The historical urban studies for this period bear little of the gratuitous prose of the amateur studies that dominated the earlier eras. Some of the best examples include Howard L. Preston, *Automobile Age Atlanta: The Making of a Southern Metropolis, 1900–1935* (Athens, Ga.: University of Georgia Press, 1979). Although the book covers a relatively small portion of the modern era, it is more than an analysis of the automobile's impact on the city's spatial development (though Preston does a fine job with this theme). It demonstrates how racial and economic mores molded a major southern metropolis. As Preston writes: "If the auto did anything at all, it better equipped white Atlantans to carry out their racial prejudices against blacks" (p. xvii). Atlanta followed a typical southern urban pattern, where significant technological change was merely superimposed on regional traditions. Blaine A. Brownell's *The Urban Ethos in the South, 1920–1930* (Baton Rouge: Louisiana State University Press, 1975) focuses on five southern cities during the height of booster mania. Brownell strips the facade of booster rhetoric and demonstrates the changes that did not occur in that decade of Progress. The book is probably the best-documented study confirming Cash's view that, in the South, Progress upheld Tradition and vice versa. As Brownell concludes, southern cities were communities "fashioned more out of wishful thinking than out of reality." Brownell's article, "Birmingham, Ala.: New South City in the 1920s," *Journal of Southern History*, XXXVIII (February, 1972), 21–48, brings the coexistence of the Klan, fundamentalism, and boosterism into sharper relief.

Dana F. White and Timothy J. Crimmins have applied their skills as historians to improve the life of contemporary Atlantans through a greater understanding of that city's past. Their History Group, Inc., has worked with such diverse groups as subway-builders and schoolchildren in a fine example of the type of historical activism that Cash sought from the profession in the 1940s. An appropriate example of their work appears in "Urban Structure, Atlanta," *Journal of Urban History*, II (February, 1976), 231–52, which traces the city's spatial development and the forces affecting that development through the twentieth century and then identifies "key locales and neighborhoods to represent significant stages in the development of Metro Atlanta." White and Crimmins hope that these neighborhood accounts will be the basis for future policy making in a city that has kept its history in cheap reproductions such as Underground Atlanta and in Cyclorama, an oozing, smoking mural of the Battle of Atlanta. The two Atlanta historians have also contributed to a useful volume of the *Atlanta Economic Review*, XXVIII (January–February, 1978), which in nine essays assesses past development, present performance, and future growth and financial prospects of the city in a realistic analysis.

In addition to accounts of specific cities, writers have recently generated a number of useful works on portions of the urban-regional experience in the modern era. The values of rural migrants in the urban environment have attracted several studies of interest, though, again, the question of cultural transference remains more implied than proved. Religion persists as the most dominant cultural feature, now institutionalized and affluent. Kenneth K. Bailey, *Southern White Protestantism in the Twentieth Century* (New York: Harper & Row, 1964), presents a not-very-encouraging account of the evangelical sects in this century, ending with the Southern Baptist Convention's questioning the suitability of a Catholic for high office in 1960. Bailey takes a rueful view of the boosterism and social inaction of the post–World War II church. "Most Baptist preachers," Bailey writes, "largely confined their homilies to the traditional gospel of spiritual redemption" (p. 154). Erskine Caldwell, *In the Shadow of the Steeple* (London: Heinnemann, 1967), presents a revealing personal account of his father, a Presbyterian minister, and the difficulties encountered by a man with liberal views and conservative congregations. Caldwell's father eventually resigned his ministerial position to become a secular teacher, convinced that the South required education more than the gospel. Lillian Smith, *Killers of the Dream* (New York: W. W. Norton, 1949), is another reminiscence of the stifling aspects of evangelical religion and how it upheld the biracial society. The book ranges much beyond discussions of religious culture and has particularly good material on the impact of biracialism on white children and the emptiness of southern women's lives up on the pedestal.

There are few works that deal exclusively with southern religion in an urban setting, but Wayne Flynt, "Religion in the Urban South: The Divided Mind of Birmingham, 1900–1930," *Alabama Review*, XXX (April, 1977), 108–34, is a good model for such a study. Flynt chronicles the growing conservatism and bigotry of the city's churches in the 1920s, coincident with the flourishing of boosterism, which overwhelmed the fragile liberalism that appeared in the early 1900s. Kenneth T. Jackson, *The Ku Klux Klan in the City, 1915–1930* (New York: Oxford University Press, 1967), depicts the church's general support of the movement in southern cities and also the persistence of rural value systems in urban residents of relatively long duration. The Klan was strongest in those cities undergoing the most rapid changes. Though a national phenomenon, the Klan took on a particular virulence and power in its southern setting in the 1920s.

John Shelton Reed, *The Enduring South: Subcultural Persistence in Mass Society* (Lexington, Mass.: D.C. Heath, 1972), presents a convincing portrait of the uniform persistence of rural values throughout southern society, sufficient to distinguish the region from the North. Though he takes most of his data from the 1950s and sixties, Reed argues that, despite the great changes that have occurred in the region since World War II, its people still adhere to traditional concepts, including "the right to private violence" and the precepts of evangelical religion. A recent study that tends to support Reed's conclusions is Robert Emil Botsch, *We Shall Not Overcome: Populism and Southern Blue-Collar Workers* (Chapel Hill: University of North Carolina Press, 1980). Botsch characterizes contemporary white workers as highly individualistic, concerned about reverse discrimination, indifferent to collective activism, and suspicious of government.

Country music has been part of the cultural baggage carried by rural migrants to the southern city. Although urban versions of this musical genre may be called "Countrypolitan," and Mickey Gilley's Urban Cowboy Band may be one of the leading country acts, the basic themes of the music—the sense of place and of rootlessness, family ties and domestic strife, salvation and sin—are essentially unchanged even if the musical accompaniment sounds more like Mantovani than Mountain Dew. But the southern city has always been a regional music-mixing machine. Not only country music but gospel and blues in its various forms have drifted into city hotels and bars from sharecroppers' shacks and mountain hollows. Jazz emerged out of this mélange, and so did rock and roll. The music of Buddy Holly from Lubbock, Texas, and of Elvis Presley of Tupelo, Mississippi, wove the themes of country music to the beat of the blues and delivered the result with gospel fervor. Though Bill C. Malone has successfully chronicled the evolution of country music in the South in his *Country Music, U.S.A.: A Fifty-Year History* (Austin: University of Texas Press, 1979) and *Southern Music, American Music* (Lexington: University Press of Kentucky, 1979), there is no scholarly treatment of the different forms of southern music in the urban milieu—a treatment that would provide insight into the impact of another rural cultural tradition on southern urbanization.

The secular urban leadership must be given some credit for transmuting the forces of change to its own traditional ends. In fact, most of the writing concerning boosters in their first twentieth-century heyday during the 1920s subscribes to this view. Blaine A. Brownell's "The Commercial-Civic Elite and City Planning in Atlanta, Memphis, and New Orleans in the 1920s," *Journal of Southern History*, XLI (August, 1975), 339–68, is a good exposition of this interpretation, particularly on the conservative uses to which urban leaders put the new profession of city planning. As Preston's study of Atlanta indicates, racial motives informed numerous planning decisions, and the growth ethic vision of urban planning eventually helped to destroy the vitality of the city center. The narrow and misguided purpose of urban leaders is also a theme in Charles Paul Garofalo's "The Sons of Henry Grady: Atlanta Boosters in the 1920s," *Journal of Southern History*, XLII (May, 1976), 187–204.

The attraction of urban expansion and major projects—territorial and structural monuments to urban leaders—was perhaps nowhere more evident than in the person of William B. Hartsfield, who, except for a brief period during the early 1940s, was mayor of Atlanta from 1936 until 1961. Yet Hartsfield was a new type of booster, more similar to the turn-of-the-century Progressive mayors in northern cities than to the heirs of Henry W. Grady. This is the view of Hartsfield presented by Harold H. Martin in *William Berry Hartsfield: Mayor of Atlanta* (Athens, Ga.: University of Georgia Press, 1978), one of the few scholarly biographies of a big-city southern mayor. Hartsfield expressed concern for the city's black population and improved the generally wretched quality of city services, though, like big-city mayors all over the country, he was proudest of his expressways and the new international airport. The chronicle is different in Memphis, according to David M. Tucker's *Memphis Since Crump: Bossism, Blacks, and Civil Reformers, 1948–69* (Knoxville: University of Tennessee Press, 1980). The reformers who took over from the Crump machine were hardly that, generally ignoring demands of blacks and providing little better public services.

Public services, in fact, remained the weakest area of booster policy. Social welfare in particular was the most neglected aspect of urban policy. Wayne Flynt's *Dixie's Forgotten People: The South's Poor Whites* (Bloomington, Ind.: Indiana University Press, 1979) covers the region's neglect of poverty, which has been chronic to the point where the poor whites have become a definable caste. Flynt expertly recounts the irony of the region's periodic rediscovery of poverty, yet its unwillingness, even in the midst of new-found prosperity, to alleviate its causes. Flynt also scores federal policies for perpetuating this culture, despite good intentions, because they ignored the unique problems and values of southern poor whites. This plea harkens back to the studies of the Regionalists, who also pointed out that distinctive regional cultures of poverty challenged traditional policy treatments.

In a less passionate discussion of urban service quality and human capital investment, Peter A. Lupsha and William J. Siembieda, "The Poverty of Public Services in the Land of Plenty: An Analysis and Interpretation," in David C. Perry and Alfred J. Watkins, eds., *The Rise of the Sunbelt Cities* (Beverly Hills: Sage, 1977), 169–90, presents valuable statistical material on the scandalously low service expenditures, especially in education and welfare, despite Sun Belt prosperity. On a similar theme in the same volume, see Robert E. Firestine, "Economic Growth and Inequality, Demographic Change, and the Public Sector Response" (pp. 191–210).

Both articles imply that the rapid annexation practiced by southern cities has further reduced service levels and quality in the core, where most poor people reside. There is growing resistance to annexation, both from within the city and its minority populations, and from outside the city, as the New York *Times* related on March 18, 1978, in "Suburb Is Fighting Annexation by Houston," on the efforts of affluent Clear Lake City residents to avoid Houston's voracious land appetite. Also on the increasing disenchantment with expansionist politics, see Arnold Fleischmann, "Sunbelt Boosterism: The Politics of Postwar Growth and Annexation in San Antonio," in Perry and Watkins, eds., *Sunbelt Cities*, 151–68. Perhaps because of the growing resistance and of the questionable fiscal soundness of indiscriminate annexation, southern urban leaders are beginning to turn inward in their quest for economic expansion. Their objective is to capitalize on the history and traditions of their communities. Historic preservation and urban redevelopment in a historic mode have become popular and financially rewarding endeavors for numerous southern cities. Although certainly an improvement over the destructive policies of renewal, they often carry with them a similar insensitivity to local poor and minorities. For some discussion of the preservation trend, see Don H. Doyle, "Saving Yesterday's City: Nashville's Waterfront," *Tennessee Historical Quarterly*, XXXV (Winter, 1976), 353–64, and David R. Goldfield, "Preservation for Whom?" New York *Times*, November 4, 1980. The typical media response, however, has been uncritical acclaim, understandable perhaps given the innate charm of southern cities to begin with. Two typical renditions in this vein are "A City Reborn: The Move to Save Old Savannah," Washington *Post*, October 2, 1977, and Philip Morris, "Five Southern Towns Change and Stay the Same," *Southern Living*, XIII (January, 1978), 3–12.

The recent upsurge of boosterism indicates that there may have been less change in the region's urban political leadership than was forecast in Jack Bass and Walter De Vries, *The Transformation of Southern Politics: Social Change and Political Consequences Since 1945* (New York: Basic Books, 1976). A review of some of this literature, especially as it pertains to southern cities, is found in James C. Cobb, "Urbanization and the Changing South: A Review of Literature," *South Atlantic Urban Studies*, I (1977), 253–66.

The region's novelists and essayists have lavished considerable attention upon the persistence of the booster ethic and the values it represents in southern cities. In fact, the Southern Renascence beginning in the late 1920s, was, in part, a response to the hollow men masquerading as regional saviours. In many respects, the best insights into southern history and mind in the twenties and thirties are in the novels of the great southern writers sensitive to the implications of regional change and traditional encrustations. Lisa Alther, the Tennessean who wrote the bestselling *Kinflicks*, presented a lively summary of the Renascence and its demise in "Will the South Rise Again?" *New York Times Book Review*, December 16, 1979, pp. 7, 34. Thomas Wolfe provided perhaps the best insights into the southern mind, probing and dissecting the personal and collective foibles of his native Asheville in four novels through the eyes of Eugene Gant in *Look Homeward, Angel: A Story of the Buried Life* (New York: Scribners, 1929) and *Of Time and the River: A Legend of Man's Hunger in his Youth* (New York: Scribner's, 1935), and of George Webber in *The Web and the Rock* (New York: Grosset & Dunlap, 1937) and *You Can't Go Home Again* (New York: Harper & Bros., 1938). The novels represented also a personal search, a spiritual home for a man alienated from his home yet drawn to it. The confusion, wandering, guilt, and revelation were as much the southern condition of the 1930s as they were the personal conditions of Eugene, George, and of Thomas Wolfe. In the power and frustrations evident in the novels, it is possible to see how the region tortured not only Wolfe, but Cash and Faulkner as well.

William Faulkner, like Wolfe, sought to understand, cope with, expose, and reject the conflicting trends in southern life during and after the depression years. Though Faulkner's foothold is more rural, the transformation of the small towns, such as Frenchman's Bend in *The Hamlet* (New York: Random House, 1940), and the increasing pervasiveness of the urban booster ethic are major concerns, particularly in his later writing. By the early 1950s, Faulkner was stumping around university campuses warning about depredations to the southern environment in the name of Progress, as the Fugitives did, and as Faulkner himself did in "The Bear" in *Go Down, Moses* (New York: Random House, 1942). He recognized that racism and illiteracy were regional millstones but hoped that Progress would not destroy other more positive aspects of the southern environment along with bigotry and ignorance or, worse yet, keep the bad and destroy the good.

Robert Penn Warren, unlike Wolfe and Faulkner, belonged to the Nashville Agrarians. The Agrarians' views are presented collectively in Twelve Southerners, *I'll Take My Stand: The South and the Agrarian Tradition* (1930; reprint ed., Baton Rouge: Louisiana State University Press, 1977). Although his works continued beyond the thirties and forties, some of his best writing occurred during that soul- and mind-searching era. Especially in *All the King's Men* (New York: Harcourt, Brace & World, 1946), whatever its merits as a fictive rendition of Huey Long's rise and fall, Warren was concerned with the past—its meaning and relevance. Jack Burden, the narrator, is a renegade historian fleeing from a profession where knowledge of facts does not give knowledge of either people or truth, and where, in the context of such ignorance, the past becomes distorted. But if, as Warren believes, "only out of the past can you make the future," then the historian's incomplete rendition of the past will threaten the future. This is the dilemma raised by modernism, which disdains the past and therefore provides no future, as the Agrarians argued. In reality, however, southern urbanization and industrialization (synonyms for modernism) were very much a part of the regional past, and so the Agrarians believed that the southern future could only be its past, which in many respects was a stagnant, stifling legacy to leave to future generations, rather than the creative molding of tradition to human regional advances as the Chapel Hill Regionalists sought. Perhaps Warren himself was uncomfortable with the position he took in *All the King's Men*, because in *Flood* (London: Collins, 1964) the juxtaposition of a tradition-laden southern town and the technology of a modern dam seem to provide a classic Agrarian confrontation between "good" and "evil." Yet as the story unfolds, the town reveals its hypocrisy, racism, and neglect. Warren makes the conflict more complex because, even with its faults, the town provides a strong sense of place—a basic southern tradition—that would drown with all the negative aspects of life. If there could only be some compromise.

The difficulty of compromise, though, was put strongly by Flannery O'Connor twenty years ago: "The anguish that most of us have observed for some time now has been caused not only by the fact that the South is alienated from the rest of the country, but by the fact that it is not alienated enough, that every day we are getting more and more like the rest of the country, that we are being forced out, not only of our many sins but of our few virtues." Which may explain why the Southern Renascence has trickled away. The potential southern writers, as Lisa Alther stated, have either "decamped for the North" or "are busy running Burger Kings."

Critics have occasionally accused southern writers, even latter-day authors such as Walker Percy and William Styron, of exaggeration and distortion of southern life as it really was or is. Leaving aside the question as to whether fiction should merely be a reflecting pool of society, the grotesqueries of Faulkner, the exaggerations of Wolfe, and the impossible lives depicted by O'Connor are not distortions. They are merely southern. Any rendition of booster rhetoric, racism, civic projects (the Parthenon in Nashville and Stone Mountain outside Atlanta come immediately to mind), religion, violence, cotton, purity of women, to mention only a brief catalog, must note the southern deviation from the rest of the country, an exaggeration. Of course, southern history, in great part, is a deviation from American history, and, as I have indicated, so is southern urbanization. In large measure, the unreal, the unbelievable are the real and believable for the South, which made the Renascence writers' search for reality so difficult because there was no "real" there. As poet Elizabeth Bishop wrote in response to a critic who accused Flannery O'Connor of exaggeration: "I lived in Florida for several years next to a flourishing 'Church of God,' where every Wednesday night Sister Mary and her husband 'spoke in tongues.' After those Wednesday nights, nothing Flannery O'Connor ever wrote could seem at all exaggerated to me." Perhaps all of us can share O'Connor's own dismay at signs that this deviate region was beginning to melt into the national mass. The South, after all, is so interesting, while there is so much in the rest of the nation that is so prosaic.

The biracial society was one exaggerated regional tradition whose passing southern humanists would not mourn (and how it is possible to excise the negative traditions while keeping the positive is a theme that has pestered literati and social scientists alike). There is not, unfortunately, a work for the modern period comparable to Rabinowitz's survey of the three decades following the Civil War. The civil rights legislation of the 1960s inaugurated a new era for blacks in cities and regions, and the Voting Rights Act helped to extend political power to blacks. But Chandler Davidson's call for a New Populist coalition of lower-class whites and blacks in *Biracial Politics: Conflict and Coalition in the Metropolitan South* (Baton Rouge: Louisiana State University Press, 1972) now seems naïve in view of general white desertion of black candidates, a movement observed and documented even earlier by Numan V. Bartley, "Atlanta Elections and Georgia Political Trends," *New South*, XXV (Winter, 1970), 22–30, and Virginia H. Hein's almost sarcastic "The Image of a 'City Too Busy to Hate': Atlanta in the 1960s," *Phylon*, XXX (Fall, 1972), 205–21.

There has been little historical assessment of economic advances by southern blacks since the protests of the early 1960s, though the census continues to give eloquent testimony of continuity in that sphere. There is no adequate sequel to Carl Grindstaff, "The Negro, Urbanization and Relative Deprivation in the Deep South," *Social Problems*, XV (Winter, 1967), 342–62, which indicates that the economic gap separating blacks and whites was greater in the southern city than in the rural areas, though city blacks were generally doing better than their rural counterparts. Does the burst of Sun Belt prosperity and the accompanying inflation maintain this gap? Data from the Southern Growth Policies Board indicate that wide income differentials remained in some cities during the 1970s.

Some review of the impact of such momentous events as the sit-ins in Greensboro, the demonstrations in Birmingham, and the march on Selma exists. David J. Garrow, *Protest at Selma: Martin Luther King, Jr. and the Voting Rights Act of 1965* (New Haven: Yale University Press, 1979), contends, for example, that the Selma march pushed a reluctant Congress and administration to complete work and passage on the Voting Rights Bill. John R. Salter, Jr.'s *Jackson, Mississippi: An American Chronicle of Struggle and Schism* (Hicksville, N.Y.: Exposition Press, 1979) is an insider's view of events up to and including the assassination of Medgar Evers in 1963. The value of the study is Salter's insight into the philosophical, generational, and tactical divisions in the city's black community. As for open-housing legislation, Robin Flowerdew, "Spatial Patterns of Residential Segregation in a Southern City," *Journal of American Studies*, XIII (April, 1979), 93–107, indicates that, at least for Memphis, the type of housing succession and ghetto formation patterns common to the large black ghettos of the North may be the future southern pattern as well. The article also contains a historiographical survey of blacks and housing in contemporary southern cities.

The civil rights movement has significance for the southern woman. One of the frustrations I encountered in preparing this book was the relative absence of quality material on women in southern cities. We already know about the pedestaled, sexually misused, crinoline-crimped southern woman of yesteryear, but what about the urban working woman? The best material on the working woman is Sherwood Anderson's description of women's living and working conditions in a textile mill village in *Beyond Desire* (New York: Liveright, 1932). Julia K. Blackwelder has undertaken investigations of women in several southern cities during the depression years, but these are only brief impressions of a much larger picture that needs uncovering. Blackwelder's findings appear in "Quiet Suffering: Atlanta Women in the 1930s," *Georgia Historical Quarterly*, LXI (Summer, 1977), 112–24, and "Women in the Work Force: Atlanta, New Orleans, and San Antonio, 1930 to 1940," *Journal of Urban History*, IV (May, 1978), 331–58. Blackwelder's research is particularly strong in contrasting the experience of different ethnic groups and occupational categories among women. But the 1930s were an unusual decade that may have thrust more women into the urban work force than at any previous time, under extremely stressing conditions.

The changing role of southern women in the 1930s implied a broader ferment within labor generally as dozens of industrial towns and cities in the region erupted in violence in response to renewed efforts at trade-union organization. Although the textile-mill culture was successful in combating incipient unionism, other less-traditional regional industries faltered under the combined efforts of determined and long-exploited workers and the federal government. Robert P. Ingalls, "Antiradical Violence in Birmingham During the 1930s," *Journal of Southern History*, XLVII (November, 1981), 521–44, and Charles H. Martin, "Southern Labor Relations in Transition: Gadsden, Alabama, 1930–1943," *Journal of Southern History*, XLVII (November, 1981), 545–68, dispel notions of docile southern labor and reveal community-wide conspiracies to maintain the status quo and block, with violence if necessary, attempts at union organization. Again, the federal government proves an important catalyst in forcing southern industrialists to comply with national legislation.

The poor—black and white—and the women may, along with the declining cities, be the forgotten elements in the southern resurgence. The memories of the colonial economy seem just that, and George B. Tindall, "The 'Colonial Economy' and the Growth Psychology: The South in the 1930s," *South Atlantic Quarterly*, LXIV (Autumn, 1965), 465–77, is the last historical marker before the subsequent Sun Belt surge silenced historical research on the subject. There are, nevertheless, new signposts erected by social scientists that point out the persistent colonialism in the region, however masked by soaring buildings and profits. Some examples include Robert B. Cohen, "Multinational Corporations, International Finance, and the Sunbelt," in Perry and Watkins, eds., *Sunbelt Cities*, 211–26; "South Carolina's Imported Boom: A State Transformed by Outside Investment," Washington *Post*, April 30, 1978; and Jim Overton, *et al.*, "The Men at the Top: The Story of J. P. Stevens," *Southern Exposure*, VI (Spring, 1978), 52–63.

Fifteen years ago, Willard Thorp's "Southern Literature and Southern Society," in Edgar Thompson, ed., *Perspectives on the South: Agenda for Research* (Durham: Duke University Press, 1967), 95–112, expressed surprise at the relative dearth of historical research on southern cities. This, he thought, was particularly unfortunate in view of "the present time of rapid urbanization" (p. 101). Since that time, southern urban history has received some exposure in a field dominated, like the movie versions of the South, by blacks and plantations. As this essay has indicated, there are a great many topics that remain lightly covered or untouched entirely. By returning the southern city to its regional roots, this book will perhaps provide increased contact and flow between the more traditional fields of southern historiography and the urban South.

Index

Agriculture: and southern urbanization, 3–4, 5–6, 15–20, 29–37, 69, 86, 88, 90, 91, 131, 141–42, 146; labor systems, 25, 46, 105–106, 140; and philosophy, 33, 164; and diversified farming, 139, 140, 141; and Agricultural Adjustment Act, 140, 142; mechanization of, 140, 141
Anderson, Joseph R., 48
Anderson, Sherwood, 130, 146
Arrington, Richard, 176
Asheville (N.C.), 9, 162
Atlanta: early years of, 35; Civil War in, 82, 83–84; reconstruction of, 85, 120–21; as rail center, 89, 91, 127; streets in, 92; health services in, 96; social services in, 97, 101, 150, 166; housing in, 97, 168; leadership of, 98, 100, 116, 128, 159; planned suburbs of, 102; compared with northern cities, 103; blacks in, 104, 109, 110, 112, 113, 114, 115, 166, 168–69, 170, 171, 173, 176; immigrants in, 106, 110; sectional reconciliation in, 119–20; physical impact of railroads on, 128; expositions in, 129; downtown of, 129, 154, 156–57; annexation by, 129–30; and southern urban system, 144, 145; rural aspect of, 146–47, 196; religion in, 149; and city planning, 152, 168; urban renewal in, 168, 169; Great Depression in, 180; population decline in, 193
Augusta (Ga.), 82, 83

Barr, Stringfellow, 10, 11
Baton Rouge (La.), 29
Behrman, Martin, 100
Biracialism: and southern urbanization, 6–7, 25–26, 56–58, 177; and services, 38, 165–66; and New South Creed, 115; and politics, 116
Birmingham: early years of, 89, 91; streets in, 92; industry in, 122–23, 183, 184; annexation by, 130; social services in, 149; Great Depression in, 180; violence in, 180; military expenditures in, 182, 183
Blacks: and protest, 7–8, 114–15, 172, 175; migration of, 103–104, 105, 165; and agricultural labor, 105; and laws to control labor, 109; occupations of, 109–10, 116, 165, 166; businesses of, 110–11, 170; and segregation, 111, 114, 117, 167, 171–75; and social services, 111, 165–66; residential patterns of, 111–12, 152, 166–69, 171; property holding of, 112, 170; and religion, 112–13; leadership of, 113–14, 176–77; and education, 113; and class divisions, 113; and riots, 115; and black-white differentials, 166–67, 169; and poverty, 166, 179; and urban renewal, 168–69; and school desegregation, 172–75; and political power, 175, 176–77; and Sun Belt prosperity, 177–78; rural ties of, 178. *See also* Free blacks; Slavery
Boosterism: as conservative, 8, 9, 160, 162; attacks on, 9, 10, 160; and growth ethic, 99, 128, 153, 190; attracting northern investors, 119–20, 189, 190; and cheap labor, 124–25, 185, 189; and downtown redevelopment, 156–57, 168–69

Camden (S.C.), 19
Cash, W. J., 32, 39, 94, 130, 161, 163–64

Charleston (S.C.): as colonial rice capital, 17–18; architecture of, 18; social life in, 18, 35; and commerce, 19, 21; and finance, 26; beauty of, 29, 85; decline of, 31, 87, 128; disease in, 41; services in, 41–42, 45; police in, 45; and free blacks, 52; immigrants in, 55; and secession, 76, 77–78; Civil War in, 84; violence in, 93; historic preservation in, 157; blacks in, 166; military expenditures in, 182; and World War II, 183
Charlotte: Civil War in, 82; city planning in, 101–102; and Cotton Mill Campaign, 123; and conurbation, 145; annexation by, 152; urban renewal in, 168; textile mill wages in, 186
Coles, Robert, 178, 179
Colonialism: and national economy, 8, 58–61, 69–70, 73–79, 126, 132, 192; British, 26; and capital accumulation, 38, 69, 182, 192; and sectionalism, 62, 73–79, 119; and railroads, 62, 73, 120, 121, 127; and direct trade, 62–63, 64, 69–70; and coastwise shipping, 65; and industry, 62, 67, 68–69, 121–22, 123, 180, 189, 192; and secession, 76
Columbia (S.C.): Civil War in, 82, 84; reconstruction of, 121; rural migration to, 143
Columbus (Ga.), 64
Cotton: cultivation of, 30, 31, 34, 140, 142; and southern economy, 30, 86; and urbanization, 30, 34, 88; marketing of, 30, 86, 87; processing of, 34, 64, 67, 68, 88, 123, 185; and mechanization, 141
Crump, Edward H., 99, 100

Dallas: streets of, 92; and southern urban system, 144, 145; leadership of, 159; military expenditures in, 182
De Bow, J. D. B., 35, 62, 64, 122
Draper, Earle S., 188
Du Bois, W. E. B., 103, 113
Durham (N.C.): blacks in, 112; and regional airport, 145; impact of inflation on, 178

Edmonds, Richard H., 108, 118, 119, 131, 180
Environmental exploitation, 4, 125, 152, 190
Evangelical Protestantism: theology of, 5, 38, 95; growth of, 38–39, 147; impact on southern mind of, 39, 147; as conservative force, 39, 95, 148, 162, 187; and urban

slavery, 49–50; and Lost Cause, 95; and social services, 95, 147; connections with business of, 147, 149, 187

Faulkner, William, 10, 125, 162
Federal government: antebellum southern fear of, 70–78; economic power of, 70–73, 78, 119; and Pacific Railroad, 73, 78, 119; and urban renewal, 168; federal courts and desegregation, 172; and Voting Rights Act of 1965, p. 175; and Community Development Act of 1974, p. 177; and New Deal legislation and assistance, 181–82, 188; and military expenditures, 182–84; and aid to industry, 183, 184, 185
Fitzhugh, George, 9, 62, 69
Free blacks: demography of, 50–51; property holding by, 51; occupations of, 51–52, 109; residential patterns of, 52–53; relations with slaves of, 53; religion of, 53

Galveston, 107
Gastonia (N.C.), 188
Glasgow, Ellen, 139, 154
Grady, Henry W., 115, 118, 120, 121–22, 128
Greensboro (N.C.): local government of, 101; city planning in, 102; school desegregation in, 173–74; sit-in demonstrations in, 175
Greenville (S.C.): Cotton Mill Campaign in, 123; rural migration to, 143; and regional airport, 145
Gregg, William, 66, 68, 76, 125

Hartsfield, William B., 159
Hattiesburg (Miss.), 183
Historic preservation, 155–59
Houston: immigrants in, 106; federal aid to, 119; spatial growth of, 144; social services in, 150, 153, 165, 166; housing in, 151; annexation by, 152, 153; residential segregation in, 167; military expenditures in, 182, 183; industry in, 183, 184
Hurt, Joel, 102, 129

Immigrants: in colonial era, 20; demography of, 53, 106; occupations of, 54–55, 110; and competition with blacks, 55, 107; family life of, 55; German, 55, 56; Irish, 55–56; residential patterns of, 56, 108; and crime, 93; campaigns to attract, 106, 108; Jewish, 106, 107–108

Industry: importance of, in combating colonialism, 62, 67, 121–22; textile mills, 64, 67, 68, 123–25, 130, 185–89; iron and steel, 64, 122–23, 180, 183; antebellum failures of, 66; lack of home patronage for, 66; rural location of, 68, 124, 185; and labor, 68, 129, 130, 185–89; and Civil War, 82; and Cotton Mill Campaign, 123–24; failure of, in New South, 124, 126; and World War II, 182–83, 184; petro-chemical, 183; high-technology, 184; and company towns, 68, 125, 130, 186, 188; and New Deal legislation, 188; and foreign investment, 189, 190–91; and industrial development campaigns, 190

Jackson, Maynard, 176
Jacksonville (Fla.): blacks in, 114, 165–66; military expenditures in, 183
Johnson, Governor Robert, 14, 15, 20, 21

King, Martin Luther, Jr., 1, 172, 173, 175
Kingsport (Tenn.): and regional airport, 145; and labor, 185
Knoxville: annexation by, 130; city planning in, 151
Ku Klux Klan, 139, 148

Labor: rural industrial, 68, 124–25, 185, 186; and strike breaking, 116; low wages for, 124, 185–86, 187, 189, 191; and New Deal, 182, 188; working conditions of, 186, 187; and housing, 186, 188; and unions, 187; and strikes, 188; skill levels of, 188–89; and subemployment, 191
Local government: leadership of, 37, 98–99, 100, 102, 159–60, 164; constraints of, 38–39, 98; and cost-benefit formula for services, 39–44, 99, 151, 153; and streets, 39–40, 92; and health services, 40–42, 95–96; and social services, 42, 96, 97, 111, 126, 149, 150, 164, 165–66, 191, 192; and railroad investments, 43, 63; and taxes, 43–44, 98; and police, 93; and annexation, 99, 152–53; and Progressive reforms, 101; and city planning, 101–102, 151, 152, 167; and housing, 150–51, 168–69; and downtown redevelopment, 156–57, 168–69; and Community Development Act, 177; and Great Depression, 180; and industrial development plans, 189–90
Louisville: police in, 45; immigrants in, 55;

health services of, 97; blacks in, 167; Great Depression in, 181

Macon (Ga.): railroad investments in, 43; blacks in, 113; social services in, 149; and labor, 185
Memphis: as cotton center, 34, 90; growth of, 34; Civil War in, 81, 82; as rail center, 90, 127; streets in, 92; violence in, 93, 115; disease in, 96; social services in, 97; bankruptcy of, 98; annexation by, 99, 130, 152–53; textile milling in, 124; downtown of, 129, 154–55; and city planning, 151; housing in, 160; blacks in, 166; subemployment in, 191
Miami: growth of, 144; Great Depression in, 181; military expenditures in, 182
Miami Beach, 181
Mobile: founding of, 22; as cotton port, 30, 87; streets of, 40; free blacks in, 52; immigrants to, 54; decline of, 87, 88; federal improvements in, 119; and World War II, 183–84
Montgomery: description of, 1; Civil War in, 84; blacks in, 104, 109, 172, 179

Napier, J. C., 113
Nashville: Civil War in, 81–82; annexation by, 99, 130; blacks in, 104, 113, 167; commerce in, 127; physical impact of railroad on, 127; social services in, 149; downtown of, 154; military expenditures in, 182
Nashville Agrarians, 10, 162–63
Natchez: beauty of, 29, 146; architecture of, 29; theater in, 35; immigrants to, 53; industry in, 67; and secession, 76
New Orleans: founding of, 22–23; beauty of, 29; commerce in, 30, 60–61; growth of, 30, 31, 34; as cotton center, 34, 35, 87; streets of, 40, 91–92; disease in, 40, 95, 96; police in, 45, 93; free blacks in, 52; immigrants in, 53, 54, 55–56, 93, 106; and railroads, 64–65; and secession, 76; Civil War in, 81, 82; decline of, 87, 126–27, 193; density of, 96; social services in, 97; leadership of, 100, 116; blacks in, 110, 115, 176; city planning in, 151–52; downtown of, 157; historic preservation in, 157
Norfolk: in colonial era, 16; disease in, 40–41; social services in, 42; decline of, 88, 193; and World War II, 183

Odum, Howard W., 163
Oglethorpe, James, 21–22

Perry, Heman E., 170
Portman, John, 156, 157
Progress and tradition, 11, 160, 162–64

Quivers, Emanuel, 48

Railroads: local government investments in, 43, 63; and colonialism, 62, 65; construction of, 63; competition for, 64–65; dependence on agriculture of, 65; and changes in marketing patterns, 86–87, 89, 127; northern takeover of, 120, 121, 127; physical impact on cities by, 127
Raleigh: city planning in, 102; blacks in, 104; and regional airport, 145
Ransom, John Crowe, 10, 11, 162–63
Regionalists, 163, 193
Richmond: as tobacco center, 16, 32, 34; streets in, 40; railroad investments by, 43; slavery in, 47, 48; immigrants in, 55; industry in, 64, 67, 181; exports of, 64; Civil War in, 80, 83, 84; annexation by, 99; blacks in, 104, 111, 112, 165, 169; reconstruction of, 121; city planning in, 152; downtown of, 154, 155; historic preservation in, 158; housing in, 164; Great Depression in, 181; and New Deal, 181
Robb, James, 73, 76
Rural migration, 38, 94, 131, 142–43

San Antonio: social services in, 150, 153; annexation by, 153; downtown of, 156; leadership of, 159; military expenditures in, 182
Savannah: founding of, 21–22; beauty of, 29, 146; growth of, 34–35, 63; disease in, 41; railroad investments in, 43, 63–64; exports of, 64; decline of, 87; bankruptcy of, 98; blacks in, 113, 114, 166; housing in, 150, 151, 169; historic preservation in, 158, 159; Great Depression in, 180; military expenditures in, 184; and industrial development plan, 189–90
Selma (Ala.): Civil War in, 82; historic preservation in, 155; blacks in, 175; industry in, 190
Shreveport (La.): cotton and, 34; blacks in, 167
Slavery: and southern urbanization, 6, 25; character of urban, 45–46, 48–49; and urban occupations, 46; agricultural, 46; and slave hiring, 47–48; and residential patterns, 48–49; and religion, 49; and recreation, 50
Smith, Lillian, 141, 148, 171
Spartanburg (S.C.): and Cotton Mill Campaign, 123; rural migration to, 143; and regional airport, 145; labor in, 185; foreign investment in, 190–91
Suburbs: annexation of, 99; planned, 102; commercial development in, 154–55; black residence in, 167; growth of, 192–93; and industrial development, 193

Tampa-St. Petersburg: growth of, 144; New Deal in, 181; military expenditures in, 183
Thompson, Edgar, 2, 32, 95, 194
Tindall, George B., 139, 143, 162, 169
Tobacco: marketing of, 15, 16; cultivation of, 15, 16, 31; processing of, 64, 181

Urban systems: in colonial South, 19–21, 23–25; in antebellum South, 30–32; after Civil War, 87–90; in twentieth century, 143–45; in Sun Belt, 143; and conurbations, 145
Urbanization: theories of, 2, 3, 193–94; and agriculture, 3, 131; and geography, 12, 14–15, 16; British policy toward, 13–14, 15, 23; and density, 29, 96; rate of, 32, 86, 90, 103, 142, 143, 144; and secession, 76–78; and Civil War, 80–85; and World War I, 130; and Great Depression, 142; and World War II, 142; as liberal force, 194

Warren, Robert Penn, 11, 152
Watters, Pat, 4, 9, 172, 174, 178, 190, 196
Williamsburg (Va.), 16–17
Wolfe, Thomas, 9, 10, 130, 147, 160–61, 162
Woodward, C. Vann, 90, 110, 144